Varsy Arsy

Proclaiming The Gospel
in Second Corinthians

by

Phillip A. Ross

Pilgrim Platform
Marietta, Ohio

ISBN: 978-0-9820385-4-3

Published by

Pilgrim Platform
149 E. Spring St., Marietta
Ohio, 45750
www.pilgrim-platform.org

Biblical quotations are from the *English Standard Version*, Standard Bible Society,
    unless otherwise cited.
ESV refers to the English Standard Version, Standard Bible Society, 2008.
MKJB refers to the *Modern King James Bible*, Sovereign Grace Publishers, 1993.
LITV refers to the *Literal Translation of the Holy Bible*, Sovereign Grace Publishers,
    Third Edition, 1995.
KJV or AV refers to the *King James Version of the Holy Bible*, public domain in the
    United States.
ASV refers to the *American Standard Version*, Thomas Nelson, 1929.
WCF refers to the *Westminster Confession of Faith*, 1646.
Strong's refers to *Strong's Exhaustive Concordance of The Bible*, Hendrickson
    Publishers.

Printed in the United States of America

For the people who have elected
Barack Obama as the
44th President of the United States of America
in the hope for
change they can believe in

TABLE OF CONTENTS

INTRODUCTION

This should be considered to be volume two of *Arsy Varsy—Reclaiming the Gospel in First Corinthians*, Pilgrim Platform, Marietta, Ohio, 2008, in the same way that Second Corinthians needs to be read in the light of First Corinthians. Not that the two cannot stand apart or alone, they can. But in the sense that the second is built upon the foundation of the first, and will be best understood in light of the first.

As *arsy varsy* was an old Puritan phrase meaning *ass-backwards*, *varsy arsy* is the putting backwards the notion of ass-backwardness—or putting the matter rightly. Paul argued vociferously against all that arrayed itself against Christ, but he was not merely *against* things. He was preeminently *for* things, *for* Christ and *for* all that Christ stood for. And Christ stands for the things that the world and Satan stand against. There was, is and will always be a fundamental opposition between the forces of good and the forces of evil. It cannot be otherwise.

The dedication of this volume may require some explanation because the theological perspective that inhabits it is not the theological perspective of President Obama, and therefore not of those to whom he appealed.[1] These volumes are directed at the correction of a mindset, a worldview, more than they are directed at any particular person or group. So, it must be understood that the dedication is only what it says. This study of Corinthians is *for* President Obama, but even more so *for* his supporters—for the edification of the American people, for their conversion, for revival, for reformation, for growth in grace, for sanctification in the hope of repentance and restitution in Christ's covenant. However, it should not be assumed that these volumes are simply a corrective for liberals and/or Democrats—not at all! The theo-

---

1 The President and I share some history in the United Church of Christ. So, I am familiar with the theology that he has been exposed to—Liberation theology and its variants. The United Church of Christ is the most liberal of the denominations that still use the name *Christian* and has led the liberal attack within the Christian camp since its inception in the 1960s.

1

logical perspective and teaching herein is for Twenty-First Century America (and the West generally) regardless of any perceived political rightness or leftness. What is more, these volumes will encourage Christians everywhere to think more deeply about what they believe, and the implications of their beliefs. These books are more about depth, than direction. They are not about right or left, but profundity, sapience and lucidity. They serve as a call into the deep waters of Christianity.

I have attempted in these volumes to provide a faithful gospel perspective, to show that Paul's letters were real—not to divest them of their spirituality, but to demonstrate that Paul's spirituality was earthy and fleshy more than it was of a detached, abstract, ethereal or imaginary quality. Unfortunately, the Christian faith has been blurred and/or diluted by the forces of modernism and Postmodernism in our day, by the lingering forces of the Enlightenment and the French Revolution of the Eighteenth Century, and by the tenacious forces of Gnosticism and Platonism that have claimed common ground with the gospel from the very beginning of Paul's ministry, from the beginning of Christ's ministry, and even from time immemorial, reaching back into the fog of ancient history.

Hope

The hope for change that was stirred up by Barack Obama's presidential campaign in 2008 was an unspecific hope, a mantra of change that appealed to a deep-seated but unclarified fear. Hope always shines brighter against a backdrop of dread. One of the arts of political success involves the ability to equivocate, to be deliberately ambiguous or opaque in order to appeal to as many diverse people as possible in such a way as to allow them to impose their own meanings and agendas upon one's words. Political success involves appealing to as diverse an audience as possible in order to capture as many votes as possible. Barack Obama appears to be a master of this art.

Nonetheless, my contention is that Obama's rhetoric of hope led people to impose their own hopes for change upon his campaign. People know at some deep, unconscious level that something is very wrong, that we have taken a wrong turn somewhere, that our current lifestyles and the values that support them are fundamentally unsustainable. We are like a herd of cliff-bound lemmings, and the course we are currently on is not likely to turn out well. A course adjustment is needed. People know it, and Obama's rally cry for hope has ignited this concern. It is a good concern, a necessary concern, fraught with danger and opportunity.

My hope is that the desire for change that was given public voice in the midst of the recent election will find its way to the deeper considerations of our sin and the good news of the gospel as Paul proclaimed it at Corinth. Paul's words were for the Corinthians without a doubt, but they are also for us because Paul's words are for the church, for the people of God, whosoever they are, wheresoever they live and whensoever they exist.

People today often think that we live at the very pinnacle of human civilization because we have extended science and technology farther than any other culture in history—and we have! But, while it is true that our science and technology are genuine wonders of the world, at the same time we have gutted the very heart of civilization, the heart of human concern and human culture by converting everything that people do into profit making opportunities. Consequently, we are not at the pinnacle of human civilization at all. We are on the verge of an unprecedented world-wide catastrophe that only a serious, wide-spread cultural change will avert—and only by the grace of God. And God is the real issue. Will we, can we acknowledge God's role in our lives, in our world? We will, of course, one way or another, sooner or later.

CRISIS

At this writing the financial markets of the world are in the midst of unparalleled crisis. Originating on Wall Street in America, toxic credit has poisoned the financial markets of the world. Governments of many countries are following America's lead in "bailing out" various corporations—banks, lenders, governmental hybrids (the twins, Freddie Mac and Fannie Mae), etc.—by "injecting" them with capital to keep them from collapsing. Governments are printing fiat money to prop up institutions that the forces of the market and history have determined to have failed, institutions that would go bust except for the bailouts.

At the time that market forces would collapse various institutions of the world culture in which we live, government forces are scrambling to prop up the failing institutions in the hope of their continuation and/or in the hope of profiting from their demise. Or perhaps the purpose of the capital injections is not their survival, but something else, something unknown, something unspoken.

It has been in the midst of this crisis that the Presidential campaign of Barack Obama issued promises of hope for change. And it is my contention that the kind of change that the whole world wants and needs at this time in history is substantive change, real change, cultural change, and not the propping up of failed institutions. Indeed, the changes that are coming to the world will sweep many people and institutions from the stage of history through a cascade of events—some intended and some unintended—that are already upon us. Like it or not, understand it or not, Christ actually is our only hope.

The crisis that has swamped the world financial systems is a symptom of a deeper problem. Money is not the problem. It is a symptom. Ground zero of our financial crisis is credit. And what is credit? It is a promise to repay a loan. It is a covenant, a compact, a contract, an agreement. The real source of toxic credit, the acknowledged source of the financial crisis, are the unfaithful promises of borrowers and the immoral practices of lenders. The world is in the grip of a crisis of faithlessness, not just concerning money, but generic and wide spread unfaithfulness. Our promissory notes rest upon a foundation of promissory rot. To fix the crisis, we must first face and fix the covenantal rot with the covenantal God.

Substantive change cannot and should not be engaged in one fell swoop as if someone has *the* answer—I certainly don't, Rather, such changes must be engaged with great care and caution. The social and cultural changes that are needed at this time should get a lot of public discussion and engagement. Now is not the time for political correctness or the denial of Christ's historic impact upon the world. It is toward such a discussion that these volumes are offered in the hope that public discussion will include the voice of Jesus Christ, whose gospel speaks directly to times like these. Rather than rejecting the wisdom of Scripture in the midst of crisis, we need to rediscover the wisdom of Scripture because the Bible has been given to us precisely for times such as these.

Paul and the Corinthians were standing on the verge of historical changes that were similar to the kinds of changes that we ourselves in our time are facing. Thus, Paul's words to the Corinthians have some helpful application for us in that the crisis at Corinth that Paul faced is not dissimilar from the crisis that we face today. Of course there is not a one-to-one correspondence between the First and the Twenty-First Centuries, but there are important similarities.

The Corinthian church was successful, large and influential. But it didn't realize that its success had been built on a misunderstanding of the gospel that Paul had planted among them. False apostles had been teaching false hopes and false beliefs in the name of Jesus Christ, under the guise of Christianity. Many of the Corinthians didn't realize the problem, though increasingly church members were becoming aware of a problem of some kind. Some of the church members had written Paul for his advice in the matter. Paul, of course, recognized the problem immediately because it was his teaching that had been contravened.

BACKWARDS

Part of the backwardness in Corinth and of our own world today is the fact that Satan and the world have arrayed themselves against the things of the Lord. It is not that God is out of step with the reality that science documents, but that Satan's secularism is out of step with that reality. The Lord is first or primary in order and immanence. The Lord is always *for* life, Satan and the world mitigate against life. Satan and the world stand *against* the preeminence of God and of life. So, it is not that Christianity is always *against* things, but that Satan and the world are always against what God positively stands *for*. So, whether Christianity seems to stand *for* things or *against* things depends upon where the observer is standing. To stand with the Lord is to stand *for* the things of the Lord, and to stand against Him is to stand *against* what He is *for*.

Paul found himself somewhat flabbergasted in Corinth because the church that he had planted there years earlier had veered so far from its inception as to be completely *arsy varsy*—backwards. Again, it wasn't so much that the gospel was in contradiction to the world, as it was that the values and ways of the world were in contradiction to—*against*—the values and ways of the gospel. The gospel did not do the opposing because it was the original impetus of God come to fruition in Christ Jesus. The gospel seed that Paul planted at Corinth was the original. It was the world and the false Corinthian apostles who were against the Lord of the universe. Paul had set them on the right course at the founding of the church, and the false apostles opposed what Paul had taught.

Paul's Second Letter to the Corinthians continued the themes of his first letter and introduced others. Written from Macedonia, Paul expressed thankfulness for the repentance and renewed obedience of the Corinthian church. He wrote about completing their collection for the Jerusalem church and defended himself against accusations and slander from the false apostles at Corinth.

Thanks to Stephanie, my wife, and Paul Williams for proofing and feedback.

Phillip A. Ross
Marietta, Ohio
April 2009

1. COMFORT

Paul, an apostle of Jesus Christ by the will of God, and Timothy our brother, to the church of God which is at Corinth, with all the saints who are in all Achaia. Grace be unto you, and peace from God our Father and from the Lord Jesus Christ. Blessed be God, even the Father of our Lord Jesus Christ, the Father of mercies and the God of all comfort, He comforting us in all our trouble, so that we may be able to comfort those who are in every trouble, through the comfort with which we ourselves are comforted by God. For as the sufferings of Christ abound in us, so our consolation also abounds by Christ. And if we are troubled, it is for your consolation and salvation, being worked out in the endurance of the same sufferings which we also suffer; if we are comforted, it is for your consolation and salvation. And our hope of you is certain, knowing that as you are partakers of the sufferings, so also of the consolation.   —2 Corinthians 1:1-7

Scholars conclude that First Corinthians was probably written from Ephesus before Pentecost (late spring) and that Second Corinthians was probably written from Macedonia later that same year before the onset of winter. About six months separate the two letters. It seems that Paul sent several letters to the Corinthians in an effort to help get them back on the gospel track.

The common format for letters of Paul's time was to indicate who the letter was from at the beginning. So, we see Paul identify himself and his position or authority as an apostle, and Timothy, who was with him. Timothy may have served as Paul's scribe or secretary at that time. Note two things about the first verse: that Paul identified himself as an apostle "by the will of God" (v. 1), and that Timothy is not identified as an apostle.

Paul was conscious of his position as a significant Christian leader. He was aware of his responsibility to get the church started correctly, and so he pressed hard to correct the Corinthian church. He also seems to have known that his letters would receive significant attention by other Christians in other churches because he seems to have been aware of various of the apostolic letters being circulated among the churches at the time. He certainly would have been aware of the gospels—at least some of them—and their importance to the churches of the day.

God's Will

The mention of the "will of God" (v. 1) as the authority of his apostleship was not a statement of self-confirmation, as if people can just claim the will of God as the justification for whatever they want to do in God's name. Rather, it indicates the nature of a call to Christ, that the call must originate in the will of God and not simply in one's own heart. A call to Christ takes more than personal desire and the approval of the elders of a church, though both of these things also happen. Paul's mention of God's will did not/does not eliminate the necessity of examination and election to church membership and/or church office. It only places the primary locus of such a call in the court of God. The point is that those who are called need to know that they are called by God.

The middle clause of verse 1 provides an interesting statement about the Corinthian church. Paul addressed the church as a whole, a unit, as if it were one, not many. It is important to note that the church in Paul's day was nothing like the churches we know in our day. Almost everything is different, from our technological lifestyles to the structure or organization of the churches and the way that we do church. It is different because we are different people than the people of the First Century. One of the fundamental differences pertains to the definition and character of the church(es).

The Greek word is *ekklēsia* and literally refers to a calling out, or a calling together—actually both a calling out and a calling together. At the time the Greeks used the word to indicate the governing body of a city (a polis, from which the word political is derived). The *ekklēsia* was a governing body, the gospel of Jesus Christ provided for an alternative governing body—the church. Paul wrote to the Philippians, "But our citizenship is in heaven, and from it we await a Savior, the Lord Jesus Christ" (Philippians 3:20). Christians are citizens of heaven.

Paul was not writing to everyone in Corinth, nor to all of the people who worshiped at the Corinthian church. First of all, he wrote to those who could read. He was not aiming that the lowest classes of society. He was aiming at Christians in any and all classes of society. Those who could read would read his letter(s) to others. Christians are

people of the Book, and can, therefore, read. As we know, his arguments are often complex and require diligent study. But Paul was not
being an intellectual snob, not showing off his intelligence. Indeed, the
simplest Christian could then and can still benefit from his letters. At
the same time Paul's letters continue to provide insights and challenges to the most erudite Christian living in the Twenty-First Century.

And while Paul was not writing to everyone in Corinth, he was
writing to every Christian in Achaia. By including all of Achaia, Paul
emphasized the unity of the church. Those who were in unity with
Christ were in unity with each other and were designated as one
church in Achaia.

INDEPENDENCE & COOPERATION

According to Herodotus, the Ionians founded twelve cities along
the southern shore of the Corinthian Gulf, many of which retain their
original names to this day. These cities formed a confederation of
smaller communities, which in the last century of the independent history of Greece attained to great importance and was known as the
Achaean League. In Roman times the term Achaia was used to include
the whole of Greece, exclusive of Thessaly. In 146 B.C., the league
erupted into open revolt against Roman domination, shortly thereafter
the Romans under Lucius Mummius defeated the Achaeans, destroyed
Corinth, its capital, and dissolved the league.

Why is this important? Because it suggests two things: the people
in Achaia had 1) a spirit of independence, and 2) a spirit of cooperation. Paul was writing to the *ekklēsia* in various cities in Achaia as if
they comprised a unity, as if they were one. This is important because
it suggests that Christian unity can occur across a region in such a way
that neither independence nor cooperation are lost.

To this church, these various *ekklēsia* groupings, Paul invoked
grace and peace. The order is important, first grace then peace. Paul
wished, acknowledged, sent grace to them and then peace from God.
He acknowledged that both grace and peace issue from God, and that
grace preceded peace. No doubt Paul was aware at this point (after his
first letter) that his message to the Corinthians was a message of both
unity and division (1 Corinthians 11:19) He was not asking all of the
Corinthians to dwell together in peace, but had already suggested that
there may need to be a division among them. He will repeat that senti-
ment in chapter six. And yet his purpose was to establish genuine
peace through the restoration of unity by the exclusion of those who
were not in Christ, as he communicated in his first letter: "To the
church of God that is in Corinth, to those sanctified in Christ Jesus,

called to be saints together with all those who in every place call upon the name of our Lord Jesus Christ, both their Lord and ours" (1 Corinthians 1:2).

Paul identified himself as being in unity with them by speaking of God as "our Father" (v. 2). And he added that Jesus Christ was in unity and/or harmony with God, as well. His first message was that God is merciful because He provides comfort in the midst of affliction. And secondly, that those who have received God's comfort in the midst of their own affliction receive it not simply for themselves, but in order that they may pass God's comfort along to others who are similarly afflicted. The comfort that the saints receive is given to them, not simply for themselves, but as a means of facilitating their service to others. This suggests the importance of the element of service in the Christian faith. Everything that God gives is to be shared, and every opportunity for service is to be engaged.

Afflicted & Called

The message is not simply that God provides comfort for the afflicted, but that the afflicted are called into service. How did Paul know this? Because he himself had been afflicted because of his faith in Christ. And he had been called into service, not merely as a result of his affliction, but by it and because of it. The purpose of the affliction was not to cause suffering among the saints, but to call and equip them for service. The affliction was the calling, and it was also the equipping. God uses affliction as a means of call and a means of sanctification—spiritual growth.

Of course, this is not the only use of affliction. God also uses it for discipline and chastisement. And for those who reject Jesus Christ, affliction provides a real-time prelude to the vicissitudes of hell as an end-of-the-line or last opportunity to turn from sin and embrace Jesus as Lord and Savior.

Every occurrence of the word *tribulation* in the KJV is a translation of *thlipsis*, which is here translated as *affliction*. Tribulation is one of God's tools. The purpose of tribulation for the faithful in Jesus Christ is the calling to and equipping for ministry, which means that Christians are definitely not spared tribulation, but may even be more susceptible to tribulation experiences than those who are not Christian. This insight has application to the Dispensational doctrine of the rapture. God's intention is not to save Christians from pain and difficulty, but to save them for ministry in the midst of it.

Christians are to experience God's comfort in the midst of personal affliction and tribulation, and then to comfort others in the same way that God has comforted us. We are to learn how God's comfort works in the midst of our own pain. And we must note that God's comfort is not usually the elimination of the pain of affliction, but the proper understanding of it. Knowing that the purpose of my affliction is to help me provide comfort for others does not eliminate or lessen the pain. Rather, it tends to increase my tolerance for pain, knowing that it has a purpose that serves the glory of Jesus Christ, a greater purpose, even an eternal purpose that promotes the cause of Christ.

To actually be useful to Jesus Christ in the accomplishment of God's purposes is a great comfort to the saints. Others may belittle such service, lamenting that it falls to them, but not those who are faithful. The faithful treasure whatever service they can provide for the cause of Christ. Large or small, great or insignificant, it doesn't matter because it pleases the Lord. This is the comfort about which Paul speaks, and can be seen again in verse 5: "For as we share abundantly in Christ's sufferings, so through Christ we share abundantly in comfort too." There is a correspondence between sharing Christ's sufferings, suffering with or because of Christ, and sharing in the comfort provided by Christ through faith.

We see it again in verse 6: "If we are afflicted, it is for your comfort and salvation; and if we are comforted, it is for your comfort, which you experience when you patiently endure the same sufferings that we suffer." Here Paul is showing us how it works. His suffering was for the Corinthians (and others), as was his comfort. It was not for him, but for them. It flowed through him. His affliction called him into service to Christ in order to learn how Christ comforts His people in the midst of affliction, and in order that he may then extend that comfort to the afflicted Corinthians. And in the same way, by imitation, the afflicted Corinthians were called into service to Christ by their affliction. And they were similarly trained by Christ Himself, who comforted them, in order that they may serve other saints who are or would be afflicted for the cause of Christ.

The same thought is extended in verse 7: "Our hope for you is unshaken, for we know that as you share in our sufferings, you will also share in our comfort." The faithful saints at Corinth experienced affliction and distress, which was no doubt exacerbated by their adherence to the gospel as Paul had expounded it to them. And the common concern in the face of difficulty and affliction is to wonder why God would do such a thing, why God would allow his faithful people to experience the pain and difficulties of tribulation. Our natural minds lead us to think that God should reward faithfulness with ease and pleasure. But Paul, conveying the supernatural mind of Christ, does not suggest that.

STRENGTHENED

Rather, Paul finds that his hope is all the more strengthened by the fact of their suffering because he knows that in Christ their suffering will result in the comfort that only Christ provides, and will call them into service as it has called him. He knows that the comfort is not a function of the suffering, but of faithfulness—that faithfulness to Jesus Christ and the comfort of Christ are the same thing. No degree of suffering can dislodge the comfort of Christ. Jesus proved that on the cross. Paul knows that no human experience, no matter how painful or traumatic, can undo God's covenant with Jesus Christ or derail the salvation that Christ has secured for His people. So, Paul's hope for the afflicted Corinthians was unshaken. Suffering for the sake of Christ cannot undo the comfort provided by Christ. Rather, it increases it.

This is a great hope, greater than anything that we in our natural minds could ever conceive of, greater than any sin, surely greater than our personal discomforts in the midst of the difficulties of this world. Christian comfort is not a respite from struggles and difficulties, nor from pain and hardship. Rather, Christian comfort is faithfulness in the midst of struggle and difficulty, faithfulness in the face of pain and hardship. I'm not saying that pain and struggle are necessary. God is not a masochist. I'm only saying that they are ordinary experiences in this fallen world, and that God uses them for His purposes.

Things will be different in heaven. There "He will wipe away every tear from their eyes, and death shall be no more, neither shall there be mourning nor crying nor pain anymore, for the former things have passed away" (Revelation 21:4). That will be then. Here and now we live between the already and the not yet. Here sin is real, and it generates pain and difficulty. So God uses it for His purposes and our benefit in Christ. And we will do well not to disparage God's ways, not to ignore God's tools, nor to lament our difficulties. Rather, Christians are called to embrace God's way, to use and to be used by God's tools, and to see our difficulties as opportunities for ministry.

2. THE BOAST

For, brothers, we would not have you ignorant of our trouble which came to us in Asia, that we were pressed out of measure, above strength; so much so that we despaired even of life. But we had the sentence of death in ourselves, so that we should not trust in ourselves, but in God who raises the dead; who delivered us from so great a death, and does deliver; in whom we trust that He will yet deliver us, with you also helping together by prayer for us, so that the gracious gift by many persons be the cause of thanksgiving through many for us. For our rejoicing is this, the testimony of our conscience, that in simplicity and godly sincerity; not with fleshly wisdom, but by the grace of God; we have had our conduct in the world, and more abundantly toward you. For we write no other things to you than what you read or recognize, and I trust you shall recognize them even to the end, even as you have recognized us in part, that we are your rejoicing, even as you also are ours in the day of the Lord Jesus. —2 *Corinthians 1:8-14*

Paul had promised to visit the Corinthians as soon as possible, but it seems that he had not been able to get there as soon as he had hoped. There is some speculation that Paul's enemies at Corinth used this situation to accuse Paul of not following through on his promises. So Paul spoke here to suggest that there was a good reason that he had not been able to get to Corinth. He had experienced affliction and almost lost his life.

Some scholars suggest that Paul was referring to the whole of his apostolic journeys as he had been chased around the Mediterranean fleeing for his life. Paul's former friends among the Pharisees and Sadducees had put a contract out on his life. There was an active conspiracy to murder Paul (Acts 25:3), which was one of the primary reasons for his journeys. Others suggest that Paul was talking about the situation involving Demetrius at Ephesus.

Demetrius had been a silver smith who had accused Paul of blasphemy against the mother goddess Diana, also known as Artemis (Acts 19:21). Demetrius correctly understood that the gospel threatened the Temple of Diana (Artemis) and the many local jobs that the temple provided. A riot broke out and Paul nearly lost his life. That was likely the situation to which Paul referred here. As reported, Paul and company were "so utterly burdened beyond (their) strength that (they) despaired of life itself" (v. 8).

RELIANCE

As their lives were threatened by the mob in that situation they found themselves relying not on themselves but on "God who raises the dead" (v. 9). The fact of the affliction and threat of death thrust them into greater reliance on God. That is exactly what Paul wanted the Corinthians to learn: that affliction and tribulation force God's people into increasing reliance upon the God who saves. Paul had not reneged on his promise to visit Corinth, he had been detained by circumstances beyond his control, circumstances that threatened his life.

Verse 10 is a little convoluted, but the idea is that God had delivered Paul and company from deadly peril time and again. And because God had been faithful to do that Paul would trust that God would provide the final deliverance that He had promised through Jesus Christ. In spite of the difficulties and discomforts of affliction, Paul set his hope on God, trusting—knowing through personal experience—that God would deliver on His promise.

Paul then asked the Corinthians to pray for him, for Paul, but also to pray that many people would give thanks for the blessings that Paul had received, and would also pray that the kind of comfort experienced by Paul would be widely known, widely experienced. Paul set up a kind of prayer chain that would reach back into the past in thankfulness for grace received and would also reach into the future and cause other people, future people, to be similarly thankful—thankful for Paul and his ministry, of course. But also thankful that they too would be able to receive and pass on God's comfort in the midst of affliction.

Verse 12 provides a summary, clarification and call to faithfulness for the Corinthians, and for all Christians henceforth. "For our boast is this: the testimony of our conscience that we behaved in the world with simplicity and godly sincerity, not by earthly wisdom but by the grace of God, and supremely so toward you" (v. 12). Paul summarized his concern in his previous letter (First Corinthians), that concern being the difference between Christian wisdom and practice and worldly wisdom and practice. And by summarizing it, he clarified it by reiterating that there is a significant difference between Christians and non-Christians that impacts both belief and behavior. The clarification, then, becomes a call issued to the Corinthians (and all Christians henceforth) to imitate Paul and the apostles in this regard.

SANCTIONS

By calling it a *boast* (*kauchēsis*) Paul suggested that he planned to tell everyone about it in order to create a kind of social expectation regarding the Corinthians (and all Christians henceforth), that Christians, imitating Paul, will behave in the world "with simplicity and godly sincerity, not by earthly wisdom but by the grace of God" (v. 12). Paul set out here three positive behavioral sanctions and one negative sanction.

The positive sanctions are to behave with simplicity, sincerity and grace. The Greek word translated as *simplicity* (*haplotēs*) literally means singleness, sincerity, and mental honesty. It is the virtue of one who is free from pretense and hypocrisy, one who is not self-seeking, but other-directed, a person with openness of heart that manifests itself by generosity. It is the emphasis on generosity that caused some translators to sometimes translate the word as *liberal* or *liberality*. However, like the word *gay*, the word *liberal* has a different meaning than it used to, and we need to take care not to impose a modern understanding on an ancient term. The term suggests a consistent application of love— *charity* in the Authorized Version, where charity is the outworking of *agape*. You've heard of "tough love." Here we have dumb love, love that doesn't second guess motives, but just responds with kindness.

Godly sincerity (*eilikrineia*) differs from simple sincerity in that it focuses on purity. The Greek word literally means cleanness and implies purity. It is the opposite of a foul-mouthed response. Unlike people who swear without thinking, so that trash just jumps out of their mouths as a first impulse, Paul wants Christians to have purity and innocence jumping out of the mouths of Christians as a first impulse in every situation. It is an application of Matthew 5:8, where Jesus taught, "Blessed are the pure in heart, for they shall see God." But we must remember that Jesus also said, "Behold, I am sending you out as sheep in the midst of wolves, so be wise as serpents and innocent as doves" (Matthew 10:16). We are to be dumb to evil, as in naive —without worldly wisdom. We are to be simple-minded or singularly focused on Christ. But we are not to be so stupid or foolish as to put our faith in danger.

Resisting Evil

Paul used the word *sincerity* (*eilikrineia*) in his previous letter, "Let us therefore celebrate the festival, not with the old leaven, the leaven of malice and evil, but with the unleavened bread of sincerity and truth" (1 Corinthians 5:8). Our world teaches us to be cool, to be knowledgeable in the ways of the world, and not to be saps because saps are easily taken advantage of by the wicked.

Kindness is exploitable. We usually think that it takes a hard-nosed person to resist the advances of a hard-nosed person, so we find that the common attitude in the world is that of dog-eat-dog. We think that in order to protect ourselves from evil we must become like those who would exploit us, but this is exactly the opposite of what Paul counsels here.

Paul does not want Christians to be taken advantage of, but neither does he want us to become just like the dog-eat-dog world in which we reside. The world teaches that the only way to resist evil is to become familiar with it, to fight it with its own tactics. If you don't know when you are being taken advantage of, you will always be on the losing end. To defend ourselves we think that we must meet cunning with cunning and evil with evil. In order to know when evil threatens us, the world teaches that we need to anticipate evil intentions in order to meet force with force, evil with evil, cunning with cunning. But that is not what Paul thought.

Paul here taught that we must distinguish between trust and purity. We are not called to blindly trust everyone we meet. Knowing the depravity of sin, we need to be wiser than that. Rather, we are to meet evil with good. Jesus taught, "Love your enemies, do good to those who hate you, bless those who curse you, pray for those who abuse you" (Luke 6:27-28). But don't be stupid. Be faithful!

The last in this trio of responses is grace (*charis*). We are to meet the world with grace—gratitude expressed through the excellence of manners and social conduct. And because grace is a gift of God, it also carries an obligation of thankfulness. We should be thankful in everything.

This is much of what Paul has been talking about regarding the experience of God's comfort in the midst of affliction. Because God unleashes His comfort in Christ in comparable measure to the intensity of the affliction, we need to respond to the difficulties of affliction with increased thankfulness, not for the affliction, but for the comfort that accompanies it in Christ. Yet, because of our sin we fail to tap into the comfort of Christ apart from the pain and difficulties of tribulation. Indeed, the comfort is always available, but we tend to ignore it when we don't feel a particular need for it. Fortunately, the greater our need the greater Christ's comfort is available to us.

DISCRETION

The negative sanction Paul gave is to respond, "not by earthly wisdom" (v. 12). Here discretion points out the difference between Christians and non-Christians through the denigration of earthly or worldly wisdom, a theme that Paul has been pressing hard. His point is not to belittle the character of others, but to accurately illuminate the character of the world, Satan's playground.

From our reading of First Corinthians we understand this to be a call to separation from the values and aesthetics of worldliness, to not entangle the self-centered humanism of unregenerate thinking in the simplicity and purity of God's Word. It is a high calling, yet it is not above the reach of the lowest, most ignorant Christian. And yet, having grasped it, the highest and most erudite believers will never drain God's Word of its full meaning and implications. It is a call for discrimination, the distinguishing between two similar but different things—godly wisdom and worldly wisdom.

Paul then testifies that he has behaved in this manner toward the Corinthians, even though he has been denigrated by the leaders who oppose him. He has set his behavior as a model for Christians to emulate, and he calls all Christians to behave similarly in order to call others to emulate them in the midst of their own situations, *etcetera ad infinitum.* It is a process of discipleship replication and multiplication through imitation, and it has been very successful.

It is a wonder how the early church fathers and Christian mystics have failed to understand verses 13-14, and twisted their plain meaning. Granted, these verses are a little obtuse, but the plain meaning is not difficult to see, unless you don't want to see it. "For we are not writing to you anything other than what you read" (v. 13) means that there are no hidden messages, nor has Paul given anyone any oral teaching that is in any way different in character than what he has written—no secret messages, no separate oral tradition or "deposit" other than what is here in plain sight.

RECOGNITION

Paul seems to have anticipated that his words would be misunderstood. Indeed, he had already been misunderstood by the Corinthians and was working to correct that misunderstanding. So he added that the Corinthians needed to add their acknowledgment to their reading, and he then repeated his hope that they would fully acknowledge (*epiginōsko*) what they had read. The Greek word literally means *recognize* and in my opinion would be better translated by this word. Paul hoped that they would read what he wrote and recognize the message and meaning as coming from the apostles, those in harmony with Paul, in conformity with the true gospel of Jesus Christ. It cannot be overemphasized that he was arguing against the Corinthian teachers of worldly wisdom. And if they didn't recognize the whole of what he was saying, he hoped that they would at least recognize some of it.

The acknowledgment or recognition here applies to both what has been said and who has said it. In the case of Scripture the two things cannot be separated, what is said is dependent upon who said it, and, visa versa. The Person who is speaking through Scripture is what makes what is said important. What is said is valuable because it is authoritative, and conversely because it is authoritative it is valuable. These two things cannot be separated, but it is possible to only partially understand a thing. So Paul hopes that the what and the Who will be fully acknowledged or recognized.

Paul knew that people love to be proud, people love to boast about various things that give them a critical edge, a leg up or advantage. So, he prayed that the Corinthians would boast about the apostles, about Jesus, about Paul and Timothy because that boasting would help to spread the gospel of Christ. It would create buzz, in contemporary marketing parlance. It would get people talking about Jesus.

So, said Paul, "on the day of our Lord Jesus you will boast of us" (v. 14). The traditional understanding of the "day of the Lord"[2] was that it was a day of judgment, a day of calamity because of God's judgment against sin. On the day of judgment, said Paul referring to the impending destruction of Jerusalem that he had spoken of in First Corinthians, they would boast of him because he would have called it correctly.

They would be spared because they listened to him and made preparations—and that would be their boast. *Paul had been right*, they would boast! On that day Paul and the apostles would also boast of the Corinthians (and all Christians) inasmuch as they listened and heeded Paul's words. Using the natural tendency of people to boast, Paul then used that tendency to help promote the gospel, both before and following the dreaded day of the Lord that would soon come upon Jerusalem.

That was their boast, but what is ours? What can we boast about?

---

2   Isaiah 13:6, 13:9, 58:13; Jeremiah 46:10; Ezekiel 13:5, 30:3; Joel 1:15, 2:1, 2:11, 2:31, 3:14; Amos 5:18, 5:20; Obadiah 1:15; Zephaniah 1:7-8, 1:14; Malachi 4:5; Acts 2:20; 1 Corinthians 5:5; 1 Thessalonians 5:2; 2 Thessalonians 2:2; 2 Peter 3:10.

Only Christ. As the ancient Corinthians could boast in Christ, so can we. As the ancient Corinthians could imitate Paul by discerning the comfort of Christ in the midst of affliction, so can we. As the ancient Christians anticipated the great and awful day of the Lord, so can we. It (the judgment) will come again. He (the Judge) will come again. As the ancient Corinthians abandoned the ideals and methods of worldly success in order to cling to Christ alone by faith alone, so can we. Our calling is their calling.

What calling? To recognize the value of behaving in the world with "simplicity and godly sincerity, not by earthly wisdom but by the grace of God" (v. 12).

3. SECOND GRACE

And in this confidence I intended to come to you before, so that you might have a second benefit, and to pass by you into Macedonia, and to come again out of Macedonia to you, and to be brought on my way toward Judea by you. Then purposing this, did I indeed use lightness? Or the things that I purpose, do I purpose them according to the flesh, so that with me there should be yes, yes, and no, no? But as God is true, our word toward you was not yes and no. For the Son of God, Jesus Christ, who was preached among you by us; by me and Silas and Timothy; was not yes and no, but in Him was, yes! For all the promises of God in Him are yes, and in Him Amen, to the glory of God by us.
—2 Corinthians 1:15-20

We are here faced with what some people purport as the absolute proof of a so-called second work of grace in the tradition of John Wesley. And no Bible makes this more clear than the English Standard Version, "so that you might have a second experience of grace" (v. 15). It looks like this Holiness doctrine is clearly taught here. We need to examine both the context and the actual Greek to be sure.

Paul set this idea up by saying, "Because I was sure of this" (v. 15), the vast majority of the other versions translate the phrase as "in this confidence." Either is fine. It is not the translation here that is of concern. Rather, we need to understand what this phrase refers to in order to determine the context. Of what was Paul sure? What was Paul confident in (or of)? What had Paul been talking about?

He had been talking about the grace of suffering, the grace of affliction, or more accurately, the grace that comforts our troubles and tribulations. We are not far into this letter, and up to this point that has been Paul's primary subject. So, we can trust that Paul was referring to that grace, the grace (blessing, comfort) that accompanies affliction.

19

HOLINESS

In order to understand the issue we need to examine this so-called second work of grace that has been so controversial since Wesley. Some scholars have contended that Wesley's doctrine of entire sanctification, the reason for existence of Methodism and the Holiness tradition, was a natural filling out of certain deficiencies in Reformation doctrine. They conclude that his teaching of the possibility of the believer's freedom from willful sin and perfection in love in this life wedded the Reformation's concerns for salvation by faith alone with the Roman Catholic ethic of love. Consequently, Wesley stood directly in the line of the "magisterial" reformers. This Reformed-Anglican-Methodist rootage of the holiness revival is one factor which tends to tie the movement to the now existing "mainline" churches of the Christian tradition.

...The holiness revival in America was born in the 1830s out of the efforts of its Methodist founders to restore the experiential knowledge of Wesley's evangelical perfectionism to the central position which the doctrine traditionally had held in Methodism. At the same time, the movement's conviction that the grace of Christian perfection—or entire sanctification, or the Baptism of the Holy Ghost—was Biblical and was to be the normal expectation of every believer's experience aroused a sense of evangelistic responsibility among its ardent advocates to spread their gospel of "Full Salvation" to Christians of every ecclesiological, theological and social stripe. The extensive Arminianization and Methodization of American religion prepared the field for a more ready acceptance of the holiness revivalist's message among non-Methodist evangelicals than might otherwise have been possible.[3]

Here we see that perfectionism (or entire sanctification—the belief that perfect or complete sanctification is possible in this earthly life) is a central doctrine of Methodism. The Holiness doctrine that the "Baptism of the Holy Ghost" brings the Holy Spirit into the life of the believer and that the power and perfection of the Holy Spirit eventually eliminates the believer's sin, that the perfection of God in the Holy Spirit overcomes all of the believer's sin(s)—all of which is, of course, true. But the controversy involves the timing of all of this. Do Christians attain to sinless perfection in this life? Or, according to the tradi-

---

3   *Primitivism In The American Holiness Tradition*, by Melvin E. Dieter, Wesleyan
Theological Journal, Volume 30, Number 1, Spring, 1995, Wesley.nnu.edu.

tional understanding, in future glory beyond this life?

There are other verses that Holiness scholars use to make their case, but this one seems to be irrefutable to them. However, the Holiness position is not the traditional position inherited by the church. The traditional understanding of this verse, as exemplified in John Gill, is that Paul's visit to the Corinthians would provide the Corinthians with a second grace, meaning another benefit or blessing. The Corinthians would benefit from receiving and reading this letter, and then when Paul got there, they would receive a second (or another) grace (another benefit or blessing). They would be blessed by reading Paul's letter, then they would be blessed again when he visited them.

I suppose it could be argued that they would grow by reading Paul's letter, then when Paul visited them he would help them grow more, grow deeper in the faith. Such a reading is fine, even probable in that in his first letter Paul had been calling the Corinthians to a deeper maturity in the faith. If this suggested second blessing refers to an increased maturity through sanctification by the presence and power of the Holy Spirit, then it's true. Christians can and do continue to grow and mature in faithfulness all their lives.

However, this does not mean that Christians attain to perfection in this life, though there is no doubt that Christ calls us to perfection. Christ's call to perfection in this life does not establish that such perfection is actually possible, any more than Christ's call to follow Him means that we are able to perfectly follow Him.

Please listen carefully.

Growth In Grace

Here is my best understanding of how this works: Christ calls people to follow Him in perfection because God's law requires us to be perfect because God cannot tolerate sin. God is perfect and calls us to be perfect so that we may have fellowship with Him. However, perfection is beyond our best abilities. We are caught in a river of sin that was unleashed by the sin of Adam. We cannot escape from this river. The current is too strong and the river is too wide.

So, God sent His Son, Jesus, to rescue us by fulfilling the requirements of perfection for us, on our behalf, as a surety or down payment on the perfection that Christ purchased for us on the cross through His perfect obedience. Consequently, the call to obedience and perfection is a call to rely upon Jesus Christ through the power and presence of His Holy Spirit through regeneration. But, and this is the important point, it is a call issued to us while we are yet sinners.

Consequently, this call is not a call to moral perfection in this life, but is a call to increasing faith in Jesus Christ in this life in the sure and certain hope of fellowship with God. That fellowship with God will require our perfection. But since perfection is not true of us now, it will come to us in the future, assuming God's promise of fellowship is true. We live in the world and the world is full of sin. Because of our current weakness and sin's current tenacity, the complete elimination of sin will require a kind of cultural reboot or retooling of humanity, an imposition of God's order on this earth that John speaks of as a new Jerusalem coming down from heaven (Revelation 21:2). As long as humanity is caught in the current world system (culture, government, etc.), which has been growing since Jesus walked the earth, we are caught in sin. "If we say we have no sin, we deceive ourselves, and the truth is not in us" (1 John 1:8). We are called to perfect holiness, and yet perfect holiness will only manifest itself when God's earthly mission is complete.

Of course, we are called to increasing holiness, even to complete sanctification in Christ and in God's time. But the conclusion of that process will not happen in this life (Westminster Confession of Faith 13:2; Romans 7:18, 7:23; Philippians 3:12; 1 John 1:10). It can't because it requires the perfect holiness and complete sanctification of all of extant[4] humanity, not just various individuals and/or churches. It requires the complete perfection of the whole of humanity because we are trinitarian beings, made in the likeness or image of God. Our identity is tied up with our families, friends, culture and nation. So, as long as there is sin in any of these, there is sin in us as individuals. Perfect holiness will require the complete eradication of sin in the whole world.

The outer edges of our personal identities as individuals are porous to the culture in which we live. Characteristics of the culture in which we live leach into our lives, and our personal characteristics leach into the culture in which we live. This is only to say that we are influenced by culture and culture is influenced by us—of course, some of us have more influence than others. Nonetheless, we are not who we are in and of ourselves. Rather, we are who we are in the context of our family, friends, church, culture and nation—and most importantly in the context of Jesus Christ, in whom we live and move and have our being (Acts 17:28). So, look around and tell me if you see any sin in our world! If you do, we are still a long way from perfection.

Of course, God could zap the world and fix everything, and eventually He will. But that is not the way that God has chosen to work with us in this time and in this place. Scripture is full of God's miracles, and yet miracles are not God's chosen means of operation in our time (the

---

4 *Extant* means still in existence; not extinct or destroyed or lost.

New Testament time). Miracles are possible, but not likely because God now uses Word and Sacrament as His preferred means.

We still live in the midst of the unfolding of the New Testament period. God has chosen to work His plan, not ours. And His plan is detailed in Scripture. We are called to faith in Christ as God's means of salvation and sanctification, for our good and for God's purposes, which will be increasingly revealed as we comply and grow in faithfulness. God is working through faith in Christ, not by miracles. Christ is our miracle! And in the light of Christ, other miracles pale in significance.[5]

BUILDING BLOCKS

God uses the people in His church as building blocks by which to build His church (1 Peter 2:5). This is critically important. Each member must be placed, aligned and mortared (attached and in relationship) to his or her nearest neighbors through the exercise of his or her gift(s). This model for the church requires a specific, geographic, local church model and mindset in order to function. Each member needs to reach and establish a gospel relationship with six others.

Why six? If you think about how bricks are laid, you see that each brick touches two other bricks on top, and two on the bottom, and one on each side. The specifics of this analogy are not important, but the general character is. Each one reaches several others. That's the point. This is the foundation for exponential growth. And that's the model.

The point of all of this is that the biblical model for church growth requires individual spiritual growth and maturity. So, if you insist on calling your initial movement into a relationship with Jesus Christ a work of grace, you will be correct. And if you insist on calling your continued spiritual growth and maturity in the faith a work of grace, you will again be correct. Salvation is all of grace, as is sanctification. And, therefore, if you insist on calling your initial coming to the Lord a first work of grace and your continued growth and maturity a second work, that's okay. Traditionally, these are referred to as salvation and sanctification and are differentiated. I suppose there is nothing wrong with calling them a first and second work of grace, though we need to be careful not to import by suggestion all of the unbiblical Holiness baggage attached to the latter term.[6]

And while it is ultimately true that God's plan is to eliminate sin

---

5   For more on miracles see *Arsy Varsy—Reclaiming The Gospel in First Corinthians*, Phillip A. Ross, Pilgrim Platform, 2008, chapter on God's Endowment/Miracles and Paul's List/Miracles.

6   That baggage being the unbiblical idea that people can attain perfection in this life. Such an idea is very dangerous and liable to abuse by prideful sinners.

from human experience, and it is true that God will complete that plan, it is not true that you or I or our great grandchildren will experience the complete elimination of sin in our lifetimes—unless God zaps it all in place. And, of course, that is not beyond God's power.

But since we know that God has taught us through His Word that such zapping is not His ordinary means of accomplishment in this New Testament era, and that God sent Jesus to live among us as our only Savior and established His church for the accomplishment of his will, and intends to use His ordinary means—Word and Sacrament—to accomplish His will in this world, we need to distinguish between the very real hope in the incremental accomplishment of God's purpose and the unreal and wistful hope that God will just miraculously and instantaneously zap everything in place apart from our active obedience, growth and involvement in His church.[7] There is a real hope and accomplishment that is progressive in nature, and there is a false hope for the instantaneous accomplishment of God's will that is imaginary in nature. Please be careful to note that I am not using the word *progressive* in the contemporary liberal sense, nor am I suggesting that God cannot work miracles—He most assuredly can, and still does! Rather, I am suggesting that many—maybe most—people have a false understanding of miracles. But that is another subject for another time.

The reason that the traditional understanding of the second grace mentioned in verse 15 is related to Paul's visit to Corinth is in part that verses 16-20 are a defense regarding some confusion that had developed about Paul's visit. Remember that Paul had promised to visit the Corinthians and was then delayed when his life was threatened by circumstances beyond his control. At that point Paul's enemies criticized Paul for not being responsible, for not following through on his promises, and suggested that Paul was not trustworthy. It appears that Paul was responding to such accusations in these verses.

Trustworthy

He mentioned that he did not treat his promise to visit them lightly, his promise was not fickle. Rather, he suggested that his promises—and ours by extension—are made in Christ and that Christ's promises are trustworthy, as should ours be. When God says *yes*, He means yes. God's promises are always trustworthy. Paul used the opportunity of his accusation of not following through on his promises to preach about the trustworthiness of God, who always follows through on His promises.

---

7   Sorry for the long sentence, but it's a big idea.

Based upon God's trustworthiness, Paul then suggested that because he was a disciple (or servant or steward) of God through Jesus Christ, his own (Paul's) promises would also be true, even if there were sometimes mitigating circumstances that were beyond his control. It had been Paul's intent to have an extended visit with the Corinthians to provide them with the additional blessing (grace) of his presence, his perspective and faithfulness in order to help them get back on the gospel track. And in spite of the setbacks and difficulties, he would follow through, even if his original time estimates proved to be impossible to keep.

Paul's concern here has been the faithfulness of God. God will fulfill His promises—even His promise of the ultimate perfection of His people. But, suggested Paul, that's a big promise and will take a long time. However, just because it will take longer than we want, doesn't mean that it won't happen. And neither does it mean that there aren't any benefits to the long strategy of progressive salvation by faith alone in Christ alone through Scripture alone.

There are great benefits in this life, even though we continue to wrestle with sin all our lives. Over time there is real growth and maturity in Christ's people. And the blessings of genuine Spiritual growth and maturity in Christ are greater than the first blessing of conversion. There is a second grace because sanctification—maturity in Christ—is real. Praise be to God!

4. FIDELITY

But He confirming us and anointing us with you in Christ is God. And He has sealed us and having given the earnest of the Spirit in our hearts. And I call God as witness to my soul that in order to spare you I have not yet come to Corinth. Not that we have dominion over your faith, but we are helpers of your joy; for by faith you stand.
—*2 Corinthians 1:21-24*

P aul had established that God's promises are trustworthy. God will not forget His people, nor renege on His promises. What God has promised will come to pass. And because Paul was a servant of God, because Paul had been called by God to proclaim and clarify God's promises to the Gentiles—people who did not previously know God or His trustworthiness—the promises that Paul made on God's behalf were also trustworthy, because they were God's promises, not merely Paul's.

In verse 21 Paul set out the foundation of his relationship with the Corinthians. It was God Himself who had authorized and established that relationship. Paul called attention to three things. First, he wrote that the relationship was between *us* and *you*. Obviously, the *you* was the Corinthian church, those to whom Paul was writing. And the *us* was the people whom Paul represented and/or traveled with. At this point only Timothy had been named. So, the *us* was Paul and Timothy. There was a special relationship between Paul and Timothy and the Corinthian church.

Second, there was also a special context of that relationship. It was "in Christ" (v. 21). The relationship was between people who were in Christ. To be in Christ is not simply a time or location, as if someone was in Pittsburgh or was in the year 2008. Rather, to be in Christ suggests that those who are in Christ are also of Christ in the sense that they are working toward the purposes of Christ, that they are doing what they are doing, acting, behaving with Christ or because of Christ or through Christ. All of these prepositions point to the meaning of being in Christ. A person in Christ is subsumed by Christ, his purpose and actions are motivated and empowered by Christ. Such a person is overshadowed by Christ, driven by Christ, dominated by Christ. Being in Christ is like being in a vehicle in which Christ is the driver.

Paul was not simply saying that he and Timothy were in Christ, but that he and Timothy and the Corinthians were together in Christ. They were all in Christ together, all motivated, subsumed, empowered, overshadowed and dominated by Jesus Christ. Christ was the context of their relationship. They may have been friends, maybe some were blood relatives, but the significant thing about their relationship was not the friendship, nor their family ties, but the fact of their being in Christ together. They were in fellowship with Christ together. This is important because those in Christ have a different relationship than those who are not in Christ. Christ is the context of their relationship, and being in Christ makes an important difference, and that difference is real.

ANOINTED

Third, Paul said that God "has anointed us" (v. 21). There are three things of importance to note here. First, that it was God who did the anointing. God was the authority who established the relationship. Second, the "us" who were anointed were Paul and Timothy. There may have been others, but who they were is lost to antiquity at this point. Third, Paul and Timothy had been anointed by God to a special relationship with the Corinthians.

What does it mean to be anointed? From the oldest records we find that people in the Middle East applied oil—vegetable oil or animal fat—on their skin. This application was referred to as anointing. People were anointed for health reasons and for hospitality—skin care in desert climates is important. Over time people began to use better oils, scented and other upscale oils. The word literally means rub or smear and implies contact. It came to mean appoint, or qualify for a special dignity, function or privilege. And we find that Israel's kings were anointed with oil as a symbol of their authorization for office. In the New Testament anointing was associated with sickness and health. Sick people were anointed with oil as part of their treatment. And church officers were anointed into office in the same way that Israel's kings had been anointed into office. Luke wrote that "God anointed Jesus of Nazareth with the Holy Spirit and with power" (Acts 10:38).

Paul used the word *anoint* (*chriō*) here to suggest that he and Timothy had been given a special office among the Corinthians. It is interesting and of some significance that he said that it had been God

Himself who had anointed them to office, and not the Corinthians. Whether or not the Corinthians had participated in that anointment is not known, and because of God's involvement it is of less significance. Nonetheless, the point was that it was God Himself who had called, prepared, facilitated, anointed and empowered Paul and Timothy for office among the Corinthians.

Sealed

Paul went on to say that God had "also put his seal on us and given us his Spirit in our hearts as a guarantee" (v. 22). A seal is a mark of ownership. Think of a king who seals a letter by imprinting the image of his signet ring into hot wax to hold the letter closed and to identify it as being authentically his. It was a way of authenticating and guaranteeing that the message contained in the letter came from the king. To say that Paul and Timothy had been sealed by God meant that they had God's stamp of ownership upon them, that God Himself had authenticated them and their message of the gospel.

To identify exactly what that seal was is more difficult. But whatever it was it would be recognized by those who were familiar with God. Just as a person could know the sender of a letter by the particular seal it bore, so the Corinthians would know Paul and Timothy because they bore God's seal, God's identifying mark or image. That the seal was nothing other than the message of the gospel itself. The message of the gospel of grace is uniquely recognizable by God's people. And we know that Paul understood that the gospel itself "is the power of God for salvation to everyone who believes" (Romans 1:16). The gospel is the image and likeness of God Himself in that it is the power of God's grace.

Yet there is another element of the seal that Paul mentioned. God had put His seal upon them and had also put His Spirit in their hearts. This is a reference to regeneration, wherein the Spirit of God, God's Holy Spirit, comes alive in the life or heart of a person. That Spirit animates and marks a person in a way that is uniquely identifiable. Anyone who is familiar with the marks of the Holy Spirit, who is familiar with how the Holy Spirit works and the changes that result from regeneration is able to identify someone so marked, not perfectly but usually.

There is also a caveat. Not everyone will recognize God's Spirit. Why not? Because it takes one to know one. I can identify another regenerate person because I know what God's Holy Spirit has done to me. I know how God has changed me, so I can recognize similar changes in other people. But if a person has not been regenerated by the Holy Spirit, he will not know or recognize or value regeneration in others. Because the marks of regeneration are personal and subjective, and because regenerate people are intimately aware of how God has changed them, because they know that the changes in their own lives are real, they can trust that similar marks—changes—in other people are similarly real—again, not always, but usually. The reality of the Holy Spirit in our own lives provides a guarantee of the reality of the Holy Spirit in the lives of others who are similarly marked.

MY PROOF

The guarantee of God's reality and of the power and presence of the Holy Spirit is found in the hearts of believers. My own changed life is the proof and guarantee of God's reality for me. Your own changed life is the proof and guarantee of God's reality for you. We are the proof of the existence of God. Such proof is not found in an argument. It is not found in the text of the Bible. It is not found in history. It is found through my own regeneration, and through your own regeneration. And if a person is not regenerate, it is not found at all—not apart from God's judgment.

The whole world stands under the judgment of God as a result of Adam's sin, and our personal guilt is exacerbated by our own sin. When God's judgment is manifest, all doubt about God's reality is quelled because God's judgment has a drastic effect upon this world and the world to come, in eternity. Every so often God brings change to everything by the imposition of His will in judgment.

But by grace alone God moves to rescue people from this context of judgment in this fallen world. God's plan will take many generations to unfold in its full glory, and when it is complete all evil will be destroyed and all extant[8] people will live in the context of God's salvation. The process of salvation will be progressive in that evil will be eliminated over time as increasing numbers of people find themselves regenerated by the grace of God.

Paul called upon God to witness the truth of what he had said. God knows the truth of every person in every situation. No one can hide anything from God. So, to call upon God to witness something is to invite God's scrutiny. At the very least it is to say that, to the best of your ability to understand and speak truth, you believe that what is being said is the truth, that it is not wrong or deceitful. Because God knows everything and cannot lie, to call God as a witness is the strongest confirmation possible that you are telling the truth. By calling God as a witness, you are putting your life on the line.

Some people may rashly call upon God to be such a witness,

---

8   See footnote 3, p. 22.

without full consideration of the consequences of such action, but not Paul. Paul knew full-well that calling God to witness to the truth of something was a very serious matter because it brings the full weight of God's judgment to bear upon the situation. If there is any deceit or error in something, God will find it out.

HESITATION

Paul said that he had been hesitant to return to Corinth in order to spare (*pheidomai*) them from something. The Greek suggests that his concern was to treat them leniently. The implication was that a previous visit had been a source of strife and difficulty in that Paul had taken serious exception to much of what the Corinthian leaders were doing and teaching, and that his previous visit had been a source of strife and conflict. So, he was hesitant to return in order to spare them additional difficulties. I suspect that Paul did not want to return before the conflict had been sorted out because he would likely call down God's curse upon the Corinthian church for the horrendous sins of the leaders (and others). Rather, he probably hoped and prayed that God would correct the situation before his next visit, without Paul having to lose his temper in righteous indignation.

Exactly what Paul was concerned about is implied rather than stated. All we have are various hints. It seems that he was afraid that if he came and confronted them about their faith, they would come out in a bad way. He didn't seem to be threatening any particular action on his part. Nonetheless, in the light of Christ they—at least some of them—would not measure up. We see this in verse 24, "Not that we lord it over your faith, but we work with you for your joy, for you stand firm in your faith."

Paul said that the concern was not some consequence that he would impose upon them because he had authority over them. He reminded them that Christian authority was a function of service, not administrative power or political manipulation. Gospel authority is not a matter of domination over another person, nor over their faith, neither their practice nor their understanding of it.

TRUTH

Gospel authority is not a matter of imposition but of inspiration. Gospel truth does not need to be imposed upon others, neither with their willing compliance, nor against it. Truth doesn't need to push people around. Rather, truth draws people into itself. Truth is inspirational. It is liberating and contagious. The authority of truth is like the power of light over darkness. It is dispelling, it dispels the illusions that tend to dominate our lives.

We know about the psychological power of denial, and how denial can alter a person's perception of reality. Denial is a defense mechanism by which a person who is faced with a fact that is too uncomfortable to accept simply rejects it, insisting that it is not true despite overwhelming evidence. A person in denial about something will bend over backwards in order to avoid seeing unpleasant truths. Such people will intentionally blind themselves to things that they don't want to accept. They fail to see certain things because they will not allow themselves to see them, though they are in plain sight. Such is the case with those who deny God.

When God speaks, truth happens. God spoke and the world was created. But we don't have that kind of power. When we speak God's truth, it is more like turning on a light. The light doesn't create what is in the room, it simply reveals it. It makes known what was previously unknown. It makes clear what was previously unclear. Similarly, God's authority makes things happen. And when we speak on behalf of God's authority, things are revealed for what they are. God's authority, like God's Word, is a light in the darkness.

Paul was worried that if he visited Corinth before they got some of the concerns that he had been writing about under control, the light that he would bring them through a personal visit might be more than they could bare. Sometimes too much light too soon can have a blinding, rather than a revealing effect. A bright light after a long period in darkness can be hard on the eyes. He did not want to lord over the Corinthians, and have them feel inadequate in the light of his genius. He knew that those endowed with the Holy Spirit would grow from the exercise of their faith. Like learning to swim, they needed to jump in and splash about. You don't learn to swim by reading a letter or a book. But he didn't want them to get in over their heads too soon.

Paul understood himself as a co-laborer (*sunergos*) with them, not as an instructor over them. He was working with them to increase their joy in the Lord, not simply to get them to think right, though thinking right is certainly valuable. If they found no joy in the faith, they would soon leave it. He wanted to increase and enhance their joy in the Lord as a way to draw them into deeper sanctification.

By Faith

The English Standard Version (ESV) has reversed the word order of the last phrase in verse 24. Most of the other versions put *faith* before *stand*, and do so in a causative way—suggesting that it is the exercise of faith that results in standing firm. The ESV makes it sound like Paul was affirming them as having been faithful, "for you stand firm in your faith" (v. 24). But that is not what he was doing, not what he was saying. His letters to the Corinthians were not an affirmation of their faithfulness, but quite the opposite. So, in the larger context of the letter the traditional word order is to be preferred, "for by faith ye stand" (AV). He was not celebrating their faithfulness, but pointing them to it.

It is by faith that we are saved, and by faith that we are able to stand, to hold our ground, to maintain our position in the Lord. Of course we hold onto Christ by faith, but He also holds us by His faith. And it is His grip on us that saves us, not our grip on Him, though our grip on Christ is not unimportant. We need to hold on to Christ with all our strength, but trust that it is Christ's strength that will hold on to us in the final analysis.

5. SUFFICIENT INSTRUCTION

*But I determined this within myself, that I would not come to you
again in grief. For if I make you sorry, who then is he who makes me
glad, but the same who has been made sorry by me? And I wrote this
to you, lest when I came I should have sorrow from the ones of whom I
ought to rejoice; having confidence in you all, that my joy is the joy of
you all. For out of much trouble and anguish of heart I wrote to you
with many tears, not that you should be grieved, but that you might
know the love which I have more abundantly to you. But if anyone
has caused grief, he has not grieved me, except in part; so that I not
overbear all of you. This punishment by the majority is enough for
such a one; so that, on the contrary, you should rather forgive and
comfort him, lest perhaps such a one should be swallowed up with
overwhelming sorrow. So I beseech you to confirm your love toward ·
him. For to this end I also wrote, that I might know the proof of you,
whether you are obedient in all things. But to whom you forgive
anything, I also forgive. For if I forgave anything, for your sakes I
forgave it to him in the person of Christ; so that we should not be
overreached by Satan, for we are not ignorant of his devices.*
—2 Corinthians 2:1-11

This second chapter shows that Paul was very aware of the critical content of his previous letter(s), He knew that many of the Corinthians personally felt the sting of his criticism. And until they resolved the issues that he had communicated in those letters, he did not want to return. If those issues were not resolved, he would have to rehash things that he had already covered. Paul knew that God's method was to provide people with additional truth as they required or needed it, as they adapted to what had already been given.

God gives us truth, and as we learn from it and accommodate it into our lives, He gives us more. But if we fail to learn from what He has already given, He stops. Until we learn to handle what He has already given us, He won't give more. To do otherwise would be a waste of His time and ours because truth is accumulative.

Speaking of the truth being accumulative Isaiah asked, "To whom will he teach knowledge, and to whom will he explain the message? Those who are weaned from the milk, those taken from the breast? For it is precept upon precept, precept upon precept, line upon line, line upon line, here a little, there a little" (Isaiah 28:9-10). Coming to understand God's truth is a function of maturity in Christ. It takes time, patience and perseverance.

REMEDIATION

In the same way, if Paul were to personally visit the Corinthians before they had digested and implemented what he had already given them, they would not be ready to learn more. So, at that point all Paul could do would be to rehash what he had already given them. His chastisement of them for their failure to apply what he had already taught them would be increased in order to spur them into additional growth or remediation. Paul did not want his relationship with them to be overly colored with admonishment, when it should be full of joy in the Lord. And he told them so plainly.

In verse 3 Paul said that he wrote critically so that they would fix the problems he addressed before he got there. That means a couple of important things. First, it means that they were able to fix them, to apply what he had taught them, without his physical presence, without his having to personally mollycoddle them. It means that his first letter provided sufficient instruction. It means that Scripture is sufficient. That is good news because it means that we, too—Christians of every age, don't need Paul to be physically present to make good use of his words. Paul knew that his words—God's words—needed to be sufficient unto themselves through the power and presence of the Holy Spirit.

Paul used the phrase "you all" twice in verse 3. His point was that the joy that he expected from them was a function of "you all." It was a corporate thing, a function of their unity in Christ, and as long as that unity was as broken as it was because of the sin in their midst, the result of his meeting with them would not be joy but pain. He would be pained by their sin and brokenness, and they would be pained by his response to their sin. But later, when he would see them, after they had addressed the problems by applying the instructions he gave them in First Corinthians, his joy in their unity, in their wholeness, in the reconciliation that would result from following those instructions, would then be their joy.

THE PROCESS

The pain of their sin would become the joy of their reconciliation as they applied Paul's instructions. Their joy in the reconciliation and unity that resulted from their obedience to God's Word would be all the greater. Then, when Paul's joy in them was added to their joy of reconciliation in Christ, the joy of his visiting with them at that point would be even greater. That's what Paul wanted, and that was what he was aiming for in his previous letter.

In verse 4 Paul went on to slobber all over his parchment because he was so emotionally stressed. He described it as affliction (*thlipsis*)—tribulation—anxiety and distress. But it was not an expression of grief, nor should they be grieved by his emotional state. Paul longed to share the joy of the Lord with them, but he knew that they needed to grow through the sanctification that comes through brokenness and reconciliation. They needed to experience the power of God's call to righteousness—and its difficulty, the power of their own sinfulness—and their helplessness before it, and then experience the propitiation and reconciliation in Christ through obedience to God's Word. This process would give them a greater understanding of Christ's way and God's mission. Paul's emotional pain was a consequence of his love for them. He was hurting because they were hurting.

If there was blame to attribute in the midst of their situation, it did not belong to Paul. It did not originate with Paul. Paul did not cause the problem, though he had responded to it. If anyone has caused you grief, said Paul, implicating the errant leaders whom he had been striving against, and knowing the pain and grief that had been caused by their situation, it had hurt them more than it had hurt Paul. He was saying that their efforts to discredit him and to cause him personal pain had failed.

Sure, it hurt him some, "in part," he said, but not much, not really. It didn't hurt him enough for him to blame (*epibareō*) them. Not a single translation uses the word *blame* in verse 5, but it is the best word to describe what Paul said. *They were trying to get at me,* said Paul, *trying grieve me, and they did a little. But not so much that I blame all of you* (my paraphrase). He was not about to blame the many for the actions of a few, but neither could he ignore the sins of a few. Discipline was needed and discipline had been given (1 Corinthians 5:11). That was enough.

Young's Literal Version best expresses the meaning of verse 6, "This censure by the majority is enough for such a one." In his previous letter, Paul told the Corinthians "not to associate with anyone who bears the name of brother if he is guilty of sexual immorality or greed, or is an idolater, reviler, drunkard, or swindler—not even to eat with such a one" (1 Corinthians 5:11). That was enough. If the person was reformable, he'd reform.

There are several lessons here. First, church members don't have to go chasing after each other, and bend over backwards to try to get someone caught up in sin to come back to church, as if church attendance will resolve the problem. Yes, reconciliation is important. But if the reconciliation doesn't happen with the Lord first, it won't happen with anyone else. So, said Paul, just excommunicate the offending person and allow the Holy Spirit to either draw him back into fellowship through repentance, or confirm him as unrepentant.

THE TURNAROUND

But once the person has demonstrated repentance, we should beat a path to his door and welcome him back into fellowship. Once repentance breaks out it needs to be encouraged and rewarded because repentance is the heart of Christianity.

It appears that the punishment had been instituted in the church, and that the offending person had turned from his sin. This is seen in verses 7-8, "so you should rather turn to forgive and comfort him, or he may be overwhelmed by excessive sorrow. So I beg you to reaffirm your love for him." Christian discipline must be quick and consistently applied by all of the church members. And then, when repentance is demonstrated, the church must also be quick and consistent in its application of forgiveness and reconciliation.

Paul went on to say that the purpose for his writing this second letter was two-fold. First, to test the obedience of the saints, to see if they would actually follow the instructions he had previously provided. This was not only a test of them, but also a test of the sufficiency of Scripture, to see if his instructions were adequate. And second, the purpose was to outwit Satan, who is a master strategist. Satan would have the Corinthians believe that it was necessary for Paul himself to personally deal with the sin in their midst. After all, the guilty party had been a church leader, an elder. How could they, who were not elders, discipline an elder? How could an elder discipline an elder of equal rank?

They may have been thinking that it would take someone in a higher administrative position to discipline an elder, which would make sense from a chain of command perspective. In such a situation, a lower ranking person could not bring discipline to bear upon a higher ranking person. If the church was an administrative, chain of command, top-down organization, then disciplinary measures would have to be bumped up the chain of command so that higher ranking officers could adjudicate and impose the necessary discipline. This was how it worked in the rest of the world. Governments, like armies, had their chains of command.

Mutual Accountability

But, because authority in the church didn't work like authority in the world, that was not how Paul recommended dealing with the situation. In the world, in the domain of Satan, that would be the way to handle it because in the world the power of authority flows from the top down. But, as Jesus said in Matthew 20:25-27, the power of authority in the church is derived, not from lording it over people, but from service. Church authority is not top-down, nor bottom-up. Rather, church authority is trinitarian. It issues from the power and presence of the Holy Spirit, and blows where it will (John 3:8).

Church authority is interdependent, and has three centers or sources of power: 1) one is through the governors, the officers. Church elders have authority. 2) Another aspect of church authority comes through the governed, the laity. Those who are governed authorize their own leaders. And 3) another aspect of church authority comes through the Holy Spirit. Truth is power. Both the governors and the governed must be attentive and responsive to the authority of the Holy Spirit, the authority of the truth.

If the Corinthians had bought the line that all church authority is top-down, chain of command authority, Satan would have had the upper hand because he would have removed, obscured or undercut the other authority centers of the church. The worldly model of authority would have been applied to the church. In a top-down system, Paul or another high-ranking apostle would have to go to Corinth and supervise the discipline, or intervene in some way. But God needed a governing system for the churches that would be self-correcting. God needed a trinitarian government for the church because God is trinitarian, and the church, even more than man himself, is an institution made in God's own image, a trinitarian image.

So, the test that Paul mentioned was a test of the effectiveness of the self-government of the Corinthian church. When operating in obedience to Paul's righteous instructions about how to handle errant sinners—regardless of their rank or position in the church—the Corinthians established that Paul's instructions were themselves sufficient to both apply the necessary discipline and to extend the gracious forgiveness and reconciliation in the face of repentance.

Paul was building upon Jesus' teaching in Matthew 6:1, "For if you forgive others their trespasses, your heavenly Father will also forgive you." Jesus also said, "Pay attention to yourselves! If your brother sins, rebuke him, and if he repents, forgive him" (Luke 17:3). And most importantly, toward the end of His ministry, Jesus "breathed on them and said to them, 'Receive the Holy Spirit. If you forgive the sins of anyone, they are forgiven; if you withhold forgiveness from anyone, it is withheld'" (John 20:22-23). So, when Paul said, "Anyone whom you forgive, I also forgive. What I have forgiven, if I have forgiven anything, has been for your sake in the presence of Christ, so that we would not be outwitted by Satan; for we are not ignorant of his designs" (vs. 10-11) he was simply teaching what Jesus had taught. Paul put Jesus' teaching into practice.

The situation in Corinth had been resolved by following Paul's instructions. The errant sinner(s) had been admonished and excommunicated. So, Paul now told them that when the disciplined sinners demonstrated repentance, they should be immediately welcomed back into fellowship. No grudges should be held. God's forgiveness, grace and mercy should be immediately extended. God does not hold it back, and neither should we. God is always after repentance and reconciliation.

6. Smelling Christ

When I came to Troas to preach the gospel of Christ, even though a door was opened for me in the Lord, my spirit was not at rest because I did not find my brother Titus there. So I took leave of them and went on to Macedonia. But thanks be to God, who in Christ always leads us in triumphal procession, and through us spreads the fragrance of the knowledge of him everywhere. For we are the aroma of Christ to God among those who are being saved and among those who are perishing, to one a fragrance from death to death, to the other a fragrance from life to life. Who is sufficient for these things? For we are not, like so many, peddlers of God's word, but as men of sincerity, as commissioned by God, in the sight of God we speak in Christ.
—2 Corinthians 2:12-17

At verse 12 Paul begins a digression about his travels. Part of what Paul said here was that he had certain plans and expectations that had not been met. Though providence did not allow him to do what he had planned to do, the Lord continued to provide for his ministry by blessing what he actually did do. He went to Troas because the Lord had opened a door for ministry there, but, because Titus was not there, he did not stay. He left and went to Macedonia, hoping to find Titus there.

This is very interesting. The Lord opened an opportunity to preach the gospel at Troas, and Paul went. But then he seems to have left almost immediately to look for Titus. With a door to the gospel open in Troas, you'd think that Paul the evangelist would have stayed because of the opportunity there. But he didn't. Scripture doesn't say, but I imagine that Paul did not abandon the opportunity at Troas, but likely left someone else to preach there.

Paul was not a one man show. He was able to trust others with the gospel, as he had trusted Timothy at Corinth (1 Corinthians 16:10).

Scripture doesn't say who preached at Troas, and it doesn't really matter. The fact that there was an opportunity there, a door opened by the Lord, meant that there were people there who would be responsive to the gospel. That's an ideal situation in that the people were eager to hear the Word. It doesn't take a great preacher to reach those who are clamoring to hear the gospel. Such people will relish in any morsels of truth they can find. It seems that Paul left the low hanging fruit in Troas for others to harvest. Paul was on a mission. He was headed for Rome. He wanted an audience with the Emperor. Paul was aiming to convert the whole Roman Empire. So, he left the easier tasks for others, and set his sights on reaching the Roman court.

But first Paul needed to see Titus. So, he went to Macedonia. Titus had some primary responsibilities for the ministry at Corinth, and it appears that Paul preferred to work through the existing authority structures, rather than supersede them. Paul referred to Titus as "my true child after a common faith" (Titus 1:4), which suggests that Titus was probably one of Paul's Greek converts and a trusted associate. Being Greek, Titus could help bridge some of the cultural issues that would come as a result of Paul's teaching and preaching. And because Paul took the Greek mindset to task at Corinth, support from Titus would have been helpful.

THANKS BE TO GOD

At verse 14 we find Paul breaking out in praise for God. Was he excited about what God was doing in Troas or about his connection with Titus in Macedonia? We don't know. He doesn't really say. And it doesn't matter. Paul was excited about what God was doing everywhere and praised God often.

The first thing that he praised in this case was the fact that "Christ always leads us in triumphal procession" (v. 13). Paul was praising and celebrating Christ's sovereignty in leadership. A door of opportunity had opened at Troas, which Paul seems to have left to others so he could go find Titus. It is likely that the preaching at Troas had been fruitful and that his meeting with Titus had been helpful. So, he broke out in praise for God's leadership in Troas, and in Macedonian—and everywhere. Praise flowed freely from Paul's lips.

The triumphal procession that Paul mentioned was a reference to the Roman army parading captured soldiers after a battle as a demonstration of its supremacy and power. As they marched through the defeated town or city, the ranking general would lead the procession showing off their booty—captured soldiers and other defeated leaders in chains. The procession was a celebration and a demonstration of Roman power, intended to leave an impression on the locals, to dissuade them from further rebellion.

Paul used the term (triumphal procession) to describe Christ's power, suggesting that nothing, not even Rome itself—the most powerful force in the world of its day—could stand before Christ. Christ was conquering the world, capturing souls and taking prisoners in a mighty procession, a celebration and a demonstration of God's power. Paul had taken this term of Roman dominion, this symbol that struck terror into people everywhere, and used it for God's purpose, to demonstrate that God had dominion over Rome itself.

On The Scent

Part of the image that Paul used was related to fragrance—odor. It's a very interesting image, as if the gospel has a smell to it. Odor is a kind of universal communication that communicates unseen through the air, without words. Related to the word *oder* is the word *essence*, which can mean both the most elemental aspect of a thing in a philosophical sense and the smell of a thing. *Essence* is a philosophical word used to indicate the heart of a thing, as well as a special part of a thing. The two words—*smell* and *essence*—can sometimes be used interchangeably.

Here's another connection: The frontal lobe of the human brain, the part of the brain that is responsible for the higher functions of thinking, is directly connected to the olfactory sensors. It appears that the frontal lobe may have developed as an extension or outgrowth of the olfactory bulb, the part of the brain responsible for interpreting smell. Or at least there is a proximal relationship. This idea suggests a biological link between knowledge and smell.

And we find that dogs and other animals "know" a thing by smelling it. I don't want to make too much of this, but neither do I want to ignore it. Smell offers an additional dimension of knowledge, it conveys information. It communicates something understandable at some level. For instance, have you ever experienced the smell of death? We can identify similarities and differences in smell, but more generally we find that we either like a smell or we don't. Smells are pleasing or they aren't. Some smells are attractive, and some are repulsive. And that seems to be part of what Paul meant here.

This triumphal procession that Paul mentioned, the procession of Christ conquering the world, "spreads the fragrance of the knowledge of him (Christ) everywhere" (v. 14). Note that as Christ moves through a town or city or area or whatever awakening, reviving, reforming, regenerating people, everyone becomes aware of Him, of His smell. Proximity increases the intensity of the smell.

But not everyone has the same reaction. Paul said, "We are the aroma of Christ to God among those who are being saved and among those who are perishing" (v. 15). Everyone can smell Christ as He sweeps through an area captivating and changing people. But not everyone interprets the smell in the same way, not everyone has the same experience, not everyone likes what they smell. People have different responses to the essence of the gospel.

LIFE OR DEATH

Paul's language is startling as he describes different impressions or experiences of Christ, "to one a fragrance from death to death, to the other a fragrance from life to life" (v. 16). The Greek suggests a causal link, as if to say that the smell of death leads to actual death and the smell of life leads to actual life. To one person Christ smells like death because his rejection of Christ points to his own ultimate death through damnation apart from Christ. And to another, Christ smells like life because his acceptance of Christ points to his own ultimate life in Christ through salvation.

In spite of anything said, the smell of Christ communicates the judgment of God on the basis of Christ alone. Believers are grateful, unbelievers are incensed. It is not that the gospel of Jesus Christ sometimes succeeds and sometimes fails to reach people. No! Christ never fails. Rather, it is that the gospel is successful in different ways among different people. To some, the success of gospel communication is the sweet smell of salvation, and to others the success of gospel communication is the rancid smell of rejection—their own rejection of Christ, and Christ's rejection of them. To some people the gospel provides energy, drive, purpose, incentive and direction. For others it does not. Unbelievers find it frustrating, confounding, confusing, offensive and useless. But everyone reacts to it, everyone perceives it, everyone interprets it one way or the other. Everyone can smell it when it draws near.

Note also that it is not simply the gospel that smells, but that it is we who "are the aroma of Christ to God among those who are being saved and among those who are perishing" (v. 15). We smell. Those who have been regenerated in Christ smell. Christ smells through us. Yes, the gospel smells, but the smell gets attached or associated with particular people, people who represent the gospel, who re-present Jesus Christ.

We might think of the smell of the gospel as attraction or distraction. Those for whom it smells of life are attracted to it. They like it. But those for whom it smells as death, those who don't like it, are distracted from it. To them it smells bad, like rotten eggs, and they are repelled by it.

This whole smell issue is curious. Paul said, "Who is sufficient for these things?" (v. 17). The Greek word translated sufficient (*hikanos*) suggests competency and greatness. The idea indicated here is, "Who can understand or explain it?" One person says it smells like life and another says it smells like death, but it is the same gospel and the same smell—at least it should be. All we can do is love Christ and preach the gospel. And in doing that some people will be attracted and some will be repelled by the same message.

WHAT ABOUT THEM?

But there is another concern. Paul said, "For we are not, like so many, peddlers of God's word, but as men of sincerity, as commissioned by God, in the sight of God we speak in Christ" (v. 17). We are not to fret about who is attracted to the gospel and who isn't. When people get worried about that, and think that someone or some group of people ought to come—or ought not to come—to Christ, but who, for whatever reasons don't, they can be tempted to change or soften the gospel message in order to make it more appealing, in order to attract or repel certain people, or a certain group. We see a lot of that kind of thing today. And Paul said here that it is wrong to do that.

Paul said that Christians are not to be peddlers of God's word. We are not selling the gospel message. The Greek word *kapēleuō* can also be translated as *huckster*. The word refers to retailers and those who sell for a living. There is a great temptation to think that the job of the preacher or evangelist is to sell the gospel and that the better the sales presentation, the more people will buy what he sells. But that is not what Paul said here.

Of course, we want the gospel to be effective. We understand that the promise of the gospel is to convert the whole world, that in the fullness of time "every knee shall bow" (Roman 11:14) to Christ. And, indeed, these promises are true. But that does not mean that we are to market the gospel, to use a contemporary idiom. The gospel is not for sale, nor do people buy it, or buy into it. The gospel is not for us to have or possess. Nor is it an investment. It is not ours.

Arsy varsy, the gospel belongs to God. Gospel ownership is not transferred, nor is it transferable. The gospel does not belong to the church, rather the church—the people of God—belong to the gospel. This is very important because it means that we are not to dress it up or tone it down. We cannot argue people into a position where they will receive it. People are not converted through our argumentation. The gospel is not an argument. Preaching is not a debate. The gospel of

Jesus Christ is an announcement, a proclamation, a statement of fact.

Our job is to speak the gospel correctly and let the chips fall where they will. The more we try to talk people into becoming Christians, the more we distort the gospel. Why? Because those who perceive it as an aroma of life unto life don't need to be convinced. They are convinced already. And those who perceive it as an aroma of death unto death will not be convinced. It is disgusting to them, and the more clearly it is presented the more disgusting it appears.

We can't change people's minds. Oh, we can sometimes influence some trivial, shallow things, but not the deep things, not essential beliefs. Of course, by the grace of God, the Holy Spirit can change hearts—and does. But you and I can't change someone else's heart. God can! But we can't. We can only present the gospel correctly, accurately, historically, and pray that God will change the hearts of those who hear it.

RELEVANCE

Contrary to popular opinion, one of the worst things that we can do in the face of unbelief is to try to soften or make the gospel more palatable to unbelievers. As we do that, unbelievers watch us mold the gospel to fit their expectations and they come to think that the gospel is what they falsely expect it to be—and it isn't! Or they come to think that people can make the gospel whatever they want it to be. We see a lot of this today. A lot of people do this, but it is wrong. The gospel is not whatever we want it to be. It is what God has given us in Scripture.

This is not a new problem that has only recently come about. Paul said that there were many in his day who peddled the gospel. That is undoubtedly what they had been doing at Corinth. Indeed, this is a huge temptation because it is the perspective of the flesh. It is our natural understanding asserting itself. And the natural man is a proud man, proud of his intelligence and understanding, proud of what he can do. He thinks that he can understand everything and do anything. And, indeed, people are indeed smart. But understanding the gospel is not a function of intelligence. It is a function of regeneration. Smart unbelievers misunderstand the gospel, and they do it intelligently. In fact, it is usually their intelligence that misleads them.

Rather, said Paul, we are to be people of sincerity (*eilikrineia*)—purity, cleanness, integrity. It's okay to be smart, but apart from regeneration, all people are lost and cannot understand the gospel of Jesus Christ.

We are to announce the gospel to everyone, and sell it to no one. We are not to withhold it from anyone, but to proclaim it to everyone.

We are not to sell it, nor to try to convince people that they need it by turning the gospel into some sort of self-improvement tool or some kind of life insurance policy. But we are to do what we can to help people understand it correctly. So when we hear false versions of the gospel, we are to speak up and correct them. We are to do everything we can to insure that false understandings of the gospel are not communicated, that people don't mistake the gospel for something that it isn't.

Rather, we are to get the gospel right under people's noses, and make sure that people get a good whiff of it. And to some it will smell sweet. To some it will be like ammonia nitrate and will wake them up from their stupor. Others will recoil in revulsion. Some wake up refreshed and want more, and some wake up grouchy and want none of it. Nonetheless, at that point, clarity will prevail as some people are attracted to Christ and others are distracted from Christ.

Regardless of their reaction, all will serve the glory of God through the Person of Jesus Christ. Some will serve God's glory by receiving the mercy of God through the grace of Jesus Christ. Here God's mercy is glorified through Christ's propitiation on the cross. Others will serve God's glory by receiving the unmitigated judgment of God by rejecting the mercy of Christ. Here God's righteousness is glorified through the damnation of unrepentant sinners who refuse to acknowledge the superiority of God's righteousness. The fact that God cannot tolerate unrighteousness is not a divine character flaw, but contributes to the reality of God's perfect goodness.

"He who has ears to hear, let him hear" (Matthew 11:15).

7. SPIRITUAL INK

Are we beginning to commend ourselves again? Or do we need, as
some do, letters of recommendation to you, or from you? You
yourselves are our letter of recommendation, written on our hearts, to
be known and read by all. And you show that you are a letter from
Christ delivered by us, written not with ink but with the Spirit of the
living God, not on tablets of stone but on tablets of human hearts.
Such is the confidence that we have through Christ toward God. Not
that we are sufficient in ourselves to claim anything as coming from
us, but our sufficiency is from God, who has made us competent to be
ministers of a new covenant, not of the letter but of the Spirit. For the
letter kills, but the Spirit gives life. —2 Corinthians 3:1-6

Paul began this chapter by denouncing self-commendation as an
act of pride. The clear communication here is that Christians do
not need to boast of themselves. But there is more. In the second
verse he went on to say that Christians don't need letters of recommendation to or from anyone because such letters may not express the
truth. They can be mistaken and misleading. They are not always trustworthy.

And yet, Paul has not completely abandoned the use of letters to
introduce and/or accompany Christians as they travel. Paul recommended Timothy to the Corinthians in 1 Corinthians 16:10-11, and similar letters were used in response to the Jerusalem Council in Acts 15.
So, we need to balance Paul's statements here with other verses that
provide justification for the use of such letters. And, that being the case,
we need to understand what Paul was objecting to here, if not the
wholesale abandonment of such letters.

Given that Paul had a legitimate concern, and that some letters of
recommendation were in use, we can surmise that Paul's concern was

the abuse of such letters. And what constituted such abuse? They were abused when the content of the letters did not match the character of those that were recommended. The letters were okay as long as they accurately portrayed the character and faith of those who were being recommended.

Paul's Recommendation

Putting this concern in the larger context of Paul's letters to the Corinthians we can see that Paul's concern was that some of the people who were leading the Corinthian church astray, either had letters of recommendation regarding themselves, or had themselves produced some letters of recommendation for some of the people they approved of—people who would have been against Paul, or who had letters of discommendation against Paul. Paul's concern may have been that there was a discrepancy between what those letters said and the actual character and/or faith of the people they mentioned. Or perhaps that those letters were critical of Paul and those who worked with him. Thus, Paul was arguing against the value of those letters. It was an integrity issue.

So, Paul asked the Corinthians to pay less attention to the letters of recommendation or criticism and more attention to the actual character and faith of people. It was as if the leadership of the Corinthian church had been recommending unfit people for leadership and ministry for whatever reasons, or discommending fit people, and Paul argued that those letters were as corrupt as the people who wrote them. Whether they argued for particular people or against particular people, the values, beliefs and worldview of the authors permeated the letters and, in this case, rendered them corrupt and useless.

Therefore, said Paul, fix your attention on the values, beliefs and worldview—the character and faith—of people, and make your own decision upon that criteria. Because, said Paul, "you yourselves are our letter of recommendation, written on our hearts, to be known and read by all" (v. 2). Further, Paul instructed the faithful Corinthians to demonstrate that they were themselves letters "from Christ delivered by us, written not with ink but with the Spirit of the living God, nor on tablets of stone but on tablets of human hearts" (v. 3). In other words, said Paul, your lives, your character and faith are the recommendations of Christ.

Paul was arguing that truth was not simply a matter of writing something down, because words can always be twisted one way or another. Just as Scripture itself can be made to appear to support any argument whatsoever—and has been used to do just that all too often. So, any written argument can be twisted beyond recognition by skillful orators, philosophers and/or lawyers. We see this kind of thing all the time, particularly in matters involving truth and integrity, character and faith. In fact, Paul's primary concern regarding the Corinthians and running through both of his letters to them was that there were leaders among them who had been hoodwinked by Greek philosophy and paganism who had been doing just that—twisting the truth, the gospel—to suit themselves, arguing that the gospel was an abstraction rather than a reality and justifying every sort of belief and behavior in the name of Jesus Christ. Leaders in the Corinthian church were doing just that.

CHARACTER

So, Paul asked the Corinthians to compare the faith and character of those who opposed him with the faith and character of those who supported him. He told them not to depend completely on the various letters that had been generated in the midst of their conflict—neither his own nor those of his opponents. Rather, he was arguing for the consistency of the gospel of Jesus Christ with the Spirit of those who were arguing about that gospel. He knew that the correct and orthodox assessment of various written arguments was difficult. It would require more than trusting someone's recommendation. It would require reliance upon the power and presence of the Holy Spirit, and in the fact that the Spirit would correctly lead those who were truly animated by the Spirit, that the Spirit would lead correctly beyond what they themselves could understand.

The Holy Spirit always does this. He always leads us correctly beyond what we can understand because no one can completely understand the gospel of Jesus Christ in its fullness. Is not the mystery of the Trinity beyond the smartest and most erudite people? Of course it is—and yet the Holy Spirit is trustworthy. Faithfulness is not a function of intelligence. It is not opposed to intelligence, but intelligence alone—apart from the faithfulness of regeneration—will always lead a person astray. Only when intelligence takes its cues from God, from Scripture, and from the power and presence of the Holy Spirit through regeneration does it faithfully become a trusted servant of the Lord.

So, said Paul, do not commend yourselves, do not get caught up in defending your own integrity or faithfulness because one's own arguments about one's own integrity and/or faithfulness are worse than useless. Self-justification is never trustworthy because self-justification is at the heart of original sin. Sin has twisted our perception of self and of reality. People can justify anything, any behavior and/or belief, and a brief review of the various world religions will confirm this important fact.

In addition, Paul said that the Corinthians themselves served as letters of his recommendation in the flesh. Paul had taught them correctly and set them on the path of faithfulness before this latest conflict had erupted. And Paul knew that the Spirit of truth would overcome this conflict and that the true Spirit of Christ would prevail among them. So, said Paul, inasmuch as you actually believe the truth and are actually filled with the Holy Spirit, you yourselves will be all of the testimony and recommendation that I need. Your faith will commend me, said Paul. Your faithfulness will prove that my version of the gospel is correct.

CONFIDENCE

"Such is the confidence that we have through Christ toward God" (v. 4). Paul was not only confident of the gospel of Jesus Christ to accomplish all of the promises of God, but he was confident of his understanding of that gospel. How could he be so confident? Because he was aware of his own conversion. He knew of his own surrender to Christ, of his own deferment to Christ, of his own regeneration in Christ. And because of this, he was not trusting in himself. He was trusting in Jesus Christ. And that was exactly what he said, "Not that we are sufficient in ourselves to claim anything as coming from us, but our sufficiency is from God" (v. 5).

This is an interesting argument in that we today trust in the sufficiency of Scripture, and rightly so. Paul was not contradicting the sufficiency of Scripture, but he was correcting the idea that any particular book of the Bible or any particular letter—thinking of his letter to the Corinthians—was in and of itself sufficient. The Westminster Confession of Faith 1:4 says, "The authority of the Holy Scripture, for which it ought to be believed and obeyed, depends not upon the testimony of any man, or Church; but wholly upon God (who is truth itself) the author thereof: and therefore it is to be received because it is the Word of God."

God is the source of the sufficiency. And furthermore, according to the Westminster Confession of Faith (WCF) we find that sometimes the teaching of one verse needs to be contrasted and/or balanced with the teaching of another verse, and that the truth of Scripture is available to all regenerate Christians through ordinary means. God's Word is sufficient because God is sufficient.

So, as good as this second letter to the Corinthians is, it is not sufficient in and of itself, but it depends upon the rest of the Bible through the understanding of a born again reader. As such, it rests, not on its own sufficiency, but upon the sufficiency of God Himself.

Know Your Enemy

Did this mean that Paul thought that he knew everything there was to know about the gospel? Not at all. But because his own life had been so completely and thoroughly turned upside down by Christ on the road to Damascus, he was able to recognize both truth and falsehood. Why? Because he knew that his previous life, his previous worldview had been backwards, inside out, upside down, arsy varsy. Because he had been a well-educated person in that Pharisaic worldview he knew that particular falsehood well. He knew how that false worldview worked, how it thought, how it reasoned, how it justified itself. So, he was able to recognize it whenever he saw it functioning.

And because he had been so immersed in that view, because he was so familiar with it, his own conversion was all the more clear because of the contrast. The result of his conversion was so stark, so different than his previous worldview that the contrast provided a degree of clarity that was astounding. No one had traveled the worldview distance that Paul had traveled through his conversion. The clarity of his understanding of the gospel was enhanced by his education and ability to articulate the Pharisaic worldview. His training and education in the enemy camp made him a particularly valuable and astute convert because he could out argue the enemy at every point. He knew what they were thinking and where they were going with their arguments before they did. So he could anticipate their arguments and defeat them before they began. Consequently, his confidence was not a false confidence, but a real confidence.

However, it should also be noted that Paul was not out to defeat the Pharisees, but rather was out to frame and proclaim the gospel of Jesus Christ to the whole world. It wasn't that he was arguing against the Pharisees, but that he was arguing for the New Covenant of and in Jesus Christ. He was arguing for the gospel.

Paul, answering the question he asked in 1 Corinthians 2:16, "Who is sufficient for these things?" stressed that "our sufficiency" is not from ourselves or from our own abilities but "is from God" (v. 5). Because Paul had argued for the wisdom of God and against the wisdom of the world, we know that Paul's opponents at Corinth were defending and promoting the worldly wisdom of logic and rhetoric as taught by their culture. The Greek perspective, which Paul had previously called human wisdom (1 Corinthians 1:22, 2:1, 2:5, 3:19) was the worldview against which Paul argued.

Alfred North Whitehead, an influential modern philosopher wrote, "The safest general characterization of the European philosophical tradition is that it consists of a series of footnotes to Plato."[9] Indeed, Paul was arguing with much of what has come to be Western Civilization.

Paul also said that God has made us competent to be ministers of a new covenant" (v. 5). The Authorized Versoin (AV) says that God "made us able," other translations say that God made us sufficient, efficient, even worthy to be ministers. The Greek word (*hikanoō*) means that He enabled us. The point is that the source of the ability to minister is not ourselves, but is from God. God is the source, the foundation. God is our sufficiency.

OLD AND NEW

Verse 6 brings up the contrast between the old and new covenants and the corresponding action of each—death versus life. This is the contrast that Paul spoke of in Romans 7:6, "But now we are released from the law, having died to that which held us captive, so that we serve not under the old written code but in the new life of the Spirit." And in Romans 8:2, "For the law of the Spirit of life has set you free in Christ Jesus from the law of sin and death."

What did Paul mean when he said that "the letter kills, but the Spirit gives life" (v. 6)? His reference to "the letter" was not a reference to all written material in existence or ever to be produced, but was a specific reference to the Old Testament, the Bible that Paul knew. It was a reference to the whole of the Old Testament and served to provide a contrast to the New Testament, the New Covenant in Christ that he was working to articulate. He did not mean that as soon as you write anything down it becomes a spiritual killer. Rather, he meant that he and others were actively working to demonstrate that God's truth, the truth of the Holy Spirit, was greater than anything that could be written, that the Holy Spirit could not be completely captured in the written word. God's mind is greater than our minds.

The reference had to do with the fact that the function of God's law, given in the Old Testament, was to convict sinners, to show people the demands of God's law, God's way of life, and to demonstrate to us that our sin nature, resulting from Adam's sin in the garden, kept us (all humanity apart from Jesus Christ) from fulfilling or satisfying God's law. Obedience to God's law apart from Christ was and is not possible. God requires perfection and we are not capable of perfection. Thus, the law reveals our ultimate inability and consequent death apart from Christ. It is essential to understand this because it sets up or reveals the problem that Christ solves. If we deny or fail to correctly understand our situation, our problem, our status before God as sin-

---

9   *Process And Reality*, Alfred North Whitehead, Free Press, 1979, p. 29.

ners, we will deny or fail to understand our need for Christ, and our dependency upon Him to provide what we cannot provide for ourselves.

In Christ is forgiveness, propitiation—whatever you want to call it, but which Paul calls life. In Christ is life. In the Old Covenant is only death without or apart from Christ. And in contrast, in the New Covenant is life with or in Christ. The significance of this verse is the revelation of the New Testament or New Covenant in Christ, issuing out of the context of the Old Covenant. It is the death of the old and the life of the new. It does not mean that writing a thing down turns it into a death dealing legalism. Rather, it means that holding on to the Old Covenant in the face of the New Covenant in Christ leads to death. It serves to call sinners to new life in Christ. And people apart from Christ are nothing but sinners, so it calls all people to new life in Christ.

8. GLORY

*Now if the ministry of death, carved in letters on stone, came with
such glory that the Israelites could not gaze at Moses' face because of
its glory, which was being brought to an end, will not the ministry of
the Spirit have even more glory? For if there was glory in the ministry
of condemnation, the ministry of righteousness must far exceed it in
glory. Indeed, in this case, what once had glory has come to have no
glory at all, because of the glory that surpasses it. For if what was
being brought to an end came with glory, much more will what is
permanent have glory. Since we have such a hope, we are very bold,
not like Moses, who would put a veil over his face so that the Israelites
might not gaze at the outcome of what was being brought to an end.
But their minds were hardened. For to this day, when they read the
old covenant, that same veil remains unlifted, because only through
Christ is it taken away. Yes, to this day whenever Moses is read a veil
lies over their hearts.*   —2 Corinthians 3:7-15

Paul continued to distinguish between the Old Testament and the
New by contrasting the glory ascribed to each. To understand the
contrast requires understanding the biblical use of the word
glory.

The word first appears in Scripture in Genesis 49. Jacob was on his
death bed prophesying about his sons and future generations of their
children. He was speaking about the strife between Simeon and Levi,
who were brothers. Of them he said, "weapons of violence are their
swords. Let my soul come not into their council; O my glory, be not
joined to their company." (Genesis 49:5-6).

The Hebrew word translated as *glory* (*kâbôd*) literally means weight
or heavy. The term can be traced back to the tent of meeting traditions
prior to the monarchical period, which began with Saul, and referred to
the radiance, or supernatural awe-inspiring sheen that was described as

inherent in things divine and royal. It suggests that the one possessing glory is laden with riches (Genesis 31:1—gold is heavy), power (Isaiah 8:7—the heavy man defeats the lighter man), and position (Genesis 45:13—riches and power provide the foundation of social position). The term can imply both a terrible splendor and a special garment, cloak, or headgear, which are all symbols of power, position and prestige.

This ancient word also suggested the idea of reputation or honor that was associated with men of position and power. It also referred to the manifestation of light by which God revealed himself, whether in the flash of lightning or in the blinding splendor that often accompanied various visible manifestations of God (i.e., the burring bush of Moses in Exodus 3:2, the whirling wheel of Ezekiel 32:8). The same kind of thing is found in the cloud which led Israel through the wilderness and became localized in the tabernacle.

The Greek word *doxa* (glory) is a translation of the Hebrew, which provided an additional shade of meaning. Our doxology is an expression of glory to God. Sometimes the idea of glory is substituted for the person who possesses it as if the two are identical. God's manifestation is always glorious—heavy, weighty, rich and powerful.

Show Me

When Moses said, "Show me your glory" (Exodus 33:18), he was not speaking of the light by night or the cloud by day, which he had already seen, but he was seeking a special manifestation of God which would leave nothing to be desired (much like Philip in John 14:8, "Lord, show us the Father, and it is enough for us"). Moses had a desire to come to see or to know God as He was in Himself, to see or know God in His fullness.

But God could not do that without harming Moses. Moses did not understand what he was asking, much like the disciples who wanted to sit at the right and left hands of Jesus. Jesus responded, "'You do not know what you are asking. Are you able to drink the cup that I am to drink?' They said to him, 'We are able'" (Matthew 20:21-22). They had an inflated understanding of their own abilities. They were not able. The glory of God is too heavy, they could not bear it. The crucifixion and the dispensation of the Holy Spirit were still in the future, and apart from these two things the glory of God is unbearable.

Consequently, God emphasized his goodness to Moses. Upon Moses' request to see God's glory, God said, "I will make all my goodness pass before you and will proclaim before you my name 'The Lord.' And I will be gracious to whom I will be gracious, and will show mercy on whom I will show mercy" (Exodus 33:19). The word *goodness* (*ṭûb*) might be translated in this instance as moral beauty. Apart from this sense of moral beauty, the perfection of God as a subject of human contemplation could be quite depressing because God's perfection reveals our sinfulness by contrast. This incident involving Moses provides the idea that God's glory is not confined to some outward sign which appeals to the senses, but is that which expresses God's inherent majesty, His greatness, and points to what we call the spiritual realm, which is visible only to the eyes of faith.

Isaiah's vision of God (6:1ff.) included both His visual and His spiritual features, particularly his holiness (see John 12:41). The intrinsic worth of God, his ineffable majesty, constitutes the basis of warnings not to glory in riches, wisdom, or might (Jeremiah 9:23) but in the God who has given all these things, and who is greater than His gifts. In the prophets the word *glory* is often used to set forth the excellence of the messianic kingdom in contrast to the limitations of the present order (Isaiah 60:1-3). Long story short: to see God is to see His glory. And conversely, to see His glory is to see God Himself.

God's Law

Coming back to Paul we note that there was a glory exhibited in the law, in the Old Testament. This means that to see or understand the Old Testament law is to see God. The law was/is a manifestation of God. It is heavy, rich and powerful. But Paul calls the law a "ministry of death" (v. 7) and a "ministry of condemnation" (v. 9) because the purpose and function of the law is to convict and sentence sinners. According to God's law—think of the Ten Commandments—humanity as a whole, and to a person, is guilty of sin and deserving of death and damnation.

But, Paul asks, "will not the ministry of the Spirit have even more glory?" (v. 8). Here is the contrast. Jesus Christ and the gospel of salvation by grace through faith trumps the law for all people who are in Christ. Paul also calls the law "the ministry of righteousness" and says that it "must far exceed it in glory" (v. 9). The ministry of righteousness is, of course, Christ's righteousness, not ours. We don't have any righteousness apart from Christ. It is ours by virtue of our union with Christ or our participation in the unity of Christ through the gift(s) of the Spirit. Of the two glories or manifestations of God—the law and the gospel, the greater glory is the gospel of Jesus Christ.

At this point arises a significant confusion among too many Christians. The issue has to do with the "end" of the law. Here is what Paul said, "Indeed, in this case, what once had glory has come to have no glory at all, because of the glory that surpasses it. For if what was being brought to an end came with glory, much more will what is per-

manent have glory" (vs.10-11). The Bible in Basic English (BBE) translates it, "For the glory of the first no longer seems to be glory, because
of the greater glory of that which comes after. For if the order which
was for a time had its glory, much more will the eternal order have its
glory." If I may paraphrase: The glory of the temporal order (the law)
pales in comparison to the glory of the eternal order (the gospel).

Does Paul mean that there is no longer any use for the law because
Jesus has come? That the law no longer applies to anyone? No. Jesus
said that He did not intend to change a single thing about God's law.
"For truly, I say to you, until heaven and earth pass away, not an iota,
not a dot, will pass from the Law until all is accomplished" (Matthew
5:18). The references to an iota and a dot are references to letters, or
more generally to writing.

The point of this sentence is that the law, the Old Testament body
of literature generally and more specifically the Torah (first five books
of the Old Testament), needed to remain in existence as they were in
antiquity. The Old Testament as a body of literature needed to remain
available in order to demonstrate how it was that Jesus Christ fulfilled
the demands of the law and would be accurately identified as the
prophesied Messiah of the Old Testament. Nothing in the Old Testament could change, lest the importance, completion and accuracy of
the life and ministry of Jesus Christ be denied, denigrated, belittled or
altered. Because Jesus fulfilled the law, any alteration of that law
would necessitate an alteration of Christ's fulfillment.

Mercy

So, while Jesus Christ fulfilled the demands of God's law, thus fulfilling prophecy and providing propitiation, the fact of Jesus Christ and
His fulfillment of God's law unleashed God's mercy, which impacted
God's law in several ways. Some things about the Old Testament cere-
monial practice of the faith have changed because Jesus fulfilled the
law by satisfying its purpose (telos—end). Various ceremonies have
changed because Jesus, by providing the ultimate sacrifice—Himself—
ended the sacrificial system. After Jesus no other sacrifice was needed.
Further sacrifice beyond what Christ had done on the cross would denigrate the value of Jesus' sacrifice. The sacrificial system has given way
to the sacrifice of Christ "once and for all" (Hebrews 7:27).

Some of the ultimate consequences of the law—eternal damnation,
for instance—have also changed for some people, people in or under
Christ. It is not that the law itself has changed, but that God's mercy
has come into play through Christ. Violators are still guilty and liable
to the consequences of their transgression. Christians are still sinners,
of course, and still continue to sin—though less and less over time. But

Christians are forgiven. Keep in mind that forgiveness only makes sense in the light of guilt. If guilt is gone or not established, then forgiveness is not necessary. Rather, without guilt the case is simply dismissed. Christians are redeemed sinners—guilty, but forgiven, unlike those who are not in or under Christ, who continue in sin and who continue to sin more and more over time, further establishing their guilt and lack of repentance and/or forgiveness. Some sinners are not forgiven because they will not receive forgiveness and remain unrepentant, which means their ultimate course of destruction and damnation remains unaltered.

In addition, some other aspects of the law have changed—not the practice of godly morality, but the authority for the judgment regarding moral failure has been moved from the civil government to Jesus Christ (Matthew 28:18). When we begin to take this seriously, we will find that it means that unrepentant sinners must face the judgments issuing from the Old Testament alone (by themselves), while repentant sinners, covered by the righteousness and blood of Christ, have Jesus Christ as their advocate (1 John 2:1).

This is a complex issue that requires its own book length arguments. I only mention it because Paul mentioned it. The context of Paul's meaning is his larger discussion about the differences between the Old Testament and the New, between the law and the gospel, between rebellion and repentance. Paul was making macro-distinctions that facilitated the rise of the Christian church as a distinct entity, distinct from the Old Testament church (but not independent of it), distinct from the Temple culture (yet built upon it). Christ issued a worldwide cultural change, based upon the Old Testament Jewish culture, but applied to the whole world. In Christ the gospel was thrust upon the Gentiles, the nations of the world, upon all sinners who were under the ancient covenant of creation, what might be called the Garden of Eden Covenant which included the creation of humanity.

Grace

To put it in a few words, grace trumps law for the believer. But because the unbeliever rejects God's grace, God's help, he is left to his own resources to face the preexisting covenantal judgment of God that issued from Adam's sin and has been advanced by his own.

Because of the glory of God, which was manifest in the laws given to Moses, but which pale in comparison to the grace of the gospel given through Jesus Christ, we Christians have hope, and our hope makes us bold (v. 12). *Bold* (*parrhēsia*) here means outspoken, frank, blunt, clear and confident, not in ourselves, of course, nor in what we say. Rather, our confidence is in God alone through Jesus Christ alone according to Scripture alone. However, to be filled with the Holy Spirit does not give us infallibility. Rather, it allows us to trust that God will finish what He began, and use us however He pleases for the accomplishment of His will.

Paul went on to say, we are bold, so we are "not like Moses, who would put a veil over his face so that the Israelites might not gaze at the outcome of what was being brought to an end" (v. 13). God needed to hide the end or purpose of the law that God had given to Moses for the Israelites. Why? Because the end or purpose of the law was to convict Israel of sin, and conviction is a party that no one wants to go to. People don't willingly go before a judge they know will convict and sentence them to death. So, the glory of God that shown on Moses' face was veiled. Listen to this testimony:

> "When Moses came down from Mount Sinai, with the two tablets of
> the testimony in his hand as he came down from the mountain,
> Moses did not know that the skin of his face shone because he had
> been talking with God. Aaron and all the people of Israel saw Moses,
> and behold, the skin of his face shone, and they were afraid to come
> near him. But Moses called to them, and Aaron and all the leaders of
> the congregation returned to him, and Moses talked with them.
> Afterward all the people of Israel came near, and he commanded
> them all that the Lord had spoken with him in Mount Sinai. And
> when Moses had finished speaking with them, he put a veil over his
> face. Whenever Moses went in before the Lord to speak with him, he
> would remove the veil, until he came out. And when he came out and
> told the people of Israel what he was commanded, the people of
> Israel would see the face of Moses, that the skin of Moses' face was
> shining. And Moses would put the veil over his face again, until he
> went in to speak with him." —Exodus 34:29-35

The glory of God manifest in the law given to Moses was too heavy for the people of Israel. They could not bear it, so it was concealed, obscured, in order to calm the fear the people had when they were exposed to God's law. In order for them to willingly engage the law, the point of the law, its end or purpose—the conviction of sin—was veiled (obscured). The people of God did not fully understand what they were doing by engaging God's law, which then setup the coming of Christ who provided full exposure to God's law. That exposure always results in God's judgment, and apart from Christ God's judgment against sin is not good news.

And so, "their minds were hardened. For to this day, when they read the old covenant, that same veil remains unlifted" (v. 14). Wow!

God hardened the minds of the Israelites—His own people—and veiled —concealed—the sharp truth of His law from them in order to fulfill His greater end or purpose through Jesus Christ. The truth of this statement is provided by the historical fact of the destruction of Jerusalem in A.D. 70, resulting from the failure of Israel as a people to embrace Jesus Christ as the long-awaited Messiah. It is not that Jerusalem was destroyed for its part in the crucifixion. No, the crucifixion was God's idea and it could not be avoided. Rather, Jerusalem was destroyed because of the wholesale rejection of Jesus Christ, the Messiah of God—and that rejection continues to this day.

CHRIST

Why would God do that? Paul continues, "because only through Christ is it (the veil) taken away" (v. 14). God was setting up the eventual unity of humanity through Christ for the establishment of the Kingdom of God on earth (Matthew 6:10). Christ is the King! In order for humanity to celebrate corporate unity (corporate in the spiritual sense, not the worldly or legal sense of a national or global corporation), a Head must be established who represents God to His people and His people to God. Christ is, of course, the second Adam, and the current and eternal corporate Head of humanity.

Nations will continue to exist on earth because God is not a global socialist. The world is too big for men to govern from a global perspective, and much of the pleasure and enjoyment of humanity stems from cultural variety. Indeed, cultural variety cannot be eliminated because it is intrinsic to God's plan. At the same time, the vast majority of cultural variety must subsist under the Headship of Christ in the sense that a garden of diverse flowers and fruits may flourish.

As Christ removes the veil, God's judgment will be revealed and applied to all extant[10] humanity, including contemporary Israelis. This judgment will usher in a greater manifestation of the Kingdom of God on earth. No doubt, there are still many chapters to God's redemption story that are yet to be written about the cultivation and harvest of God's garden in Christ Jesus. We should look unveiled and with great hope, expectation and anticipation as the glory of God is poured out upon the nations of the earth in the precious name of Jesus Christ, now and in the future.

Paul then repeated himself for emphasis, "Yes, to this day whenever Moses is read a veil lies over their hearts" (v. 15). Someday God will lift that veil, and Israel will be regrafted into the Kingdom— not by the statutes of the law, but by the mercy of God in Christ

_____
10   See footnote 3, p. 22.

(Romans 11:25-26). On that day the Kingdom will take a giant step forward as God celebrates the return of a prodigal son (Luke 15:11-32).

9. FREEDOM

But when one turns to the Lord, the veil is removed. Now the Lord is the Spirit, and where the Spirit of the Lord is, there is freedom.
—2 Corinthians 3:16-17

The "one" that Paul speaks of here is Jewish because he has been making the case that the Jews have a veil over their hearts and minds regarding the law given to Moses. So, the one who has the veil lifted is the one who has been veiled in the first place. It is significant that Paul was talking about Jews coming to Christ. Nowhere does Paul or any of the apostles suggest that Jews should do anything other than come to Christ, who is the long-awaited Old Testament Messiah.

The idea conveyed in verse 16 is simple, but its implications are profound. Christ lifts the veil. The purpose of salvation is fellowship with God, which requires the propitiation of sin because God cannot tolerate sin. So the reception of salvation requires the acknowledgment of the reality of sin, both the reality of human sin in general and of one's own sin in particular. While it is true that salvation comes by grace through faith in Christ, and while it is true that God's grace is a completely free gift that does not depend upon us or upon anything we can think, say or do, it is also true that those who reject God's salvation do not acknowledge the reality of sin. The failure to accept the reality of sin produces the failure to accept the reality and need of salvation. These two things—sin and salvation—are linked in a dependent relationship. The need for salvation comes out of sin, and where sin is denied so is salvation.

There is more to salvation than personal experience. It is more than an emotional resolution. There is an objective element to salvation in Christ because there is more to it than one's own psyche or spirit. God is creating something objective through salvation or by means of salvation—the kingdom of God. God is building His church with living stones. As Peter said, "you yourselves like living stones are being built up as a spiritual house" (1 Peter 2:5).

GREAT AWAKENING

One of the unfortunate consequences of the Great Awakening in America in the 1700s is the fact that following the Great Awakening Christianity placed its major emphasis upon the personal experience of conversion and neglected other aspects of the faith. Please understand that I am not arguing against the reality or the importance of personal conversion. It is essential, but it is not everything, not by a long shot. Conversion is only the first step of a long journey. And while every journey begins with the first step, and no journey begins without a first step, the first step is only a small part of the journey. Granted that apart from personal conversion one's journey will be a very different journey altogether. Nonetheless, personal conversion is only the beginning.

By placing the major emphasis upon personal conversion Christians have turned their attention from their objective mission to the world, to society at large, to the subjective and personal experience of individual conversion. Where Christians used to be outwardly focused, they have become increasing inwardly focused. Where Christians used to look outwardly to Christ for the impetus for salvation, they increasingly look inwardly to themselves. Rather than trusting outwardly, objectively, in the work of Jesus Christ, too many Christians today seem to trust inwardly, subjectively, in their own personal experience or response to Christ.

And while our attention has become increasingly subjective, we have all but abandoned concern for sanctification, for growth and maturity in the faith. Our attention since the Reformation has been on justification, which according to Luther is "the article by which the church stands or falls," and according to Calvin is "the principle hinge by which religion is supported." This is true. But there is more to Christianity than its principle hinge.

INTROSPECTION

The consequence of this narrow focus has been the abandonment of the work of Christian growth and maturity—sanctification. Today we have more Christians, but they are less mature in the faith. The common practice is to confess one's faith, to experience conversion, and stop there. There are also cultural causes that are outside of the Christian church that have contributed to our dumbing down, our passion for all things adolescent. Unfortunately, in our day maturity isn't popular.

Again, while it is true that all Christians will have a particular subjective experience of Jesus Christ, it is not true that their subjective experience plays a causal or critical role in salvation. Perhaps an analogy will help. When I see a particularly beautiful sunrise, I have a subjective experience of it. It's beautiful. Wow! I am inspired and filled with awe. But my subjective experience is not the cause of the sunrise, nor does my observation of it have any effect upon the rising of the sun. The sun rises whether or not I see it, whether or not I like it, whether or not I'm inspired, whether or not I want it to.

And so it is with Christ. Christ has come to save the world, and our reaction—positive or negative—has no impact on the success of that mission. Christ will save the world with or without us, with or without our participation, with or without our faithfulness. It's a done deal, It's already accomplished, we're just working out the final details. This is the objective sense of Christianity that has been lost in the modern world.

Since the Great Awakening Christians—and, indeed all Americans —have become increasingly subjective and focused upon our personal, individual experience. Americans are known, not as a unified or common people, but as a nation of diverse and unique individuals who favor their own diversity and uniqueness over any expression of national unity, or unity of any kind. This phenomenon is found in both our religious and our secular habits, expressions and life styles. And it is not entirely wrong because each person is in fact a unique individual.

TRINITARIAN

And yet because we are trinitarian beings created in the image of the trinitarian God of Scripture, we, like God Himself, are more than mere individuals. Part of our identity is found in our corporate existence, as a church and as a nation. No man is an island, but rather humanity is a culture in which individuals participate—and our participation in human culture is not merely voluntary, but is a necessary part of our existence. To say "we" is to embrace the collective reality of our existence.

Part and parcel of the establishment of the veil upon the Jews was to hide the end or purpose of the law from them because the purpose of the law was and is the conviction of sin resulting in a sentence of death. Prior to the coming and propitiation of Christ on the cross, the conviction and sentence provided by God's law were intolerable because there was no remedy. The acknowledgment of sin prior to

Christ was a death sentence. Prior to Christ, the revelation of God's law, which showed us our sin, was a revelation of certain and hopeless death and destruction, the likes of which make the modern expressions of existential angst pale in comparison. All of humanity, as a whole and to a person, stand guilty and are condemned by God's law. Apart from Christ that is the end of the story.

Because no one of us can perfectly obey and/or abide by God's law and live in strict obedience to it, no one will escape the temporally destructive and eternally damning power of God's wrath—apart from Christ, that is. We must thank the Lord for concealing this fact from the Jews in order to establish God's law on earth because without God's law humanity would have fallen deeper into the web of sin and selfishness that so retards the development of personal character and cultural improvement.

Both personal character and cultural improvement require an attitude of genuine love and concern for others and a kind of sacrificial abandonment of self-concern for the benefit and welfare of others that no one person can find in and of himself. Such love, concern and sacrificial living issue from the corporate side of our identity. As corporate beings, people who are dependent upon human culture, whose very existence issues out of social relationships, we know that our very lives are dependent upon others. And so it behooves us to care for others as we care for ourselves because of our mutual interrelatedness.

This is only to say that humanity is itself a body. Call it a corporate body or a body politic, but understand that God has called it into being as the body of Christ. And that body is today like a building which is still in the process of construction. The foundation of the apostles and the prophets has been laid, walls have been erected with various windows and doors. The construction is in process, and there is much yet to do. The question for us today is how we will be incorporated into God's building, the church. Will we actively take part in its construction, giving ourselves wholeheartedly to the process? Or will we be ground up and used as fertilizer for the lawn? We have a choice.

Freedom

Paul said, "Now the Lord is the Spirit, and where the Spirit of the Lord is, there is freedom" (v. 17). Thank God that the Father is the Architect, the Son is the General Contractor and the Spirit provides the labor, to use the Trinity analogously. Indeed, where the Spirit of the Lord is, there is freedom, but this freedom belongs to God, who gives or shares it with His people. And because this freedom belongs to God and is ours only by His grace, it is the freedom to accomplish His will, which means that it is not the freedom to do whatever we want—and particularly not when what we want for ourselves contravenes what God wants for us.

But that's not quite right, either. Because this freedom that Paul is talking about is actually the freedom to do what we want in Christ. That is, in Christ God's people will actually want to do what Christ wants us to do. We do not follow Christ out of necessity or compulsion, but out of our own free choice. In Christ God's people want what God wants for them. And because Christ has provided the remedy for sin through the propitiation of God by His death on the cross, Christ has freed us from the consequences of sin—the judgment of God, which is death and damnation. Having been freed from the consequences of sin, freed from death and damnation, we are free indeed.

Yet, we must understand that our freedom is not ours alone. We did not earn it. We cannot steal it. We cannot buy it or somehow accomplish it. Rather, it has been freely given as a gift of God's amazing grace through faith alone in Christ alone according to Scripture alone. The freedom that we enjoy in Christ is not ours to do with what we please, except that in Christ we want to please the Lord above all things and in all things. The freedom is ours to be obedient to God in Christ. It is the freedom to live as Christ has called us to live—in Him, in community, in harmony, in cooperation, in love and service. This is our only freedom, the only freedom available to man, to humanity. Everything else is slavery to sin.

Everything that we do because of our uniqueness, everything we do because of our creativity, because of our own desires apart from Christ is not freedom. It is not freedom because it issues out of sin and produces additional sin, which results in judgment, in death and damnation.

Apart from Christ all of humanity is on a train that is hurtling through history bound for hell. And being on that train is not a function or expression of freedom. We did not choose to be on that train, but we have been born on it. Our freedom, the only freedom available to us as fallen human beings, is freedom in Christ to disembark that train before it reaches its final destination. Christ is the ticket to disembark, the only ticket.

The End

"And we all, with unveiled face, beholding the glory of the Lord, are being transformed into the same image from one degree of glory to another. For this comes from the Lord who is the Spirit" (v. 18).

We must read Scripture with unveiled faces. We must see the end and purpose of God's law in Jesus Christ. We must face the horrific implications of God's judgment. We must face the law and its perfection, and freely, willingly acknowledge our sinfulness and guilt before a wrathful and judgmental God in order that we may witness the grace of God and the power of Christ's propitiation on the cross. The refusal for any reason to stand before God in judgment—whether we refuse to acknowledge God's reality, the law's power or jurisdiction, the efficacy of Christ's sacrifice, or simply out of ignorance or apathy—constitutes a refusal to accept God's grace and a denial of the power and presence of the Holy Spirit. Such a denial is the one unforgivable sin, unforgivable, not because God has not given it, but because out of ignorance and obstinacy people turn their backs on it. And the result is that God will bring such people into His kingdom anyway—as fertilizer.

Here is the unveiled end and purpose of God's law, not that God wants people to be fertilizer for the Kingdom, but that God has graciously provided salvation for anyone who wants it, anyone who will receive it—on His terms, not ours. The kingdom of God is not barred from anyone who wants in, nor will God drag in anyone who does not want to go. Rather, those who refuse the Lord will simply continue on the train to its terminal destination, and God will collect the fertilizer to use on His garden.

Nothing will escape service to the glory of God because God is all-powerful. The only question is how you will serve the glory of God. Will you serve as a living stone? Or as fertilizer?

Paul wrote to the Ephesians, "speaking the truth in love, we are to grow up in every way into him who is the head, into Christ, from whom the whole body, joined and held together by every joint with which it is equipped, when each part is working properly, makes the body grow so that it builds itself up in love" (Ephesians 4:15-16). This is what God wants. What do you want?

10. THE LIGHT OF KNOWLEDGE

And we all, with unveiled face, beholding the glory of the Lord, are being transformed into the same image from one degree of glory to another. For this comes from the Lord who is the Spirit. Therefore, having this ministry by the mercy of God, we do not lose heart. But we have renounced disgraceful, underhanded ways. We refuse to practice cunning or to tamper with God's word, but by the open statement of the truth we would commend ourselves to everyone's conscience in the sight of God. —*2 Corinthians 3:18-4:2*

So, said Paul, summing up his argument about the veil that hid the end or purpose of the law from the Jews, "we all...." He emphasized the fact that he was speaking about all believers, not simply the apostles or the Corinthians, but all believers. Furthermore, he said that all believers see the glory of the Lord with unveiled faces. The lifting of the veil from the eyes of believers means that believers are able to see the end or purpose of the law—their own conviction of sin, and the sentence of death that it brings.

And the reason that we can see the end purpose of the law is that the remedy—Christ—has been revealed. We in Christ can tolerate the guilt and condemnation that has accrued to us from God's law because Jesus Christ, our Advocate at the bench of God's court, has received the full consequence of our sin through His propitiation on the cross. He received the sentence that we deserve, and has acquired the mercy of the Judge to grant forgiveness to all who receive and accept the plea bargain of His life for ours.

The one condition of this plea bargain is that those who receive it receive it in Christ, and continue in Christ in perpetuity. Fortunately, that condition has been met by the Holy Spirit, who has been authorized and dispensed to be the cause and ground of regeneration and sanctification into glory. This means that the Holy Spirit serves as the

guide and protector for all who are in Christ. And because of that guidance and protection, we who are in Christ can see the righteousness
and justice of God's law and our own guilt precisely because we are not
faced with the awful specter of the complete damnation of humanity.

The annihilation of humanity (our destruction, damnation and
eternal torment in hell) cannot be God's ultimate desire because God is
good and loves His people. The complete annihilation of humanity certainly goes against what we learn of God's love and mercy in Scripture.
And yet, Scripture also teaches God's righteousness and justice, the
fact that God cannot tolerate sin, any sin, and that God condemns sinners to hell (death, damnation and eternal torment—Mark 3:29), a
judgment that corresponds to the seriousness of sin. How are these
two biblical facts to be reconciled?

In the light of Christ we come to see that God's purpose is not the
annihilation of humanity, but the eradication of sin—our sin. And in
grateful jubilation we fall on our knees in thankfulness to God because
apart from the righteousness of God's law, we could not even see our
sin—and many still do not! Nonetheless, apart from Jesus Christ,
nothing can be done to alleviate that sin, the sin that is revealed by the
righteousness of God's law.

Revealed

In our own strength, in our own abilities we are not able to even
see the problem, must less solve it. But in Christ, and in Christ alone, is
salvation accomplished. In Christ the veil has been removed and the
glory of God revealed. The glory of God reveals our shame, and our
shame throws us into the arms of Jesus Christ, who turns our shame
into His righteousness through regeneration, our new birth in Christ,
who is the renewed image of God into which we are born again in
Christ.

In Christ, then, and by the guidance and protection of the Holy
Spirit, we who are born again grow and develop and mature under the
guardianship of the Holy Spirit. That is, both our regeneration and our
sanctification are precious gifts of the Holy Spirit, who leads us in ever
increasing growth and maturity in Christ, from glory to glory, from a
lesser glory to a greater glory, "until we all attain to the unity of the
faith and of the knowledge of the Son of God, to mature manhood, to
the measure of the stature of the fullness of Christ" (Ephesians 4:13).
Here's how Paul said it to the Corinthians, "And we all, with unveiled
face, beholding the glory of the Lord, are being transformed into the
same image from one degree of glory to another. For this comes from
the Lord who is the Spirit" (1 Corinthians 3:18).

Building on this idea, Paul continued in chapter four, "Therefore, having this ministry by the mercy of God, we do not lose heart" (v. 1). In spite of the awful sin and guilt that have accrued to humanity over the centuries because of Adam, and have continued even in the light of Jesus Christ, we do not lose heart. To lose heart means to stop believing that success is possible. So, not losing heart, we continue to believe that success is possible—not our success, but God's success through Christ. We continue to trust that Christ will succeed in His mission to save this dying world that is drowning in its own sin. We trust that humanity will not be snuffed out, but that God will preserve His remnant, as He has always done. But in Christ we have come to see that Christ's final remnant will actually be huge, "as the sand of the sea, which cannot be numbered for multitude" (Genesis 32:12).

We have this ministry, said Paul, that ministry being the revelation of the light of Christ, the light that both reveals the depravity of human sin and the unimaginable greatness of God's mercy. The Reformers understood their mission as the revelation of law and grace, and believed that, as the old song goes, "you can't have one without the other." Indeed, holding on to one or the other to the exclusion of one or the other produces a one-eyed and lopsided gospel. Such a gospel can be seen, but not in its fullness because a veil of sorts obscures God's purpose. Just as two eyes are necessary for depth perception, so the right understanding of both law and grace are necessary to see God's end purpose in Christ. Law and grace work together to remove the veil.

It is true, as Paul also said to the Romans, "sin will have no dominion over you, since you are not under law but under grace" (Romans 6:14). By the law we understand ourselves to be condemned sinners, but in Christ we acknowledge that God's mercy has trumped God's law for those who are in Christ because of Christ's propitiation on the cross. Christians are no longer under the jurisdiction of the law, and yet we owe allegiance to the law for two reasons: 1) it has revealed our sin and shown us our need, and 2) in Christ we are free from the damnation that is ours because of the law and we are free to live in obedience to the will of God as revealed in Christ, a will that is greater than the law, a will that includes God's end purpose of the law, which is the salvation of humanity in Christ.

In Christ we are free from the condemnation of the law, and so we are free to practice the law in the light of Christ without the fear of condemnation. Our freedom in Christ does not mean that we must avoid God's law, but rather it means that we are free to receive those aspects of the law that Christ has given us and we are free to abandon those aspects of God's law that Christ has fulfilled for us.

HONESTY

The first principle of this ministry that is ours by the mercy of God is the renunciation of "disgraceful, underhanded ways" and the refusal "to practice cunning or to tamper with God's word" (v. 2). Young's Literal Version reads, "did renounce for ourselves the hidden things of shame, not walking in craftiness, nor deceitfully using the word of God." Other versions read, "nor adulterating the Word of God" (Modern King James Bible), "nor corrupting the Word of God" (Green's Literal Version (LITV), "nor handling the word of God deceitfully" (AV), "not walking in deceit or distorting God's message" (Holman Christian Standard Bible). The idea is that the first principle of gospel ministry is honesty regarding one's self, one's own sin, and honesty regarding God's Word, apart from which gospel ministry is not possible. God's people must see their own sin, the depths of their own depravity and the ongoing temptation to sin, which is revealed by God's law. And we must also come to see the remedy that has been given by the mercy of God through the propitiation of Christ on the cross.

Paul emphasizes the need to handle or understand God's Word correctly as a foundational principle of gospel ministry—and all Christians are ambassadors for Christ and ministers of the gospel in one way or another. And because of this emphasis we come to realize that it is not only possible to mishandle Scripture, but that the strength of Paul's emphasis here and elsewhere suggests that Paul too often encountered such mishandling of God's Word. Indeed, Paul has been arguing that some of the Corinthian leaders were guilty of mishandling God's word themselves because they had confused the wisdom of the world, the wisdom of the Greeks, of Greek philosophy, with the wisdom of God. They allowed Greek habits and ideas, habits and ideas that were foreign to the gospel, to creep into their own minds and into the church.

He was saying that their break with the world that came with their regeneration in Christ, the break that represented the death of their old lives and the birth of their new lives in Christ, had not been a clean break. They had brought some of their old pagan (Greek) habits, ideas, beliefs and practices into the church. This is a common problem because the gospel of Jesus Christ is so contrary to the ways and thoughts of the world, so different, that it takes a while to adjust to God's ways. It takes a while for the truth and effectiveness of God's ways to sink into our thick skulls. Old habits are hard to overcome because they are habits. Habits are automatic reactions. Habits happen without thinking. Overcoming them takes intention, practice and dedication. It's not easy to break old habits or to develop new ones. It takes time and effort.

So, the honesty that Paul calls on is the honesty to catch ourselves in our old habits as the first step of conversion. If we are to overcome our old habits, the first thing we must do is to notice when we engage them so that we can stop and take an alternative course of thought and/or action. We must understand our old habits as sinful and catch ourselves in sin, see ourselves as guilty sinners, so that we can give ourselves anew everyday to the glory of God in Christ. We must renounce our own "disgraceful, underhanded ways" (v. 2) by bringing all things into the light of Christ, by yielding to the wisdom of Christ in all things.

Related to this, we must "refuse to practice cunning (*panourgia*) or to tamper with God's word" (v. 2). Cunning is a translation of the Greek that means adroitness—trickery or sophistry. Paul means that we must not be fooled by our own intelligence, by our own abilities, by trying to make God's Word say what it does not say. It means not reading into God's Word what is not there. And conversely, it means reading out of God's Word what is actually there.

EISEGESIS & EXEGESIS

Scholars know these two ideas, these two ways of reading Scripture, as eisegesis and exegesis, reading meaning into a text and reading meaning out of a text, respectively. Both are possible. The Modern practice in biblical theology has been to exegete the text. Beginning in Germany in the 1800s biblical scholars developed the art of textual criticism, wherein they applied a kind of scientific analysis to the text of Scripture in the hope of extracting its objective meaning, a meaning that could be agreed upon by all rational people. But it didn't work out that way because equally rational scholars exegeted mutually exclusive meanings from the same texts.

With the rise of Postmodernism toward the end of the last century, biblical scholars began taking cues from literary scholars, who discovered the value of eisegesis. Postmodern scholars found the quest for objective truth, truth that could be universally agreed upon by rational people, to be futile. Taking this tact even further, they believed that the quest to exegete the original author's meaning from a literary text to be beyond our abilities because the meaning of a particular text was always informed by its context. And the original author's context was not the reader's context. And so the reader would always, consciously or unconsciously, read his or her own context into the text because the original context was not part of the reader's perspective.

Consequently, Postmodernism focuses attention on our own sub-jective understanding or meaning of a thing. So, we talk about what a thing means *to me*, rather than simply what it means, because it means different things to different people. As Postmodern people we focus on differences of meaning rather than on meanings that we all under-stand commonly. In fact, Postmodern people deny that common meaning is even possible because people have different perspectives, different histories, different contexts. The value of life for Postmodern people, then, is not found in the things we hold and understand in common, but in our differences, in the various ways we understand the same things differently. The Postmodern focus is not on unity but on diversity.

However, both of these positions—exegesis and eisegesis, Mod-ernism and Postmodernism—are flawed because they fall short of the biblical method of interpretation. The biblical method requires us to see the larger biblical context of a particular verse or chapter by seeing the general theme (or context) of the verse or chapter as it exists within the greater sweep (or context) of history as understood and taught in Scripture. The Bible provides its own context, and there are levels of biblical context that fade back into Creation itself. The whole of the biblical story, its unity, is the context of all of its various parts.

Paul was making an application of this sort of thing to the Cor-inthians. With our eyes unveiled, in the sense that Paul has been dis-cussing, Christians are able to see God's end purpose in history, which is the context of God's involvement in history. God gave the law to reveal sin, to show us our inability, our need. God sent Jesus Christ to do for us what we cannot do for ourselves, that is, to save us from death and damnation. That is the greater purpose, the greater context of Scripture.

Regeneration

However, seeing this, understanding this, is a gift of regeneration. According to the Westminster Confession of Faith 1:5, "our full persua-sion and assurance of the infallible truth and divine authority thereof (our understanding of Scripture—ed.), is from the inward work of the Holy Spirit bearing witness by and with the Word in our hearts." This means that we can see or understand the truth of God's Word only because God's Holy Spirit reveals it to us, only because God's Holy Spirit in us through regeneration provides the proper context by making us an integral part of the greater biblical story.

God regenerates His people by the power and presence of the Holy Spirit, who thereby reveals the truth of sin and salvation to believers—

in our own lives. And such regenerated believers then read that context into Scripture (eisegesis). What context? That personal born again perspective that shows us God's plan and purpose—and our part in that plan. Through regeneration it becomes personal, which in turn allows us to see the deeper meaning, to read God's meaning out of Scripture (exegesis) in order to apply it to our own lives and situations.

Thus, eisegesis and exegesis are held together in proper biblical interpretation and application because they are mutually informative, both are necessary, both are included in the wholeness of human character. They mutually and reciprocally inform and confirm God's truth to believers. No longer are believers deceived by half truths about God's Word. No longer do believers corrupt God's Word, no longer do they adulterate or deceitfully use God's Word for their own purposes. But rather, through regeneration by the presence and power of the Holy Spirit, we are used by God's Word for the purposes of gospel ministry. Born again believers are no longer self-focused, but are God-focused. And while this initial insight or change happens immediately, the fullness of its implications, of its development within the lives of believers and of its actual practice among believers takes time to mature.

And so, said Paul, "by the open statement of the truth we would commend ourselves to everyone's conscience in the sight of God" (v. 2). We commend ourselves. It's not that I commend myself and you commend yourself. This commending is not a function of personal self-confidence and pride. No! It is, rather, that believers commend believers. Believers commend one another. Christ in me commends Christ in you, and Christ in you commends Christ in me. We stand as witnesses for one another because we see Christ in one another. Christ is our link. Christ is our connection. Christ is our bond. Christ is the light by which we see one another. And, indeed, Christ is the light by which we see everything. That is our calling. That is our ministry.

11. BELIEVING IS SEEING

And even if our gospel is veiled, it is veiled only to those who are perishing. In their case the god of this world has blinded the minds of the unbelievers, to keep them from seeing the light of the gospel of the glory of Christ, who is the image of God. For what we proclaim is not ourselves, but Jesus Christ as Lord, with ourselves as your servants for Jesus' sake. For God, who said, "Let light shine out of darkness," has shone in our hearts to give the light of the knowledge of the glory of God in the face of Jesus Christ.   —2 Corinthians 4:3-6

Paul continues his discussion of the veiled gospel. He has made the case that in Christ or because of Christ's propitiation on the cross, the veil that previously hid the end purpose of God's law given to Moses has been removed. In Christ we can see the end purpose of the law—the condemnation of sin and the damnation of sinners—because Christ has Himself received the just punishment for our sin in our place. He has taken our punishment upon Himself, and freed us from the specter of the burden of damnation.

Having been freed from that burden, the burden of personal eternal damnation as the just consequence of our sin, we are gratefully free to live in love and obedience to the One who has freed us—Jesus Christ. Christ has freed us from the consequence of our failure to live up to the demands of God's law, and at the same time He has freed us in order to live as a brood under His wings (Matthew 23:37). He wanted to do this for the Jews in Jerusalem, but they would not have it.

Christ's death on the cross has done two things. First, it paid the debt for our sin. And second, it purchased our lives so that we can live in Christ. Christ's faithful obedience to God's law is the foundation for our discipleship in Christ. We follow Christ into obedience, knowing that his perfect obedience will cover the many imperfections of our imitation obedience. Because Christ is obedient to God's law, and because Christians live in Christ, in obedience to Christ, who is Himself obedient to God, we are free from the punishment for disobedience. His perfect obedience makes up for our imperfect obedience. Even when we don't live in perfect obedience, Christ's payment for our sin covers us in a way that protects us from God's wrath. God trusts Christ to do what He said He will do, and He said that he will bring us into full compliance through the process of sanctification.

CONDEMNED

Those engaged in the process of sanctification—maturity in Christ —are protected from God's ultimate wrath, and able to see God's purpose in Christ. But, said Paul, "even if our gospel is veiled, it is veiled only to those who are perishing" (v. 3). The veil remains in place for all who reject Christ because they reject the only thing that can protect them from the intolerable wrath of God. Those who reject Christ reject Him precisely because they cannot see or tolerate the unveiled law of God apart from Christ. By denying Christ, all they see is God's law, which condemns them to eternal damnation without hope.

Such a worldview is intolerable. No one can cope with the fact that their lives are hopelessly bound for eternal damnation. Only two options are available: 1) receive God's gift of grace in Christ, or 2) reject it. Once Christ has been rejected, the natural conclusion of that rejection is to reject the validity of God and His law. Those who reject Christ do so out of their own free will, thinking that they know better than God. Because they freely decide that Christ's propitiation on the cross does not personally apply to them, they then determine that Christ's propitiation is folly because they have determined that it will not work in their case. The purpose of the Bible is to reveal Christ's remedy for God's law. When that purpose is freely rejected, the curse of the law remains. Those who reject Christ are not free from God's law, as they think they are. Rather, they are still subject to it's curse of damnation, the remnant of the creation covenant (Genesis 3:17).

Can we pray that God will have mercy on those who are perishing in spite of their rejection of Christ? No. Why not? Because God has already shown mercy by providing Jesus Christ to satisfy God's demand for justice in the face of sin by dying on the cross. And the mercy of Jesus Christ is sufficient for all of humanity. Christ is the mercy that those who are perishing reject. And for us to pray for some other kind of mercy involves us in the rejection of the mercy that has already been given. To pray that God will provide some other mercy than the grace and mercy of Jesus Christ is to deny Christ Himself.

So, rather than praying that God will have mercy on those who are perishing, we need to pray that those who are perishing will abandon their foolish rejection of Christ. That rejection is the veil! Their own stubborn rejection is their blindness to what God has so graciously provided. Just as the rejection of Christ obscures reality for unbelievers, the reception of Christ clarifies reality for believers. In both cases, Christ is at the crux of reality. Are those who reject Christ free to accept Him at will? Rejection of Christ is a function of free will, but is free will an adequate means to receive Christ?

Jesus said, "For God so loved the world, that he gave his only Son, that whoever believes in him should not perish but have eternal life. For God did not send his Son into the world to condemn the world, but in order that the world might be saved through him. Whoever believes in him is not condemned, but whoever does not believe is condemned already, because he has not believed in the name of the only Son of God" (John 3:16-18). Verse 18 is the key to understand what Jesus means here. The whole world is condemned already because of Adam's sin. That is the context of Christ. Without Christ the whole world and all of humanity is already plunging into eternal damnation regardless of what people think, say, do or decide—with or without free will. The world is a boat without a rudder or a motor that is caught in the current of sin and is about to plunge over the abyss, and there is nothing that anyone can do about it—except Jesus Christ.

Christ has come and is still in the process of grabbing all who will believe by the scruff of the neck and hoisting them into the helicopter of salvation. Christ is on a rescue mission. Those on the helicopter come to their senses once they are out of immanent danger and find themselves to be believers.

Help!

Some who have not yet been rescued call out, "Lord, why don't you save us all?" Jesus stops and turns to them and says, "you ... outwardly appear righteous to others, but within (some of) you are full of hypocrisy and lawlessness. ...How often would I have gathered your children together as a hen gathers her brood under her wings, and you would not! See, your house is left to you desolate. For I tell you, you will not see me again, until you say, 'Blessed is he who comes in the name of the Lord'" (Matthew 23:28, 37-39). Jesus made reference to a verse in the book of Job, "Naked I came from my mother's womb, and naked shall I return. The Lord gave, and the Lord has taken away; blessed be the name of the Lord" (Job 1:21).

Paul answered a similar question in Romans,

> *"What shall we say then? Is there injustice on God's part? By no means! For he says to Moses, 'I will have mercy on whom I have*

mercy, and I will have compassion on whom I have compassion.' So
then it depends not on human will or exertion, but on God, who has
mercy. For the Scripture says to Pharaoh, 'For this very purpose I
have raised you up, that I might show my power in you, and that my
name might be proclaimed in all the earth.' So then he has mercy on
whomever he wills, and he hardens whomever he wills. You will say
to me then, 'Why does he still find fault? For who can resist his will?
But who are you, O man, to answer back to God? Will what is molded
say to its molder, 'Why have you made me like this?' Has the potter
no right over the clay, to make out of the same lump one vessel for
honorable use and another for dishonorable use?'" —Romans 9:14-21

Knowing that God is not the author of sin and evil, Paul said to the
Corinthians regarding this same concern that "the god of this world
has blinded the minds of the unbelievers, to keep them from seeing the
light of the gospel of the glory of Christ, who is the image of God" (v.
4). Here Paul said that the choice to see Christ or not is not a function
of human free will, but that "the god of this world" has imposed blindness upon those who reject Christ and left them to their own
resources. That blindness is the source of the rejection of Christ. Unbelievers reject Christ, and rejecting Christ they do not see Christ's
remedy personally applied to them. And apart from Christ's remedy,
they stand in the just condemnation of God.

Believers have a hard time understanding how some people can
reject Christ because believers see with unveiled faces what unbelievers don't see at all—or at least not clearly—because their faces are
veiled. The two groups—believers and unbelievers—do not understand
or interpret reality in the same way. When they look at reality through
the crux of Christ, "to one (it is) a fragrance from death to death, to
the other a fragrance from life to life" (2 Corinthians 2:16). Paul
acknowledged the apparent contradiction that the same reality is
understood and experienced by believers in one way and by unbelievers in an opposite way. But he did not resolve the tension of that
apparent contradiction. He left it in place because God left it in place
when he dealt with Moses and Pharaoh, Jacob and Esau, Cain and Able,
etc. Rather, Paul asked, "Who is sufficient for these things?" (2 Corinthians 2:16).

Believers see Christ's position in reality as the Son of God who has
taken away the sin of the world through His sacrifice on the cross. And
we are able to see this only because Christ has atoned for our sin. God
has removed the veil from our faces. We believe in the helicopter of
salvation because we have found ourselves to be on it. The reality of
Christ's intervention into the history of the world is personal in the
case of believers.

BLINDED

But unbelievers see only a wrathful God who has condemned them to eternal damnation. They do not find themselves to be on the helicopter. Unbelievers cannot see that Christ has provided a remedy. The remedy is veiled from them by their stubborn disbelief. And, without a remedy, unbelievers discount the reality of God in one way or another. Unbelievers rationalize their disbelief by saying that God doesn't exist, or that He doesn't have jurisdiction or power over them, or they will deny or change the meaning of what He has so plainly said. All of these forms of rationalization are expressions of denial, and the psychology of denial deceives those engaged in it. As Paul said, unbelievers are blinded by their own beliefs, by the false gods who represent those false beliefs.

Paul said earlier that other gods, false gods, so-called gods, are not real (1 Corinthians 8:4). They are created by the imaginations of men on the basis of false beliefs. Nonetheless, those false beliefs produce real consequences in the world. They blind the minds of unbelievers. So, whether you want to put a spiritual interpretation on this or a psychological interpretation, the result is the same. Unbelievers are blinded by their unbelief. And their blindness keeps them from seeing the "light of the gospel of the glory of Christ" (v. 4).

Paul went on in verse 5 to clarify that while unbelievers are blinded by their own false beliefs, believers are not enabled to see because of their belief, as if belief and unbelief are the same kind of thing. Paul was not saying that seeing God's truth is a function of belief, as if people can work up some subjective, psychological state of mind called "belief" and presto, God pops into view. Not at all! It is not that the reality of God depends upon our personal, subjective belief, which is what unbelievers think. But rather, those who see the reality of God are compelled to believe by the reality. The reality invokes the belief, the belief does not invoke the reality.

People do not create reality by what they believe, but rather people adapt themselves to the reality they experience to be real. Unbelievers tend to think that reality is created by belief, probably because they experience the power of denial that blinds them to the reality of God, and so unbelievers create a kind of imaginary understanding (explanation) of the world without God and falsely call it reality. Unbelievers think that reality is created by their own beliefs because that is exactly what *they* do. That is their experience, denying God they create false explanations of reality that have nothing to do with God.

Imagine

But believers have a very different experience. Believers see God, not because of their belief but because of God's reality. When a flashlight is turned on in a dark room, people don't see it because they believe in the reality of flashlights. Rather, people see it because it is real and it has been turned on. Then, having seen the light of the flashlight, they adjust their beliefs to conform to the reality they see. Because they see it, they understand it to be real. Believers do not adjust reality to conform to their beliefs, as unbelievers do, but arsy varsy, the beliefs of believers are adjusted to conform to reality, the reality of God, and the reality of the remedy for sin provided by Jesus Christ. So, said Paul, "what we proclaim is not ourselves," (not a product of our own imaginations) "but Jesus Christ as Lord, with ourselves as your servants for Jesus' sake" (v. 5).

Paul and the apostles did not set themselves up as lords over the faith or over the conscience of others. Nor were they trying to prove how smart or eloquent or mystical they were. Nor were they trying to become wealthy by asserting themselves as the leaders of a social movement or institution. Nor were they suggesting that salvation was the result of human intelligence, superior morality or any kind of human decision. Rather, they knew themselves and the depths of their own depravity because they had read and accepted the biblical story of Adam's fall as actual history. They knew that everyone—to a person— was running from God because they could not face the specter of personal damnation in the light of God's law. They knew it because it was true in their own lives prior to their rescue by Christ. Jesus Christ changed their hearts and their minds.

Paul especially knew this, as his own conversion came—not because he decided to believe, but as the result of an unwanted and uninvited encounter with the risen Christ on the road to Damascus where his legs were knocked out from under him and he was thrown into the dust by the Lord of glory. God had grabbed Paul by the nap of the neck and thrown him into salvation while Paul was on his way to persecute God's people. Of course, Paul came to agree with and accept Christ as Lord and Savior, but his acceptance came after his encounter with the Lord, not before.

Reality

Christ is the reality, and the reality has been made manifest. And we who see the reality of Jesus Christ understand ourselves to be His servants. We did not create God or Jesus Christ for our own benefit, our own salvation. We are not "into Jesus" for our own good. Our relationship with the Lord is often painful and costly. But we persist because we are into it for God's glory. God has broken into history to show us His reality, and seeing that reality, we acknowledge His greater power through our submission and service.

"For God, who said, 'Let light shine out of darkness,' has shone in our hearts to give the light of the knowledge of the glory of God in the face of Jesus Christ" (v. 6). This is another statement of the divinity of Christ. Paul said that the knowledge of the glory of God is seen in the face of Jesus Christ. We identify people by their faces. Of course the rest of the body plays a role in one's identity, but faces are our primary means of personal recognition and identity. To see someone's face is to recognize the person. So, to see the glory of God in the face of Jesus Christ is to recognize God's face in Jesus Christ. It is to identify God in Christ. It is to see the light of Christ against the backdrop of the darkness of the world.

Again, believers see the light of Christ, not as a way to rationalize their beliefs about God, as if God and His Christ are figments of human imagination. But rather, the light of Christ has intruded upon our blindness. The light in the darkness forces itself into our vision. When a flashlight is turned on in a dark room, we do not see it because we choose to see it. We see it because it has been turned on. Someone chose to turn it on, and in this analogy turning it on was not our decision. It was God's decision. God sent Christ quite apart from our willingness to be saved. God turned on the flashlight, and we saw it.

But how can we explain that fact that others in the same room don't see it. Is the room still dark for them? No, the light shines. They see it, but they deny that it is God. Unbelievers concoct various scenarios that explain the light without reference to God. They devise natural explanations for it, and deny all references to God. They deny that God's salvation in Christ applies to them, and develop explanations—rationalizations—to justify that denial. And anyone who has known someone in denial knows the extent that people will go to maintain their denial. Psychologically, denial is a defense mechanism that refuses to acknowledge painful thoughts. Because thinking such thoughts is a source of pain, they refuse to think them as a way to alleviate the pain of their willful rejection of Christ and embrace of damnation.

As Paul said to the Romans, "For although they knew God, they did not honor him as God or give thanks to him, but they became futile in their thinking, and their foolish hearts were darkened" (Romans 1:21). Blinded by their lust for the world, the world blinds them to the reality of God. Are they blinded by their false gods? Or by their own false beliefs? Which came first? The chicken or the egg? Paul would answer that question by saying that we as human beings are not privy to such things. We don't know and we can't know And furthermore, that it doesn't matter because the reality is that we have chickens and we have eggs. The light of Christ shines brightly, and some see it and some don't, some will and some won't.

Deal with it!

12. Keeping Heart

But we have this treasure in jars of clay, to show that the surpassing power belongs to God and not to us. We are afflicted in every way, but not crushed; perplexed, but not driven to despair; persecuted, but not forsaken; struck down, but not destroyed; always carrying in the body the death of Jesus, so that the life of Jesus may also be manifested in our bodies. For we who live are always being given over to death for Jesus' sake, so that the life of Jesus also may be manifested in our mortal flesh. So death is at work in us, but life in you. Since we have the same spirit of faith according to what has been written, "I believed, and so I spoke," we also believe, and so we also speak, knowing that he who raised the Lord Jesus will raise us also with Jesus and bring us with you into his presence. For it is all for your sake, so that as grace extends to more and more people it may increase thanksgiving, to the glory of God. So we do not lose heart. Though our outer self is wasting away, our inner self is being renewed day by day. For this light momentary affliction is preparing for us an eternal weight of glory beyond all comparison, as we look not to the things that are seen but to the things that are unseen. For the things that are seen are transient, but the things that are unseen are eternal.

—2 Corinthians 4:7-18

Paul's allusion to a "treasure in earthen vessels" (v. 7) is a reference to the value of the gospel in relationship to the value of our own lives. We are earthen vessels and the gospel of Jesus Christ is the treasure that has been put into us. Normally a valuable treasure would be kept in a lock box or a bank vault. But this treasure has been put into ordinary jars of clay. One of the problems with putting a treasure into a jar of clay is that the jar can be easily broken and the treasure lost. Earthen vessels are storage vaults. Normally, a treasure is put into something that will protect it from loss or decay.

However, this treasure is unique. It cannot be lost. It has been given once and for all, and is of infinite value to all humanity. The danger with this treasure is not losing it, but either ignoring it because you think it is of no value, or hoarding it—trying to keep it for one's self or one's own small group for fear of scarcity. Our sinful and myopic vision suggests that this treasure is in short supply, or that Christ or God's ability or desire to save is limited. But God is infinite, not limited. God's abilities and desires are infinite, which means that this treasure can be divided into an infinite number of parts, and each part will retain its original infinite value. The regular rules of math do not apply to infinite values.

GROWTH BY DIVISION

God has given us this treasure, not to hoard it for or among ourselves, but to give it away as widely as possible. We are to share this treasure (the gospel) with as many people as possible. And by so sharing it, the value of the treasure will actually increase. How so? As the treasure is divided or shared among Christians, the "piece" that each Christian is given is of the same value as the original. So, if I have a piece and it is of infinite value, and I then share it with you, your piece is also of infinite value. So, together we have doubled the value by sharing it. Again, the mathematics of infinite values is different than the mathematics of finite values. The bottom line is that by sharing the gospel, dividing it up among as many people as possible, its value grows. That is, the gospel grows through division, through sharing it with others.

There is another valuable insight to be mined from this popular verse that is often overlooked. This verse teaches the sovereignty of God. It teaches that the presence of the gospel in earthen vessels—in our lives—is not a matter of our doing, but God's. Why has God placed this valuable treasure in feeble earthen vessels? "To show that the surpassing power belongs to God and not to us" (v. 7). And how does putting a valuable treasure into a ordinary earthen vessel show God's power? It demonstrates that the treasure is not protected by the earthen vessels, which are easily—and often—broken as the treasure is shared. In fact, revealing the treasure—sharing it—is a function of breaking the vessel. Or we could say that the treasure if best revealed, or most fully revealed, when the vessel in which it is contained is broken.

This was certainly God's method of revealing the treasure of Jesus Christ as He was broken on the cross of redemption. That's our model. He's our Lord. We are His disciples who follow Him into brokenness, death and resurrection (Romans 6:3-4). In the miracle of the feeding of the five thousand (Matthew 14:19-21), bread was broken (divided) and it multiplied (grew). Later "he took bread, and when he had given thanks, he broke it and gave it to them, saying, 'This is my body, which is given for you. Do this in remembrance of me'" (Luke 22:19). In the breaking (dividing) of the bread is the multiplication of the treasure. God's ways are not our ways. His wisdom is not the wisdom of the world. And the power to accomplish the multiplication of the treasure through its division belongs to God, not us.

Paul goes on to provide more detail about God's way. Focusing on the fact that jars of clay are easily broken, he said, "We are afflicted in every way, but not crushed; perplexed, but not driven to despair; persecuted, but not forsaken; struck down, but not destroyed; always carrying in the body the death of Jesus, so that the life of Jesus may also be manifested in our bodies" (vs. 8-10). These are the earthen vessels that hold the *treasure* (*thēsauros*—deposit or wealth) of the gospel. Paul was among those, even the leader of those, who were afflicted, perplexed, persecuted, and struck down. Paul was telling us that these things are not God's punishment for the ongoing sins of the saved. They are God's instruments of growth, maturity and sanctification.

Broken

Those who carry the gospel deposit will encounter such things in the face of those who reject the gospel. Sometimes these difficulties will be more or less intense, more or less difficult, depending on the degree of rejection by the culture in which Christians live. Christians must understand that they will be broken by the vicissitudes of life as an ordinary part of Christian maturity and growth. But difficulties and struggles are not the end or purpose of faithfulness. Rather, the purpose is the new life that comes as a result of our death in Christ.

Paul said that Christians are "always carrying in the body the death of Jesus, so that the life of Jesus may also be manifested in our bodies" (v. 10). Always (*pantote*) means at all times. The death of Christ, which includes His suffering and ours, is something that is never forgotten or neglected, but always on our minds. This is so important that Paul repeats it in verse 11, "For we who live are always being given over to death for Jesus' sake, so that the life of Jesus also may be manifested in our mortal flesh." Why is Christ's death so important? Isn't it negative to always focus our attention on Christ's suffering and death?

It is, unless one is born again. Apart from regeneration, the gospel is actually depressing because it points to damnation apart from regeneration. Christ's life in eternity was revealed through His suffering in this life as a man. The suffering and death of Christ provided the propitiation, the atonement or the satisfaction of God's demand for justice in the face of human sin. Christ's suffering and death were necessary for our salvation. No suffering and death would mean no salvation. So, Christians who are thankful for their salvation treasure Christ's suffering and death—but not in a negative, sadistic way. Rather, facing Christ's suffering and death, and our own—in Christ, results in freedom from the fear of suffering and death in life.

The regenerate see the death of Christ as the fountain of life because Christ's propitiation applies. But where Christ is rejected, there is no regeneration, no rebirth. So, the specter of Christ's death means nothing, and meaning nothing, it does not point to life. Every soldier in the face of battle knows that he must rise above his own fear of injury and death in order to perform to his fullest potential in the moment. This is part of the psychology that gives us strength and perspective in the face of life's difficulties.

This is reminiscent of Paul's previous letter, where he wrote that "God chose what is foolish in the world to shame the wise; God chose what is weak in the world to shame the strong; God chose what is low and despised in the world, even things that are not, to bring to nothing things that are, so that no human being might boast in the presence of God" (1 Corinthians 1:27-29). Paul had been arguing against the false teachers in the Corinthian church who had tried to portray Paul as a looser because of his suffering and difficulties. Paul was putting that suffering in perspective, showing that it is a necessary part of Christian faithfulness. Remember that Paul had "decided to know nothing among you (them) except Jesus Christ and him crucified" (1 Corinthians 2:2).

Calvin notes that Paul was saying that the person who manifested "a larger measure of gifts, he, in that proportion, comes so much the nearer to conformity with Christ in this respect."[11] Calvin's point was that the more Christ-like we become, the more suffering we will endure. Some people may wonder why that should be? Jesus told us. Jesus warned us in a prayer, "I have given them your word, and the world has hated them because they are not of the world, just as I am not of the world" (John 17:14). Calvin was saying that those who become more Christ-like will suffer more because they become more like what the world hates. I'm not saying that everyone hates Christians. But I am noting that Jesus said that the more worldly people are, the more they will hate Him and His followers.

Calvin helps us understand verse 12, "So death is at work in us, but life in you." There are two contrasts here: death and life, us and you. Death was at work in Paul and those who traveled with him because of

---

11 *Calvin's Commentaries XX*, The Corinthians, Volume Second, Baker Bookhouse, Grand Rapids, 1993, p. 205.

their greater sanctification. Paul and the apostles were working themselves to death for the life of the church. But this is not to be unique to Paul and the apostles. Rather, all Christians are called to give themselves for the life of the church. Some do it more, some less. And as we give ourselves, and our lives are broken open for the sake of revealing the gospel, the church grows among those to whom it is revealed.

GIVING IT AWAY

The gospel grows by giving it away. But giving it away is not as easy as first assumed because people will not want it until their hearts and minds have been changed by the Lord of glory. Giving it away is costly, and usually painful because the jars of clay must be broken in the process of giving. Why is it this way? Because the breaking of the vessel reveals the value of the treasure.

Verse 13 includes a quote from Psalm 116:5-19:

> *"Gracious is the Lord, and righteous; our God is merciful. The Lord preserves the simple; when I was brought low, he saved me. Return, O my soul, to your rest; for the Lord has dealt bountifully with you. For you have delivered my soul from death, my eyes from tears, my feet from stumbling; I will walk before the Lord in the land of the living. I believed, even when I spoke, 'I am greatly afflicted;' I said in my alarm, 'All mankind are liars.' What shall I render to the Lord for all his benefits to me? I will lift up the cup of salvation and call on the name of the Lord, I will pay my vows to the Lord in the presence of all his people. Precious in the sight of the Lord is the death of his saints. O Lord, I am your servant; I am your servant, the son of your maidservant. You have loosed my bonds. I will offer to you the sacrifice of thanksgiving and call on the name of the Lord. I will pay my vows to the Lord in the presence of all his people, in the courts of the house of the Lord, in your midst, O Jerusalem. Praise the Lord!"*

Paul has simply applied this Psalm to Christ. He was showing us how Scripture makes sense of his experience in Christ. And in the midst of difficulty, pain and struggle Paul can persevere because he "know(s) that he who raised the Lord Jesus will raise us also with Jesus and bring us with you into his presence" (v. 14). As surely as God raised Jesus from the dead, so He will raise us from our death. We can be as sure as Christ was about this. We need not fear. We need not fret. We need not worry. Soon we all shall be in the presence of God. This present death is but a fleeting moment against the backdrop of eternity.

Paul's suffering (and ours) is all for the sake of the church and "to the glory of God" (v. 15). Paul lived in a difficult time. The church was in labor, in the process of giving birth. It was a painful and bloody time. Paul knew that in time as grace extended to more people it would increase the ability of people to give thanks, and would increase the number of people who gave thanks. As more people became grateful to God it would become easier to be a Christian. The fire burns brighter when the logs are piled together. Similarly, Christian fellowship doesn't simply add to the grace of thanksgiving, it multiplies it.

Because of these things, said Paul, "we do not lose heart" (v. 16). Yes, times are hard, but the difficulties we face only encourage us to greater faithfulness. The gospel of Jesus Christ cannot be defeated because difficulties only increase the resolve of the faithful by reminding us that "we were buried therefore with him by baptism into death, in order that, just as Christ was raised from the dead by the glory of the Father, we too might walk in newness of life" (Romans 6:4).

CONFLICTED

When Paul made mention of an outer self and an inner self, we need to understand that we do not have two selves. We do not suffer the psychosis of a split personality. Yet, the war that rages within us is real, the war that Christ has inaugurated through our regeneration, which involves the death of the old man the the birth of the new. Our old man has been crucified with Christ (Romans 6:6) so that we may "put on the new man, who according to God was created in righteousness and true holiness" (Ephesians 4:24). The one is wasting away and the other is being renewed on a daily basis. Our regeneration begins in an instant, but takes more than a lifetime to complete.

The process of growth and maturity in Christ has a purpose. We are being prepared for an "eternal weight of glory beyond all comparison" (v. 17). Our struggles and afflictions are a kind of training ground. Training for what? For increased responsibility and service to the glory of God.

Our previous study of the word *glory* showed us that the idea of weight is at the center of the definition of glory. In verse 17 Paul speaks of an eternal weight of glory. The Greek word translated as *weight* (*baros*), literally means a load, an abundance, and also suggests increased authority. The idea here is that our maturity and sanctification in Christ provides additional substance (weight) to the glory of God. Each saint who comes to Christ becomes a living stone in the spiritual house that is being built by God through Jesus Christ. Each new stone adds to the structure and makes it larger, stronger and heavier. Each stone adds weight, adds glory to God and to His project of world reclamation and transformation.

Not Seen

Finally, Paul spoke about the difference between things seen and things not seen. The implication is that things seen belong to the realm of the worldly, and things not seen belong to the realm of the spirit. The concern is reminiscent of the definition of faith given in Hebrews 11:1, "faith is the assurance of things hoped for, the conviction of things not seen."

So, how do people become aware of things not seen? Do they bump into unseen things? Are unseen things only perceptible by some sixth sense? Is it that some people are abnormally sensitive and see things unseen? Or that others are abnormally insensitive, and fail to see what is before their own eyes? How can we show what is unseen to people who don't see unseen things? Exactly what is Paul talking about?

He's talking about things that are intangible, assets that are real but immaterial and not physical—like the fruits of the Spirit; "the fruit of the Spirit is love, joy, peace, patience, kindness, goodness, faithfulness, gentleness, self-control" (Galatians 5:22-23). In Galatians Paul listed these fruits of the Spirit as being in opposition to "the works of the flesh (which) are evident: sexual immorality, impurity, sensuality, idolatry, sorcery, enmity, strife, jealousy, fits of anger, rivalries, dissensions, divisions, envy, drunkenness, orgies, and things like these" (Galatians 5:19-21).

Yet, we can ask if the fruits of the Spirit—love, joy, peace, patience, kindness, goodness, faithfulness, gentleness, self-control—are any less visual than the works of the flesh—sexual immorality, impurity, sensuality, idolatry, sorcery, enmity, strife, jealousy, fits of anger, rivalries, dissensions, divisions, envy, drunkenness, orgies, and like things?

These two categories of things are simply manifestations of different values, different spirits. And that is the point, said Paul, for the crasser things are transient, but the things of God are eternal. The ungodly qualities are passing away in death, either through regeneration or through damnation, while the godly qualities will be eternally manifest in God's people.

The transient things are passing away. Nothing of a transient, temporary, sinful nature will survive in eternity. So, with our minds set on eternal things, the things of Jesus Christ, we are to let go of this momentary affliction. We are to see beyond what is passing away, beyond our own death, and beyond the death of the culture of death, that we may hold fast to Jesus Christ and the culture of life as it is revealed and made manifest in and through Jesus Christ.

13. In Or Out

For we know that if the tent that is our earthly home is destroyed, we have a building from God, a house not made with hands, eternal in the heavens. For in this tent we groan, longing to put on our heavenly dwelling, if indeed by putting it on we may not be found naked. For while we are still in this tent, we groan, being burdened—not that we would be unclothed, but that we would be further clothed, so that what is mortal may be swallowed up by life. He who has prepared us for this very thing is God, who has given us the Spirit as a guarantee. So we are always of good courage. We know that while we are at home in the body we are away from the Lord, for we walk by faith, not by sight. Yes, we are of good courage, and we would rather be away from the body and at home with the Lord. —2 Corinthians 5:1-8*

Paul's reference to "the tent that is our earthly home" (v. 1) is an allusion to the body, our bodies. Note the plural. To understand what he means requires us to look at the verse with trinitarian eyes. As discussed previously, references to "body" need to be understood as an image of God's trinitarian character.[12] God is trinitarian and we are created in His image (Genesis 1:26-27). The trinitarian character of Paul's language here helps us understand what Paul is talking about, suggesting that we think about our home, both earthly and heavenly, in trinitarian terms. A body can be individual, corporate and spiritual—or all three simultaneously.

The Authorized Version translates it "our earthly house of this tabernacle." It is a house or tent, but it is ours, not just mine or yours individually, but ours. Multiple people dwell there, in this tent, in this body. The *house* (*oikia*) could also be translated as *household*, emphasizing the relationships rather than the building. It points to the place where we

---

12 See *Arsy Varsy-Reclaiming the Gospel in First Corinthians*, chapter "The One and the Many," Phillip A. Ross, Pilgrim Platform, Marietta, OH, 2008.

dwell one with another, and is about the reality of dwelling together as much as the place of our dwelling. It's not actually a tent or a house, but refers to humanity and to the body of the church, which is the body of Christ.

HOME

The point of Paul's reference is the comparison he makes. He compares this tent or house that is our earthly home with a "building from God, a house not made with hands, eternal in the heavens" (v. 1). It is, of course, a comparison of earth to heaven, of our earthly body with our anticipated heavenly body. The one exists in the temporal realm and the other in the eternal realm. We have no idea what heavenly bodies are like. We can't know anything about them. All we know is that they will be similar enough to our bodies now that we will recognize one another in Christ, and different enough that we cannot imagine what we will be like.

The point seems to be that our current situation is temporary, but our final destination will be eternal. Though all of the translators translate the conditional (*ean*) as *if*, because of the nature of temporal bodies—the fact that all temporal bodies will in fact one day cease to exist—it could just as well be translated as *when*. "For we know that if (when) the tent that is our earthly home is destroyed, we have a building from God, a house not made with hands, eternal in the heavens" (v. 1). The point seems to be to console our fear of death with the hope of eternal life, a much used biblical theme.

Paul has been speaking of the difficulties of this life for some time now, and reiterates this concern in verse 2, "For in this tent we groan, longing to put on our heavenly dwelling." This concern is much like Revelation 21:4 where it is promised that "He will wipe away every tear from their eyes, and death shall be no more, neither shall there be mourning, nor crying, nor pain anymore, for the former things have passed away." The pain of the moment is put into context by the eternal reward of the struggle.

Part of Paul's concern may be that the pain and difficulties that Christians must undergo on behalf of the Lord could leave them without strength to persevere. The allusion to nakedness suggests weakness and vulnerability, "if indeed by putting it on we may not be found naked" (v. 3). This may be a continuation of Paul's earlier concern that "this perishable body must put on the imperishable, and this mortal body must put on immortality" (1 Corinthians 15:53). There is to be a change of clothing that marks the difference between the end of the temporal and our transition into the eternal. But it is not clothing in a literal sense, but rather Paul is using clothing as a symbol of righteousness.

Paul wrote to the Ephesians, "put off your old self, which belongs to your former manner of life and is corrupt through deceitful desires, and to be renewed in the spirit of your minds, and to put on the new self, created after the likeness of God in true righteousness and holiness" (Ephesians 4:22-24). Jesus Christ is the "the Lord Our Righteousness" (Jeremiah 23:5-6).

Mysterious

Endeavoring to share the fullness of Paul's vision he penned one of the most mysterious verses in Scripture, "For while we are still in this tent, we groan, being burdened—not that we would be unclothed, but that we would be further clothed, so that what is mortal may be swallowed up by life" (v. 4). The Greek word translated *unclothed* (*ekduō*) literally means to cause to sink out of or to take away—to recede. Paul is saying that the struggles of this life will not strip us to nothing, They will not completely undo us or destroy us, but in Christ we will continue to grow, to be further clothed in His righteousness through sanctification in order that our mortality, our death, will be *swallowed up* (*katapinō*) by life. Death will ultimately be consumed by life, and when it is finally consumed it will be gone—vanquished.

John took up this same theme, "He will wipe away every tear from their eyes, and death shall be no more, neither shall there be mourning, nor crying, nor pain anymore, for the former things have passed away" (Revelation 21:4). This is the hope that fuels Christianity, that provides strength and direction during struggles, pain, difficulty and conflict. God will prevail in spite of our weaknesses and failures. That is our hope, and not merely some abstract and distant desire, but it is in fact the greater reality because it is eternal.

Skeptics will charge that this is a false hope, or that only failures and weaklings need hope, or that hope is an escape from reality, or whatever. How do we know that our hope in Christ is not false? Paul said that "He who has prepared us for this very thing is God, who has given us the Spirit as a guarantee" (v. 5). The Spirit is the guarantee of this truth, this greater reality. Skeptics don't recognize the Spirit, so they don't recognize the guarantee. But those who have been reborn in Christ have the Spirit. And the Spirit has changed us completely and continues to bring change and growth every day, drawing us closer to God, clothing us more fully in Christ's righteousness. We who have been changed, we who have been regenerated by the power and presence of the Holy Spirit are the evidence of the Spirit. Just as rustling leaves are the evidence of wind, or shadow is the evidence of light, so we are the evidence of the Spirit who has changed us, and who does not lie and cannot fail to fulfill what has been promised.

Young's Literal Version translated this verse as, "He who did work us to this self-same thing is God, who also did give to us the earnest of the Spirit." The idea is that God gave us the Spirit as earnest. Earnest is an old fashioned word for deposit. It used to be (before credit cards) that when you wanted to buy something, you would make a down payment as a way of demonstrating your intent to buy. So, Paul is saying here that God has given us the Holy Spirit as a down payment on our salvation. It is a gesture on God's part to demonstrate His intent to fulfill His promise. When someone makes a down payment on a house, it means that they intend to buy the house. The Holy Spirit shows us God's intent to fulfill His promises, and God will not, does not and cannot default on His promises. If you have the Spirit—and Paul said that the Corinthians had it—the rest will necessarily follow.

COURAGE

Paul begins verse 6 with *so* (*oun*), which can also be translated as *therefore*. It's a conclusion. It means that what comes next is the logical conclusion of what has come before. On the basis of the previous verses, then, we—those who have the Spirit as an earnest—are "always of good courage" (v. 6). Always, at all times, means that there isn't a time that we don't have good courage. Other translations use the word *confident* (*tharrheō*) or *assured*.

But there's a rub. Many people who think of themselves as Christians are not always of good courage, not always confident or assured. Does this contradict Scripture? Not at all. Paul's word stands. It is true and can be trusted. If anything is to be doubted, it must be our own experience, our own understanding, and not Scripture. God's Word is true even if everyone else is a liar (Romans 3:4). When we are young or young in the Spirit our confidence is weak because our faith is weak. This is normal and is to be expected. As we mature through sanctification we become more confident and assured of God and of our faithfulness, our relationship with God.

And while it is true that people grow at different rates, some maturing faster or earlier than others, if someone has been a Christian for a long time—say twenty years or so, and still struggles with confidence in God's Word or their assurance of salvation, something is wrong. And it is not God or the Bible. While justification comes by grace alone through faith alone, sanctification comes by grace alone through the practice of faith. We grow as we trust the Lord, as we walk with the Lord, as we engage our faith. So, where faith is not maturing, it is the lack of practice or engagement of faithfulness that is the likely culprit.

When people claim to be Christians but don't practice the faith, one of several things may be going on. It could be that they are liars (John 8:44), or it could be that they are fooling themselves (Matthew 7:21-23), or it could be that they are stony ground Christians who have withered (Mark 4:5), or it could be that they are backsliding Christians. Christians do sin (1 John 1:8), but the Christian life is not to be identified by a life of sin.

Believers are new creations with new hearts and new life (2 Corinthians 5:17). Christians have the earnest of the Spirit which produces good fruit (Galatians 5:22-23). A Christian life is a changed life. Christians are forgiven no matter how many times they sin, but at the same time Christians should live progressively more holy lives as they grow closer to Christ over time. We should have serious doubts about anyone who claims to be a believer, yet lives a life that says otherwise, whether that life is full of intentional sin or incessant doubt.

HOME

The latter part of verse 6 is quite interesting. The English translations fail to point out that the main contrast of the verse is between two nearly identical words. The first (*endēmeō*) is translated as "while we are at home" and the second (*ekdēmeō*) is translated as "we are away from." The two words are identical except for the prefix. The first prefix means *in* and the second means *out*. The contrast is being in or out of *dēmos*, which means people or public—in or out of the body, the community, a group. *Dēmos* is the root of the word *democracy*, which literally means rule by the people (as opposed to theocracy, which means rule by God).

But the contrast is not between being in or out of a democracy, but being in or out a people group. Here we can think of the people as being a body in the plural or corporate sense. The fact that we should be thinking about this concern in terms of a body is strengthened by the fact that Paul uses the word *body*. Paul is saying that inasmuch as we are at home in the body, inasmuch as we find our identity with the people (*dēmos* not *ekklēsia*), we will not be at home in the Lord, we will not find our identity in the Lord. Paul raised the question, Are we at home with the people (*dēmos*) or with the Lord? Either/or but not both! Paul has made this an exclusive choice, "while we are at home in the body we are away from the Lord" (v. 6). It's one or the other.

In support of this contrast Paul continued, "for we walk by faith, not by sight" (v. 7). The Greek word translated as *walk* (*peripateō*) isn't just about our feet and legs. The older word to describe what it means would be *deportment*—our conduct, behavior, attitude. It's the way we live, the way we behave toward others. And we are, of course, to live by faith not sight, not on the basis of appearance or fashion, but on the basis of Scripture. We are to focus on what we learn in Scripture, not what we see in the world.

Repeating the comparison between being present or absent, Paul said, "Yes, we are of good courage, and we would rather be away from the body and at home with the Lord" (v. 8). Paul didn't ask the Corinthians if they were of good courage, he told them that they were. Because they were Christians they didn't doubt their own faith or assurance. They claimed it. Or rather, Paul claimed it for them, and then showed them how to claim it for themselves. *Furthermore,* said Paul, *Christians would rather identify with the Lord than the people.* Christians feel more at home with the Lord than with the people, the *dēmos* not the *ekklēsia.*

This is the model of Christian faithfulness, and points to the difference between the people and the church, the *dēmos* and the *ekklēsia.* It is not a pining for some imagined perfect world, nor a denial of the realities of the world in which we live. It is, rather, a source of strength that will allow us to persevere as instruments of Jesus Christ in a world that hates Him. It is also the source of protection from the acids of sin that tend to dissolve our resolve to persevere in faithfulness. While we live and move and have our being in this passing world, it is not our home. We do not find our identity in this world, not with its people, not in its comforts, not in its fads or fashions. But rather, we have been plucked out from identification with the world, and cast into identification with Jesus Christ and the people of God, living and dead, present and past.

"If you love Me," said Jesus, "keep My commandments. And I will pray the Father, and He shall give you another Comforter, so that He may be with you forever, the Spirit of Truth, whom the world cannot receive because it does not see Him nor know Him. But you know Him, for He dwells with you and shall be in you" (John 14:15-17).

14. One For All, All For One

So whether we are at home or away, we make it our aim to please him. For we must all appear before the judgment seat of Christ, so that each one may receive what is due for what he has done in the body, whether good or evil. Therefore, knowing the fear of the Lord, we persuade others. But what we are is known to God, and I hope it is known also to your conscience. We are not commending ourselves to you again but giving you cause to boast about us, so that you may be able to answer those who boast about outward appearance and not about what is in the heart. For if we are beside ourselves, it is for God; if we are in our right mind, it is for you. For the love of Christ controls us, because we have concluded this: that one has died for all, therefore all have died; and he died for all, that those who live might no longer live for themselves but for him who for their sake died and was raised. —2 Corinthians 5:9-15

After discussing the differences between this earthly body and our heavenly body, Paul said that it doesn't really matter where we find ourselves on earth or in heaven. His point is that our location makes no difference regarding our priority to serve Jesus Christ or our access to Him. Regardless of our situation or station in life, "whether at home or away from home" (on earth or in heaven), we are "to be well-pleasing unto him" (v.1—Authorized Standard Version [ASV]), to the Lord. That is to be our priority in everything.

Why is this a priority? Because "we must all appear before the judgment seat of Christ, so that each one may receive what is due for what he has done in the body, whether good or evil" (v. 10). Being a Christian does not exempt us from judgment. Everyone will stand before the throne of God in judgment, Christians and non Christians alike—and each will be judged, not by God, but by Jesus Christ (John 5:22).

While unbelievers may be terrified by the prospect of standing before Christ in judgment—and they certainly should be, believers are spared the ultimate consequences of sin. However, believers must still face the relative consequences of their actions in the body—what they have done with their lives. Believers will not burn in hell, but at the same time heaven is not a democracy. It's a kingdom.

Christians are all equal before the bench of judgment in that our sins are forgiven in Christ, who has paid the price for sin in order that believers may be granted entry into heaven. But once in the kingdom of heaven, believers are then subjected to further judgment based upon their previous lives and the experience and skills they bring to the kingdom in the light of their character and maturity in Christ.

HEAVEN

Heaven is not a summer camp, but is another place of service to God. What we have done, our deeds, our works, are not forgotten or ignored at judgment. God forgives our sins and allows us entry into the kingdom on the coattails of Christ. Once in heaven, we are not judged on the basis of our sin, but upon the basis of our growth and maturity in Christ, our Christian character. In heaven we are judged on the basis of the good works that we did (or tried to do), or the lack thereof.

Unbelievers are judged on the basis of their unrepentant sin, while believers are judged upon the merits of Jesus Christ. In Christ believers are separated into a different category than unbelievers (sheep and goats) and then further judged (evaluated) on their good works in Christ, on the degree to which the character of Christ has been able to manifest in the lives of believers and accomplish the will and work of Christ. Getting into heaven is not the end of the Christian journey, but the beginning of a new phase of the journey. Heaven is eternal, which means that there is a lot of time for growth in grace and work in Christ.

The purpose of heaven is eternal praise to the glory of God, and everyone in heaven will be intently focused on that task. Furthermore, it is not a drudgery, but a joy! We will praise God with our whole beings (our spiritual bodies) as we mature and grow in faithfulness, where the fullness of faithfulness will include growth in our understanding of God's ways and God's character, growth in our abilities to exercise faithfulness through music, art, counseling, teaching, etc. There will be plenty to do, and it will all be a great joy, full of significance and meaning, beauty and splendor.

EVANGELISM

"Therefore," continued Paul, "knowing the fear of the Lord, we persuade others. But what we are is known to God, and I hope it is known also to your conscience" (v. 11). Christians personally know the fear of the Lord. Why? Because God is fearsome. "Behold, the fear of the Lord, that is wisdom, and to turn away from evil is understanding" (Job 28:28). "The fear of the Lord is the beginning of wisdom; all those who practice it have a good understanding. His praise endures forever!" (Psalm 111:10). Luke said that "the church throughout all Judea and Galilee and Samaria had peace and was being built up. And walking in the fear of the Lord and in the comfort of the Holy Spirit, it multiplied" (Acts 9:31). People who don't know the fear of the Lord cannot be Christians because the fear of the Lord is at the very center of both conversion and faithfulness.

It is because we know the fear of the Lord that we work to per-suade others about the truth of God, Jesus Christ and the gospel. Note that God is sovereign and in control of all things, that no one comes to Christ apart from God's prior justification. People don't believe the gospel until their hearts and minds have been changed by the mighty grace of God through regeneration. And yet Christians actively work to persuade others to accept God's truth in Jesus Christ. This is not to say that Christians don't love God, we do. We love God with a fearsome love. This fear of the Lord is not incompatible with love.

Why do Christians evangelize if they know that people cannot become Christians apart from the power and grace of God? Because we know that God works through His people, and that God's preferred method of reaching the lost is through His ordinary means—Word and Sacrament. Because we are called and commanded to do so. God sanc-tifies and matures His people through service, and one aspect of Chris-tian service is evangelism.

Speaking to this issue, Peter said,

"For 'Whoever desires to love life and see good days, let him keep his tongue from evil and his lips from speaking deceit; let him turn away from evil and do good; let him seek peace and pursue it. For the eyes of the Lord are on the righteous, and his ears are open to their prayer. But the face of the Lord is against those who do evil.' Now who is there to harm you if you are zealous for what is good? But even if you should suffer for righteousness' sake, you will be blessed. Have no fear of them, nor be troubled, but in your hearts honor Christ the Lord as holy, always being prepared to make a defense to anyone who asks you for a reason for the hope that is in you; yet do it with gentleness and respect, having a good conscience, so that, when you are slandered, those who revile your good behavior in Christ may be put to shame. For it is better to suffer for doing good, *if that should be God's will, than for doing evil."*   —1 Peter 3:10-17

Paul said that "what we are is known by God" (v. 11). God knows us. He knows our thoughts and desires before we do. God knows us because He created us in the first place, and has renewed and reshaped us through regeneration. But it is not enough that God knows us. Paul hoped that we would also know ourselves as God knows us.

God's mechanism for this is our conscience (*suneidēsis*). Conscience allows us to see ourselves completely, to see ourselves as God sees us. The idea is that through conscience we become partners with God by seeing our own reflection in the light of Christ through the study of God and His Word. Conscience allows us to conform our behavior to our beliefs, our understanding of right and wrong, which in Christ is informed by God's Word through the power and presence of the Holy Spirit through regeneration.

BOASTING ABOUT PAUL

Paul continued this argument in verse 12, "We are not commending ourselves to you again but giving you cause to boast about us, so that you may be able to answer those who boast about outward appearance and not about what is in the heart." There are two ideas that Paul was communicating here. He was saying in the first clause that his purpose in writing to the Corinthians was, not to commend himself, but to provide them with material (his letters) that they could use to further the gospel. How so? Paul was giving the Corinthians cause to boast about Paul and the apostles, suggesting that they could point to his letters as a way to clarify the gospel and the mission of Jesus Christ. Again, Paul was not writing in order to show off or to recommend himself, but to provide a written witness to the truth of the gospel that the Corinthians could share with others to help them better understand the gospel. He was saying that he was not boasting about himself, but that they should boast about him and the apostles as being faithful stewards of the gospel.

In the second clause of verse 12 Paul said that the gospel was not about outward appearances but about the condition of the heart, not what could be seen—the world and its values, but what could not be seen—the Spirit and the values of the Spirit. Again, we need to remember the circumstances of Paul's letter. He was writing to an outwardly successful church, successful in the eyes of its community because it had money, members and influence. But in the process of becoming successful its leaders had compromised the gospel in a variety of ways, most noticeably they had confused the wisdom of the Greek worldview with the wisdom of the Lord. Part of that confusion led to immoral sexual practices among the leadership. Paul contrasted the outward appearance of faithfulness with the inward condition of a regenerated heart.

In part, he said that his letters should be used by the Corinthians to help people understand the contrasts between wisdom and foolishness that he had been making. He was commending his letters as vehicles for gospel clarification, the clarification of the differences between worldly wisdom and godly wisdom, between the outward appearance of faithfulness and the inward condition of a repentant conscience. He was authorizing the churches to use his letters to clarify the gospel. These letters would answer questions about why Paul and the apostles should be preferred over the corrupt leaders of the church. They would explain why Paul was discredited for speaking the truth, which opposed (and was the opposite of) the popular Greek worldview, and why the corrupt leaders were rewarded for speaking lies, which conformed to the popular Greek worldview.

RIGHT MIND

These two positions are further contrasted in verse 13, "For if we are beside ourselves, it is for God; if we are in our right mind, it is for you." The concern here is whether Paul and the apostles were out of their minds or in their right mind. Paul related being out of their minds to God, and being in their right mind to the Corinthians. To be in Christ is to be in the mind of Christ. It is to apply Christ's mind, Christ's heart, the values of Christ to one's own life. And inasmuch as we are able to do that, we mortify the mind of the Old Man, the unregenerate, unrepentant mind and nurture the mind that comes with the New Man, the mind of Christ illuminated through Scripture. Inasmuch as we are regenerate, we have left the old ways of thinking behind.

In contrast to this is "our right mind" (*sōphroneō*), which means sound, sober and sane. It is a common mind, a community mindset that is dominated by the love of Christ, concern for the community of Christ and illuminated through Scripture. The soundness and sanity of this mind, this way of thinking is that it is focused on Christ and the well-being of God's people, and is meek to the leadership of the Lord. Paul was not doing his own thing, but was singularly focused on doing God's thing in the midst of God's people. How was it that Paul could do this when the other leaders of the church could not?

SWEPT INTO GOD'S WILL

He answered this question by saying that "the love of Christ controls us" (v. 14). Paul was not operating out of his own free will, but had submitted himself to the will of God in Christ. The love of Christ constrained (*sunechō*) them (the apostles). It held them, compressed them, compelled them, arrested them, even thronged them. They were caught up in the love of Christ, swept up in it. Like flood waters it swept them into the stream of God's love. They were not under their own power.

And yet this being carried away with the love of Christ was not a violation of their free will. They wanted to do nothing else. They had not been swept up against their will. They were actively praying that the great flood waters of regeneration would pour out upon all humanity. Why were they in this situation? Paul answered, "because we have concluded this: that one has died for all, therefore all have died" (v. 14). The reason that Paul and the apostles were controlled by the love of Christ was that in Christ they had died.

Discussing this theme with the Romans, Paul said,

> *"Do you not know that all of us who have been baptized into Christ Jesus were baptized into his death? We were buried therefore with him by baptism into death, in order that, just as Christ was raised from the dead by the glory of the Father, we too might walk in newness of life. For if we have been united with him in a death like his, we shall certainly be united with him in a resurrection like his. We know that our old self was crucified with him in order that the body of sin might be brought to nothing, so that we would no longer be enslaved to sin. For one who has died has been set free from sin. Now if we have died with Christ, we believe that we will also live with him. We know that Christ, being raised from the dead, will never die again; death no longer has dominion over him. For the death he died he died to sin, once for all, but the life he lives he lives to God."*
> —Romans 6:3-10

This was not a speculation by Paul, but had been communicated directly to him through his own regeneration. He knew it was true because of the change that Christ brought to him personally. Christ was as real as the changes in his own life. Paul testified that Christ "died for all, that those who live might no longer live for themselves but for him who for their sake died and was raised" (v. 15).

Here we note that what Paul meant by "all" has been disputed over the centuries. Some say that he meant that Christ died for *all people*, and others say that Paul meant that Christ died for *all believers*, a subset of all people. Let me suggest that both ideas have merit. There can be no argument against the idea that Christ died for all believers. Let me remind you that Scripture teaches that one day every knee will bow to the Lord (Romans 14:11). In the fullness of time—someday—

everyone alive, all extant[13] people, will believe in Jesus Christ as the kingdom of God becomes fully manifest on earth as it is in heaven. Someday the set of living people and the subset of believers will be the same.

Nonetheless, the point of verse 15 is that all who are alive will someday live, not for themselves, but for Christ. The argument that he made in verse 14, that all have died because Christ died for all, must also be applied to Christ's resurrection, that all will be raised because Christ was raised for all. All of whom? Ultimately for all of humanity, and until the time that every knee bends, the "all" applies to the subset of believers. And as believers in the power and the goodness of Jesus Christ, we have both the hope and the confidence that one day all humanity will believe, and in confession and repentance through regeneration will find salvation in Christ.

---

13 *Extant*, again, means still in existence; not extinct or destroyed or lost.

15. Make It Right

Wherefore we henceforth know no man after the flesh: even though we have known Christ after the flesh, yet now we know him so no more. Wherefore if any man is in Christ, he is a new creature: the old things are passed away; behold, they are become new. But all things are of God, who reconciled us to himself through Christ, and gave unto us the ministry of reconciliation; to wit, that God was in Christ reconciling the world unto himself, not reckoning unto them their trespasses, and having committed unto us the word of reconciliation. We are ambassadors therefore on behalf of Christ, as though God were entreating by us: we beseech you on behalf of Christ, be ye reconciled to God. Him who knew no sin he made to be sin on our behalf; that we might become the righteousness of God in him. —2 Corinthians 5:16-21

As a consequence of what Paul previously said (consider both of his letters to the Corinthians to this point) he drew the following conclusion and applied it to everything that follows. "From now on, therefore, we regard no one according to the flesh. Even though we once regarded Christ according to the flesh, we regard him thus no longer" (v. 16). What Paul means by "from now on" is from Christ forward.

The manifestation of Jesus Christ in history has so changed everything that from His manifestation forward, to think of or consider anyone in terms of the flesh (*sarx*) constitutes a denial of Jesus Christ. The truth of Jesus Christ, now manifest in history, has stripped away the temporary veneer of a mere fleshly human existence and exposed the deeper and eternal reality of every person. Paul has come to several conclusions in his letters to the Corinthians, but to this point none are as significant as this one.

Why is it that we are not to consider every man, woman and child "according to the flesh" (v. 16)? Doesn't he mean that we should consider all Christians as spiritual beings rather than fleshly beings? Of course he does. But Paul's words clearly say by implication that everyone needs to be considered from a spiritual and eternal perspective—even unbelievers. This is a universal statement, and we cannot discount its universal character. But what it doesn't mean is that all people are currently to be considered Christians. The distinction between believers and unbelievers—covenant keepers and covenant breakers—continues into eternity. Believers will be saved into eternity, and unbelievers will be damned into eternity. Both are headed for equally eternal but opposite destinations. The eternal spiritual reality of both will endure.

ALL, AS IN EVERYONE

Christ came in order to facilitate this distinction, this historical and eternal divide. That's what His judgment is all about. The manifestation of Jesus Christ in history has a particular effect upon every person that has been or will ever be born. Christ is the central watershed in history in the sense that all individuals and nations have always been judged (evaluated) on the basis of the gospel of Jesus Christ. In the Old Testament judgment was based upon the anticipated Christ, and in the New Testament and beyond judgment is based on the actualized Christ. So, with the manifestation of Jesus Christ in history this judgment began in earnest. Everything prior to Jesus' birth anticipated this coming judgment, and everything following His resurrection celebrates this present judgment—a judgment that has not completely unfolded, but whose unfolding has most definitely begun.

No one is to be considered in terms of the flesh (*sarx*) alone. which can also be interpreted as body, or the fleshly aspects of the body. And in particular, Christ Himself is not to be so considered. This is not a denial of Jesus' humanity, but constitutes the recognition that He died and has been resurrected. He was known in the flesh, but that was past tense. Now that He has been resurrected, we cannot know Him according to the flesh alone anymore. His presence is now spiritual

To understand this we hearken back to 1 Corinthians 10, where Paul spoke extensively about the body of Christ, and differentiated between the spiritual body (*soma*) and the fleshly body (*sarx*), between the individual body, the corporate body and the spiritual body. From this perspective all people are to be considered in terms of the wholeness of the body of Christ, and their relationship to the body of Christ, which is His Church in its fullness—invisible and visible, triumphant and militant, informal and formal. Following Christ's resurrection He is present on earth through or as His church—spiritually. People are either in the body of Christ or they are not. That's the issue.

Jesus Christ "was conceived of the Holy Spirit, born of the Virgin Mary, suffered under Pontius Pilate, was crucified, died, and was buried. He descended into hell. The third day He arose again from the dead. He ascended into heaven and sits at the right hand of God the Father Almighty, whence He shall come to judge the living and the dead" (from the Apostles' Creed). Paul was saying that this is all historically true and that no one in the world will ever be the same because of it. He doesn't mean that only Christians will never be the same because they believe, but he means that as unbelievers confirm their unbelief in the light of Christ they, too, will be permanently effected by the reality of the judgment of Jesus Christ in history.

In this sense the manifestation of Jesus Christ in history is efficacious for all people—efficacious for believers unto salvation, and efficacious for unbelievers unto damnation. Christ is an historical watershed. The efficaciousness of Jesus Christ is a function of His judgment before which all people will stand—both the living (all extant people, people who are alive) and the dead (both those who died prior to His birth and those who died after His birth). Paul is simply confirming that Jesus Christ is a very big deal.

New Life

"Therefore, if anyone is in Christ, he is a new creation. The old has passed away; behold, the new has come" (v. 17). Here Paul said that all Christians are necessarily born again or regenerated, and those who are not born again are not Christians. Being a Christian is not different than being born again. There are no Christians who are not born again. Here, however, Paul does not use the term *born again*. He uses *new creation*. Here we must take care not to limit our understanding of what it means to be born again to the popular ideas among Charismatics or Pentecostals. The biblical truth regarding new life in Christ is much fuller, much richer, more real, more gracious and more inclusive than these popular understandings would have it.

The root of the Greek word *creation* (*ktizō*, from *ktisis*), according to Strong's, suggests the idea of the proprietorship of the manufacturer. The idea is that if anyone is in Christ he is a new proprietor of God, the Creator—not that we own Him, but that He owns us and our proprietorship. In Christ we have been installed as a new proprietorship or a franchise of the God corporation, the body of Christ, so to speak.

A proprietorship is an enterprise owned by a single person who is responsible for its liabilities and entitled to its profits (or assets). God through Christ owns the original franchise, and our franchise branch must adhere to the corporate franchise model. And at the same time we are responsible for the liabilities accrued on behalf of the franchise and are entitled to a share in the assets of the corporation, even as beneficiaries of the Owner. Individual franchises are owned by the Parent Corporation, but responsible for their own operation, which must conform to the corporate model.

NEW FRANCHISE

Each person in Christ becomes a new personal franchise composed of body, mind and spirit, and each church in Christ becomes a regional franchise composed of various personal franchises. The point of speaking in these terms is to provide a fresh biblical perspective on what it means to be in Christ. Those in Christ are creatures—creations, enterprises, franchises—of God. In Christ we are spiritual creatures, spiritual creations, spiritual franchises, whose primary relationship is to God through Jesus Christ. This relationship is spiritual, legal, personal, familial, emotional, intellectual, concrete, abstract, relative and ultimate. In other words, it's actual, real. It is not imaginary, not a construct of human imagination, but a construct of God's decree. It is real and it has real consequences in the world—and beyond.

Paul alluded to death and rebirth when he said that the "old has passed away; behold, the new has come" (v. 17). If the old does not pass away, the new has not come. And similarly, when the new has come, it crowds out the old and leaves it for dead.

"All this," said Paul, "is from God" (v. 18). Here the ESV stands alone. Other versions are almost unanimous in translating this phrase as "All things are of God." This raises the question as to whether Paul meant to say that everything in the world is from God, or that all of the things which he has been speaking about are from God. The Greek could go either way, so the context must determine the meaning. And the ESV's suggestion that Paul was referring to what he had been talking about better fits the context. Paul has made several of these kinds of references and literary transitions in this letter, so this instance fits the pattern.

And yet, the words "all this" point, not only back to what Paul had been saying, but they also point forward to what Paul said next. Namely, that "God ... through Christ reconciled us to himself and gave us the ministry of reconciliation" (v. 18). Christ reconciled us—Christians, and then showed us how to serve the process of that same reconciliation in the lives of other people. The ministry of reconciliation can also be translated the *service* (*diakonia*) of reconciliation.

This doesn't mean that only elected and installed deacons can serve in such a function. There are two senses of the word *diakonia*, two functions or kinds of Christian service. One refers to the elected, formal office of Deacon, and the other refers to the informal function of serving or helping others. The context tells us that Paul was not referring to the formal office of Deacon because he has not been discussing formal offices at all. Rather, he has been speaking broadly about service to the campaign of Christ's reconciliation that is incumbent upon all Christians.

Paul went on to explain, "that is, in Christ God was reconciling the world to himself, not counting their trespasses against them, and entrusting to us the message of reconciliation" (v. 19). What was God reconciling? Consider two Greek words that are translated as world, *kosmos* and *aion*. *Aion* refers to the world in terms of time, and is sometimes translated as age, suggesting the world defined in terms of history. In contrast, *kosmos* refers to the world in terms of expanse or space, suggesting the world defined in terms of matter. Here Paul used *kosmos*, which is the more inclusive term because it includes all historic times or ages.

Reconciliation

So, in or through Christ, God is reconciling everything—the whole world—to himself. And what does it mean to reconcile? The Greek word (*katallassō*) is a compound of two other words, *kata* and *allassō*. *Kata* often denotes opposition, and *allassō* means to change or make a difference. The idea is that Christ has made a difference regarding the opposition between God and humanity. That opposition has come about because of human sin, and Christ has taken care of the sin problem by personally taking on the consequences of sin through His death on the cross. Christ paid the sin debt, and satisfied God's terms of peace. In Christ or through Christ, God's opposition has been turned into cooperation with believers, with faithful Christians, those who follow in the wake of Jesus Christ. Properly said, it is not that God cooperates with us, but that we cooperate with God. He's in the lead, we're the followers.

Again, reconciliation mends the opposition between humanity and God by paying for the injustice that has been done to God by sin, through Christ's propitiation on the Cross, and reestablishing human cooperation with God through the dispensation of the Holy Spirit to empower the lives of believers by changing our hearts, changing our minds, changing our lives such that we become willing servants of God through Christ. We are then able and duty bound to serve the ministry of reconciliation by pointing others to the love and forgiveness of Jesus Christ.

"Therefore," said Paul, drawing another conclusion, "we are ambassadors for Christ, God making his appeal through us" (v. 20). We are all to act as representatives of Christ. When people become ambassadors, they serve in that capacity twenty-four seven. It's not a job, it's a position. It's not a task to be done, it's a status, a worldview, a mindset.

THROUGH US

As ambassadors we speak on behalf of Christ by making the appeal of reconciliation. And inasmuch as we do it right, the appeal is not ours, but Christ's. While we are to make every effort to express an appeal for reconciliation on behalf of Christ, the appeal is not ours. It does not belong to us, but belongs to Christ. Christ makes His appeal through us. And the best thing that we can do is to get out of the way. We need to keep our personal proclivities and preferences out of the appeal.

The appeal needs to be more biblical and less personal. The central relationship that is established through reconciliation is not between us and those to whom we make an appeal. Don't misunderstand me here. Reconciliation between estranged believers is important, but it is of secondary importance because, if we are not first and foremost reconciled to God, no other reconciliation can take place. The first and primary relationship that we serve is always between Christ, whose ambassadors we are, and those to whom we witness. That relationship is the key to everything else.

While evangelism often travels across bridges of friendship and relationship, we must not allow our own personal relationships with other believers to become the central focus of our faithfulness. Faithfulness always puts Christ first. Faithfulness filters everything through Christ, such that everything is understood in terms of Jesus Christ. Our relationships with one another are important, of course. But they are secondary to our relationship with Jesus Christ.

Having said all of this, Paul presses the point home, "We implore you on behalf of Christ, be reconciled to God" (v. 20). This is an excellent summation of the gospel in that the first clause is a request and the latter clause is a command. Knowing that reconciliation and salvation are gifts of God, given through Jesus Christ and the dispensation of the Holy Spirit through regeneration, we understand that the command to be reconciled is a command to receive the reconciliation that Christ has procured on the Cross on our behalf. The primary action of reconciliation is not ours to make—Christ has already made it. Rather, it is ours to receive, to accept. We do not reconcile ourselves to God, we receive Christ's reconciliation.

Those who do receive and accept Christ's reconciliation receive a gift that has been given to them without regard for who they are or what they have done. It is a gift that has no regard for them—for us, for individual Christians—personally. God is no respecter of persons (Romans 2:11). The gift of grace is not about our personal ability to accept it, because even the ability to accept it has been given to us. It might be better understood to say that God's gift of grace is, not given, but imposed upon us. It is God's gift, and God has mercy on whom He has mercy and compassion upon whom He has compassion (Romans 9:15). So those who receive it, receive it not because of who they are or what they have done, but because of what God has done.

NOT THE SAME

Contrary to our usual thinking, God does not treat everyone the same, just as the law does not treat everyone the same. The law treats law breakers differently than it treats law abiders. Law breakers are punished, law abiders are not. And the difference is a function of justice. Justice requires different treatment for law breakers than for those who abide by the law. Thus, those who refuse God's grace, who refuse God's gifts of mercy and reconciliation do so out of their own strength, their own desires, their own free will, their own stubbornness. And their refusal to receive it means that it has not been given.

How so? If I try to give you a gift of $10,000 and you refuse it, then the gift has not actually been given. You haven't received it, and I haven't given it. I may have offered it, but I never actually gave it. Neither the bank nor the IRS would consider my effort or intention to constitute the bestowal of such a gift. Though I desired to give it to you, it was never actually given because it was never actually received.

Whose fault is it that you don't have it? Yours, and yours alone. You are completely responsible for not having the gift because you don't want it. And so it is with God's gift of grace and mercy. In God's sovereignty He only gives His grace to those who will receive it. He knows better than to give it to those who don't want it. He's not about to give it to His enemies.

God's ambassadors ask, beg, implore, demand and command everyone to receive reconciliation with God through Jesus Christ. We target everyone because we don't know who has received God's gift of grace and who hasn't. God does, but we don't. Nonetheless, all who receive God's grace, do so by the mercy and power of God alone. It is His gift. He gives it to whoever He wants. Thus, God gets all of the praise and glory for the reconciliation of believers.

Conversely, all who do not believe, those who refuse God's reconciliation, do so out of their own stubbornness, out of their own free choice to deny God. And they receive all of the responsibility and blame for their own actions, for not yielding to the power and presence of the Holy Spirit. Does that mean that they are more powerful than God because they can contravene God's will for their salvation? No. It means that they are stubbornly prideful and full of themselves.

The decision to refuse God is not a decision that is made out of strength or intelligence. It is a decision that is made on the basis of sin. It does not contravene God's will at all because part of God's will is the punishment of sin and its eradication from the world.

UNFAIR

It may not seem fair to you that God withholds grace from some people and then punishes them for not receiving His grace, but it isn't because that is not the way it actually happens. If you think this way, your concept of fairness or justice is too small and it is leading you astray. You are trying to hold God accountable to your understanding of justice and fairness rather than trusting that God is actually fair and just in all His dealings. There are more pieces of the puzzle that you and I don't have access to, that God takes into consideration. Consequently, we are required to trust God rather than to know everything as He knows everything. That trust is also called faith.

Why does God want us to be reconciled to Him? It's part of His plan to eliminate sin. Paul said, "For He has made Him who knew no sin, to be sin for us, that we might become the righteousness of God in Him" (v. 21). Again, Paul captures the whole gospel in this one sentence. In Christ we are redeemed, where redemption means that one thing is exchanged for another. Our old selves are redeemed for new selves in Christ. Our old habits are redeemed for new habits in Christ. Our old ways of thinking and acting and being are exchanged for new ways of thinking and acting and being in Christ. Out goes the old and in comes the new. That's redemption.

The contrast here is between sin and righteousness. Sin is the old way and righteousness is the new way. Sin is our way, and righteousness is Christ's way. And because we are full of sin, we are without righteousness. Thus, the righteousness that comes to us through our redemption in Christ is Christ's righteousness, not our own. We don't have any righteousness to contribute. We have been so completely captured by sin that we are utterly helpless before its influence in our lives. Sin is so much a part of us that we cannot even see it without having been given new eyes. We tend to think of ourselves in terms of our sin and cannot conceive of ourselves apart from our sin. What God calls sin, we call our unique character and personality. We want to become more of who we are in our sin, and we strive to foster the growth of sin in our lives, thinking all along that our sin is our authentic identity, thinking that we are right about all of these things.

So, when we are confronted with the righteousness of Christ, His righteousness is so completely foreign to our understanding that we do not recognize it as righteousness. We call it narrow minded, bigoted pride. Unbelievers often chide believers for having a "holier than thou" attitude. Unbelievers see the righteousness of Christ in believers and recoil in revulsion. It is so completely foreign to human thinking and so utterly opposed to human sin—the sin that we love and respect —that we hate it.

Sinners experience the righteousness of Christ as something threatening, something bad. And it is threatening, but it is not threatening to Christians. It is not threatening to our humanity, nor to our real identity in Christ. But it is threatening to our sin, the sin with which unrepentant sinners so completely identify themselves. So, they flee it. Unrepentant sinners run from it, or bristle and call it evil. They deny it, and say *no* to it because they love the sin with which they have grown comfortable. They identify themselves more with their sin than with Jesus Christ.

Turn

Only when we see our own sin as sin, see it as God sees it, can we call it sin. And only as we see another option, another possibility for our own identity as human beings, can we turn to Christ and away from sin. The one turning motion accomplishes both things. Turning to is turning from—one turn, one way, one Lord, one faith, one baptism. That turn is everything!

"For our sake he (God) made him (Christ) to be sin who knew no sin, so that in him we might become the righteousness of God" (v. 21). Heavenly Father, make it so.

16. Now

Working together with him, then, we appeal to you not to receive the grace of God in vain. For he says, "In a favorable time I listened to you, and in a day of salvation I have helped you." Behold, now is the favorable time; behold, now is the day of salvation. We put no obstacle in anyone's way, so that no fault may be found with our ministry, but as servants of God we commend ourselves in every way: by great endurance, in afflictions, hardships, calamities, beatings, imprisonments, riots, labors, sleepless nights, hunger; by purity, knowledge, patience, kindness, the Holy Spirit, genuine love; by truthful speech, and the power of God; with the weapons of righteousness for the right hand and for the left; through honor and dishonor, through slander and praise. We are treated as impostors, and yet are true; as unknown, and yet well known; as dying, and behold, we live; as punished, and yet not killed; as sorrowful, yet always rejoicing; as poor, yet making many rich; as having nothing, yet possessing everything. We have spoken freely to you, Corinthians; our heart is wide open. —2 Corinthians 6:1-11

Paul turns in chapter six from the description of what it means to be a new creation in Christ to a call to action as a consequence of regeneration. He has laid out for the Corinthians the character of the conflict in which they found themselves embroiled. The false wisdom of the world, manifest in their midst as expressions of Greek culture and the philosophy or worldview of that culture, had crept into the church. It had sown its deceitful seeds among those who had come into the church from the ranks of Greek culture, and who had undoubtedly brought with them some of the attendant sins and errors of that culture. And what was worse, that false wisdom, no doubt disguised as gospel faithfulness, had also snaked its way into the hearts and minds of some of the Corinthian leaders. Church leaders in Corinth had been practicing and teaching the falsehoods of worldly wisdom as if they were the deeper insights of Christian faithfulness, as if they were some kind of higher spiritual achievement.

Paul had clarified the differences between worldly wisdom and the wisdom of Jesus Christ, clarified some of the subtleties of the Trinity as it found expression in the body of Christ, and now turned his attention to the moral imperative of the gospel. "Working together with him, then, we appeal to you not to receive the grace of God in vain" (v. 1). Now that the Corinthians knew the truth, the difference between worldliness and faithfulness, now that they had become new creations in Christ through regeneration, the life of the Spirit necessarily drew them together in fellowship with other believers—with Paul and the apostles, not merely to bask in the pleasure of good company, but to work together to accomplish God's purpose for salvation in Jesus Christ. Now that they were new creatures in Christ, they were on the gospel team. In Christ, they suddenly had possession of the ball, so to speak. They had the deposit of faith, the gift of grace in their possession.

Not In Vain

As part of the team, they had a role to play, a position on the field. They occupied a place that was important to the success of the team—and they had the proverbial ball! Paul instructed them, called them, appealed to them, urged them, beseeched them, not to just stand there, but to secure the ball and head for the goalposts. Granting them the greatest freedom possible, he provided a negative instruction, telling them not what to do, but what not to do. They were free to do anything within the bounds of propriety and faithfulness, except this one thing. They were not to receive the grace of God in vain.

This is a most important instruction, not only for what it demands, but for what it forbids. The fact that Paul said such a thing implies that it is possible to receive the gospel in vain. If it were not possible, there would be no need to include such an instruction. But it is possible to receive the gospel in such a way that nothing comes of it. That's what it means to do something in vain. It means that nothing comes from what is done. It means that the result of the action taken is nothing. It means that what is done has no meaning, that it is empty, hollow, vacant, useless. This is what it means to receive the grace of God in vain. Vanity is pride without substance, an over assessment of one's value, skills, worth, abilities, etc.

Does this mean that it is possible to lose your faith? Well, yes and no. Though it is the real grace of God that comes to such a person, no real faithfulness develops from it. A real seed cannot germinate apart from real soil, sun and water. It appears that a real seed of grace can fall where soil, sun and/or water are insufficient (Mark 4:5). It is possible that the gift of grace can be actually given to such a person, and can even begin to germinate, but then be squandered. It can fizzle out. The gift can be not properly or fully engaged. Engaging the gift of grace as a disciple of Christ is the subject of this chapter.

Paul quoted Isaiah 49:8 in verse 2. There the Lord said, "In a favorable time I listened to you, and in a day of salvation I have helped you" (v. 2). In verse 1 Paul said that we must take the gospel and run with it. Then in verse 2 he said that the strength by which we run is not our own because Christians are inhabited by Another. And yet, in spite of the inhabitation of regeneration the gospel can be received in vain. How can we understand all this?

All Christians are born again, which means that all Christians begin their walk in faith as babes in Christ. Being born again is not a sign of spiritual maturity, but of spiritual immaturity. It is the first of many steps or stages of growth in grace. The Corinthians had recently become new creatures in Christ. They were spiritually immature. All Christians become new creatures in Christ, but here in verse 2 Paul said that Christians are not to remain babes in Christ, but we are to grow in sanctification, in spiritual maturity.

GIMPING FOR GOD

And the personal discipline of maturity requires conscious and intentional engagement of the grace of God, wrestling with angels—like Jacob wrestled with the angel of the Lord at Peniel (Genesis 32:30). Jacob wrestled with God, and the angel could not prevail against Jacob. This story provides a biblical model of faithfulness in this regard. We are to engage God and wrestle Him for God's blessing.

Genesis tells us that the angel prevailed not over Jacob. The Hebrew indicates that the angel was not able, that he did not have the ability, that he could not prevail over Jacob in this sense, that he did not have the power to do so. The wrestling match was a tie. They wrestled all night and neither prevailed.

Then the angel said, "'Let me go, for the day has broken.' But Jacob said, 'I will not let you go unless you bless me.' And he said to him, 'What is your name?' And he said, 'Jacob.' Then he said, 'Your name shall no longer be called Jacob, but Israel, for you have striven with God and with men, and have prevailed'" (Genesis 32:26-28).

Something quite odd happened here. Just prior to this "Jacob's hip was put out of joint as he wrestled with him (Genesis 32:25). This was a serious wound because Jacob would limp for the rest of his life because of it. So, what does it mean that this angel could "touch" Jacob's hip and wound him for life, but could not prevail against him. Does it mean that the angel could not defeat Jacob? Unlikely. The angel was his superior in every way. So, how then are we to understand this?

Because Jacob had a major role to play in God's plan, the angel, no doubt, had been forbidden to kill Jacob. This is probably what it means when it says he saw that he prevailed not. He wrestled Jacob, but was not allowed to kill him—but neither could he prevail against him. This likely means that Jacob was willing to fight him to the death, that Jacob would not give up. It is a statement about Jacob's willingness to die to secure the Lord's blessing. Jacob would not give up and the angel could not kill him in order to win.

How, then, was Jacob's blessing secured? Jacob's name was changed. Because names represented character in the Old Testament we must assume that there was a corresponding change in Jacob's character that accompanied the name change. That change in character was a type of regeneration, a reconfiguration of Jacob's personal identity.

This is borne out by the Hebrew meaning of the names involved. Jacob (*yaăqôb*) literally means heel catcher, one who trips up others, and signifies a supplanter—one who wrongfully or illegally seizes and holds the place of another. The reference is to Jacob's tricking his brother and father in order to receive his father's blessing (Genesis 27), which would ordinarily have gone to Esau. The whole thing was actually his mother's plot, but Jacob has gotten most of the credit/blame for it. At best we might say that Jacob had been an opportunist and not a man of principle.

Then the angel changed Jacob's name to Israel (*yiśrâ'êl*), which means "he will rule as God" (Strong's Hebrew Dictionary). After wrestling with God, Jacob's character was to be caught up in God. This is quite significant. Jacob would from that day forward represent God and the rule of God. God would rule through Jacob. God would be in Jacob.

But we also must understand that the fact that people are to wrestle with God in no way suggests that people are superior or that they can actually triumph over God to secure His blessing. Not at all! Rather, like a father who wrestles with a child does not wrestle for the purpose of defeating the child, but as a method of training, exercising and developing skills and coordination, trust and intimacy. God does not wrestle with His children in order to defeat them, but to train them. By wrestling with God we learn about ourselves. We learn our weaknesses and inabilities, and strengthen our skills—and at the same time we learn, personally and intimately, about God. We encounter His strengths and abilities. This wrestling is important.

The key element regarding wrestling with God is that we must give our all, our best effort. We must be willing to die in order to receive God's blessing, and we cannot fool God about our strength or our effort. If we fail to give our all, He will know. Jesus spoke of this dying to live (John 11:25), as did Paul (Romans 8:13, 14:8; Philippians 1:21) and Peter (1 Peter 2:24).

GOD IS INFINITE

Perhaps the way to understand this is to talk about the difference between finite and infinite. The difference between Jesus Christ, who is a member of the Trinity, and a human being is an infinite difference. Regardless of how much a human being grows in sanctification. Even if he ends up one iota less than Jesus Christ, the difference between them is still infinite because infinity minus one is still infinitely smaller than infinity. Again, the mathematics of the infinite are different than the mathematics of the finite. Consequently, the power and strength of God will always be infinitely greater than the power and strength of any individual or collection of individuals, save Jesus Christ.

And yet, "Christ Jesus..., though he was in the form of God, did not count equality with God a thing to be grasped, ... made himself nothing, taking the form of a servant, being born in the likeness of men" (Philippians 2:5-7). Though Christ was coequal with God in the Trinity, He submitted to God's authority. And because Christ so submitted Himself to God, we ought all the more to live in submission to God through Christ.

The upshot of all this is that we as born again Christians must engage the Lord with all our heart and with all our soul and with all our mind and with all our strength (Mark 12:30). And though we feel like we are wrestling with God for our very lives—and we are, God is not wrestling for His life. We are as kittens to a mother cat, cubs to momma bear.

Paul said in verse 2 that though God has helped us by dispensing His marvelous grace upon us, and though all of the success of our maturity and sanctification depends upon Him and not upon ourselves, nonetheless we must engage the Lord with all we have, full bore, twenty-four seven. God has heard the cry of humanity, and has sent the aid we need in the Person of Jesus Christ. Thus, they, the Corinthians—and we as disciples ourselves—must begin now! "Behold, now is the favorable time; behold, now is the day of salvation" (v. 2). Now means henceforth, hereafter, from Christ forward.

Paul had pulled out all the stops. He assured them that he had not provided any cause for stumbling or offense, which of course means that he was aware that stumbling was a real possibility, and that the temptation to blame him as the cause of their failure to grow in grace was great. Of course, he was also aware that the gospel itself was "a stone of stumbling, and a rock of offense" (Romans 9:22) to many, to both Israelites and Gentiles. So, Paul pointed out the difference between the legitimate offense of the gospel and the illegitimate excuses that people concoct to justify their own rejection of Jesus Christ and/or their refusal to grow in grace.

Paul's ministry, Paul's letters could not be blamed for either being inadequate or leading people astray. Paul's ministry and teaching were true to the gospel. Paul could not be pitted against Jesus, as if they taught or represented different things. Paul was one with the Lord in Christ. The teachings and letters of Paul could not be used to drive a wedge between believers. Any offense that was felt in the face of Paul's admonitions was not the result of Paul's offensiveness, nor of his mis-construing of the gospel, but was the result of the offense of the gospel itself. And Paul said that people simply had to deal with the fact that it was the gospel itself that offended them, not him.

Self-Commendation

So, said Paul, "as servants of God we commend ourselves in every way" (v. 4), and went on to list the various ways that he and his troupe provided self-commendation regarding their faithful engagement and teaching of the grace of God. How could the Corinthians, or anyone, know that Paul spoke the truth and was a true instrument of God's grace? Paul listed the things that commended him and would com-mend all of God's people as instruments of grace. Those who are actu-ally motivated by the Holy Spirit through regeneration will manifest certain qualities, certain behaviors, certain fruits, certain kinds of faithfulness in the face of difficulties. Paul's list:

"by great endurance, in afflictions, hardships, calamities, beatings, imprisonments, riots, labors, sleepless nights, hunger; by purity, knowledge, patience, kindness, the Holy Spirit, genuine love; by truthful speech, and the power of God; with the weapons of right-eousness for the right hand and for the left; through honor and dis-honor, through slander and praise. We are treated as impostors, and yet are true; as unknown, and yet well known; as dying, and behold, we live; as punished, and yet not killed; as sorrowful, yet always rejoicing; as poor, yet making many rich; as having nothing, yet pos-sessing everything" (vs. 4-10).

These are the marks of faithful Christians. And what do they show? They show that faithful Christians continue in faithfulness regardless of what Satan or the world or circumstance throws at them. Christians persevere in faithfulness, no matter what. Perseverance in the face of difficulties is the sign of faithfulness. The unfaithful give up. They get distracted by other concerns. They are unwilling to pay the price of personal pain and/or struggle. They don't want to wrestle blessings from God, they want God to just give them blessings.

Perseverance is the fruit of faithfulness—not church growth, not worldly success, not many converts, not great music, not building programs. Of course, there is nothing wrong with such things, but they are not necessary consequences of faithfulness. They can—and too often do—exist apart from faithfulness, and are therefore not sure indications of faithfulness.

Of course Christians are called to joy and peace, happiness and contentment—all the warm fuzzies that God promised. But the warm fuzzies are not necessarily going to be a significant part of the Christian experience in this sinful world. Warm fuzzies may or may not come in this life, but whether they do or don't, there is no personal preparation or faithfulness or discipline required to receive them. No one will refuse these kinds of things. These kinds of warm fuzzies will most certainly manifest in heaven, and someday on the earth as it is in heaven, over time, little by little, more and more every day and every year.

But these things are not what Paul was talking about here. Paul was preparing God's people for gospel service in a fallen and sinful world. Paul was preparing Christians to follow the Lord into self-sacrificial living, to follow Paul into the kind of service to humanity that goes unappreciated—and more than merely unappreciated, it is often hated. Jesus said to His disciples, "I have said these things to you, that in me you may have peace. In the world you will have tribulation. But take heart; I have overcome the world" (John 16:33). Paul knew all to well that there would be difficulties for the faithful, and wrote to the Romans (5:3-5), "we rejoice in our sufferings, knowing that suffering produces endurance, and endurance produces character, and character produces hope, and hope does not put us to shame, because God's love has been poured into our hearts through the Holy Spirit who has been given to us."

Three chapters later he wrote,

"Who shall separate us from the love of Christ? Shall tribulation, or distress, or persecution, or famine, or nakedness, or danger, or sword? As it is written, 'For your sake we are being killed all the day

long; we are regarded as sheep to be slaughtered.' No, in all these
things we are more than conquerors through him who loved us. For I
am sure that neither death nor life, nor angels nor rulers, nor things
present nor things to come, nor powers, nor height nor depth, nor
anything else in all creation, will be able to separate us from the love
of God in Christ Jesus our Lord." —Romans 8:35-39

Christian hope is not about warm fuzzies. Christian discipleship in this fallen world is about discipline and perseverance in the face of opposition and difficulty. Both are part of the reality in which we live.

Paul concludes this thought by saying, "We have spoken freely to you, Corinthians; our heart is wide open" (v. 11). Paul did not sugar-coat the gospel, but spoke plainly of its joys and its sorrows, of its ultimate success regarding the mission of Christ and of its cost, its demands on God's people.

Like any investment, greater rewards require greater costs, a greater return involves a greater risk. The mission to which Christians are called provides great satisfaction in its accomplishment. But the completion of the Christian mission remains a hope for the future—a certain hope because God will not fail. But a hope because the completion of God's mission is always infinitely beyond our ability to accomplish it.

We are to consciously and intentionally engage the mission, knowing that we cannot complete it, knowing that there will be difficulties along the way. Nonetheless, the greatness of the mission in conjunction with the assurance of God's faithfulness, provides great joy, even in the face of difficulty. We can face those difficulties because we know that God will overcome all obstacles. He will complete what we cannot. He will do for us what we cannot do for ourselves, but He expects us to do for ourselves what we can.

The fact that the accomplishment of Christ's mission is not as near as we might hope is not a cause for resignation or abandonment. Rather, like long distance runners we simply pace ourselves for the long haul. We should be encouraged that Christ's mission is so great that it will not be easily accomplished, that it is worth, not only our lives, but our eternal commitment and vigilance in this life and the next. As the hymnist wrote,

That soul, though all hell should endeavor to shake,
I'll never, no never, no never forsake.

17. SLIP OUT

You are not restricted by us, but you are restricted in your own
affections. In return (I speak as to children) widen your hearts also.
Do not be unequally yoked with unbelievers. For what partnership has
righteousness with lawlessness? Or what fellowship has light with
darkness? What accord has Christ with Belial? Or what portion does a
believer share with an unbeliever? What agreement has the temple of
God with idols? For we are the temple of the living God; as God said, "I
will make my dwelling among them and walk among them, and I will
be their God, and they shall be my people. Therefore go out from their
midst, and be separate from them, says the Lord, and touch no
unclean thing; then I will welcome you, and I will be a father to you,
and you shall be sons and daughters to me, says the Lord Almighty."
—2 Corinthians 6:12-18

It is important to keep the context of verse 12 in mind. Paul has been
talking about the possibility of receiving God's grace in vain, and
showing how to tell if God's grace has not been received in vain, but
has been well received. In short, receiving grace in vain amounts to
nothing, and receiving grace properly yields the fruit of perseverance.
Faithfulness is both the end to be achieved and the means of that
achievement. Faithfulness is the fruit of the Spirit under consideration.

Having said to the Corinthians, then, that neither he himself personally, nor any of his teaching had provided any sort of obstacle to the
reception or practice of the gospel, he said, "You are not restricted by
us, but you are restricted in your own affections" (v. 12). He did in fact
observe that there was some obstacle that was preventing the Corinthians from growing in faithfulness. Something was restricting them,
constraining the growth of the gospel among them. And it was not him,
not Paul, not his teaching, nor that of the apostles. Rather, what
restricted them was their own affections, their own bowels, their bel-

119

lies, their feelings. The Greek word is *splagchnon*, and literally means spleen.

The translators got it right because it is an idiom for one's emotions, feelings or affections. Paul was saying that the growth of the gospel had been restricted—strangled—in the Corinthian church by the subjective, personal feelings and emotions of the church members themselves. As the cartoon character, Pogo, once said, "We have seen the enemy, and it is us!" We are our own worst enemies because we allow our emotions to get in the way of our perception. We let our feelings shape our beliefs. We not only allow our affections to determine what is important to us, but we love doing this! We prefer it. We crave it because it seems to be the very thing that will make us happy. Then we gorge ourselves upon it because it is so emotionally satisfying. First, it promises the hope of emotional satisfaction, then it actually satisfies such hope by giving in to our emotional indulgences. But there is a cost to doing this, a consequence that effects how we see things.

EMOTIONAL SKEW

To understand how this works we need to see how our emotions work. But this is not so simple. Defining and understanding human emotion is a subtle, complex and widely disputed area of study. There is little agreement between psychologists, sociologists, and philosophers. Even economists study human emotions as the cause of market fluctuations, not to mention the biblical view of emotions. There are many widely divergent views. Yet, at the same time, everyone personally knows about the reality of human emotions because we are all in constant contact with them, in ourselves and in others.

One dictionary provides a simple definition: "any strong feeling." While weak feelings may also be included, the pundits intuitively knew that when we speak about emotions, we speak about the cause of a change or a commitment. Emotions effect our moral behavior. We speak of strong feelings because we believe that emotions are not under our control, but that we are under the control of our emotions. We excuse various kinds of unusual behavior because someone is emotionally distraught. We generally understand ourselves to be people who are able to exercise our own free will, except when we are overcome by emotion. Then, we are under the influence—and often, the control—of our emotions and want to think of ourselves as somehow not responsible for our behavior or actions at such times. Our emotions drive us to act in ways that we would not otherwise act. Explaining their actions when emotionally distraught, people often say, "I had no choice."

Paul said that the Corinthians were restricted (stenochōreō), restrained, constrained, cramped, distressed by ... what? By their spleens. In 2 Corinthians 4:8 Paul used the same word, which is translated here as *restricted* and there as *afflicted* or *troubled*. The word suggests a constraint, to be in a narrow spot or to be hemmed in. To understand human emotions in terms of our spleen is to suggest that there is a relationship between our blood chemistry and our emotions. Do emotions cause a change in blood chemistry? Or does blood chemistry cause a change in our emotional state? Tough question.

I'm going to answer both questions with a "yes" because my own experience suggests that emotions and blood chemistry are in a symbiotic relationship. What I mean is that each serves as a kind of catalyst for the other, such that any change in either one produces a corresponding change in the other, and sets in motion a kind of cascade reaction as a way of preparing the body for a response of unknown kind or magnitude. It prepares the body for the fight or flight response. Once the situation is assessed and responded to, or the external conditions change, both the emotional feelings and the blood chemistry return to normal.

This analysis is mostly about the emotion of fear, but the other emotions work similarly, though the behavioral goal or response of different emotions is different and the blood chemistry is different. Nonetheless the process is very similar.

FOGGY THINKING

The point of all of this is to suggest that our emotions tend to cloud our thinking and our so-called better judgment. And that is Paul's point. The clarity of thinking, assessment and response of the Corinthians was blurred or clouded by their own feelings, their blood chemistry. They couldn't see beyond their own proverbial noses. Their thinking had been captured—limited, constrained—by their emotions.

Paul continued, "In return (I speak as to children) widen your hearts also" (v. 13). Most other versions translate the first word as *now*. It is a conjunction that serves to link two sentences together and isn't usually used in English. Paul has simply linked this sentence with what he said before about our feelings clouding our judgment. He also went out of his way to let them know that he was speaking to them as if they were children, as if they were so immature that they just didn't know any better. And finally he delivered the point of this sentence: "widen your hearts" or as the Authorized Version reads, "be ye also enlarged." The Greek is figurative and suggests the broadening of one's horizons, the taking in of the wider picture, seeing the greater context.

By implication, he was calling them narrow minded. He was saying that they were too intently focused on themselves, bigoted—blindly and obstinately attached to some belief or view of things or some particular opinion, and intolerant toward the real gospel of Jesus Christ, the gospel that had been obscured by the false teachers. And that intolerance produced a kind of blindness to the gospel.

Then he dropped the gospel bomb as a way to free them from the constraints that were hemming them in,

> Do not be unequally yoked with unbelievers. For what partnership has righteousness with lawlessness? Or what fellowship has light with darkness? What accord has Christ with Belial? Or what portion does a believer share with an unbeliever? What agreement has the temple of God with idols? For we are the temple of the living God; as God said, 'I will make my dwelling among them and walk among them, and I will be their God, and they shall be my people. Therefore go out from their midst, and be separate from them, says the Lord, and touch no unclean thing; then I will welcome you, and I will be a father to you, and you shall be sons and daughters to me, says the Lord Almighty'" (vs. 14-18).

Why have I called this a gospel bomb? Because it provided a way to break the Corinthians free from what was restraining them from seeing the gospel. Paul was destroying the false opinions of our natural humanistic beliefs, and showed that God's church grows by division as well as multiplication. The church grows in depth by division and in breadth by multiplication. Both are necessary.

The fact that Paul said this at all suggests that he was responding to what he perceived to be a problem in the Corinthian church. The church had to some extent received God's grace in vain, as he had mentioned earlier. The Corinthians had been to some extent restricted in or by their own affections. Their feelings—emotionalism—had clouded their understanding. And they had been to some extent unequally yoked with unbelievers, the false teachers. Paul was not merely suggesting that such things might happen, but that they had already happened in their midst. That was why he was addressing these issues.

UNEQUALLY YOKED

Why did Paul speak of being unequally yoked? Why did he not just say that believers and unbelievers should not be yoked at all? The Greek (*heterozugeō*) does in fact mean unequally yoked or joined together unequally. We often think of being unequally yoked as pertaining to marriage, and that it suggests that Christians should not marry non-Christians, that this is the meaning of the unequally yoked issue. And, while it is true that Christians should not marry non-Christians, is that what Paul meant here? Does marriage constitute an unequal yoke? Is marriage a contract between equals? Don't the marriage partners have equal opportunities, equal rights and equal obligations?

(Lord, go ahead of me now and tune the tympanic membranes of the ears of my readers so that what is heard are Your words, not mine.)

Biblical marriage is not an equal yoke. There are different opportunities, different rights, different obligations for husbands and wives. According to the Bible, marriage is an hierarchical or representative relationship. Paul said, "For the husband is the head of the wife even as Christ is the head of the church, his body, and is himself its Savior" (Ephesians 5:23). Husbands and wives are actually unequally yoked, by definition, according to Scripture. So, thinking of marriage when Paul talked about being unequally yoked is a good example.

But more to the point, Paul had a particular relationship in mind regarding the Corinthians. Remember that Paul had been opposing some of the Corinthian leaders—deacons and elders—in the church. So Paul wasn't just speaking about being yoked to fellow unbelieving church members, he was speaking about being yoked or in covenant with unbelieving church leaders. Paul knew well that there would be members of every church who did not believe, either from ignorance and immaturity or from defiance and denial. Unbelieving church members were not to be the norm, but neither were they unknown. There have always been unbelieving church members in every church in every era.

UNBELIEVING LEADERS

So, Paul's sharper point was to not be unequally yoked to unbelieving church leaders. When the leaders are unbelievers, or teaching falsehood as if they were unbelievers, there is little that faithful Christians can do because the leaders have the authority and power. And much of Paul's message was to respect and honor those who were in authority and power. A faithful member in such a situation is at a serious disadvantage—and serious risk. So, said Paul, if your are in that situation, break the yoke. Get out! Leave! Find another church.

Paul cited various pairs of opposites and pointed out that there is nothing in common between them. Light has nothing in common with darkness. Christ has nothing in common with Belial, who is equated with what is worthless. The temple of God has nothing in common with idols, nor a believer with an unbeliever. Where these opposites are mixed together, both doctrine and fellowship suffer. Conversely, to increase the value of both doctrine and fellowship requires an increase in the purity or a decrease in the impurity of the church.

How can this be done? By focusing on righteousness—Christ's righteousness, of course, because we sinners don't have any of our own. But we can grow in Christ's righteousness by living in His shadow, living in the historic train of His righteousness, by jumping onto His coattails. Christians can grow in righteousness. People can align themselves with Christ's righteousness through the growth of the fruits of the Spirit by lifting up Jesus Christ in worship, prayer, study and service.

But where the side of the yoke with the most authority and power is dark with misunderstanding and unfaithfulness, where the sons of Belial (Deuteronomy 13:13) reign, where idolatrous and unbelieving leaders are in charge, the disadvantage to the quality of the teaching and fellowship is greatly multiplied. It's particularly bad for believers and not conducive for growth and sanctification. So, said Paul, don't remain in such yokes, such churches. As Paul Simon said in his hit song, *Fifty Ways To Leave Your Lover* (1975, BMI):

Just slip out the back, Jack.

Make a new plan, Stan.

You don't need to be coy, Roy.

Just get yourself free.

Hop on the bus, Gus.

You don't need to discuss much.

Just drop off the key, Lee.

And get yourself free.

REFORM

But, you might ask, why not remain as a beacon of light? Why not stay and fight for God's truth and justice—for renewal? Why not make the effort to reform the church? Paul gave only one reason: because you are unequally yoked. Because the yoke you are in as a member of an heretical, dissident, unorthodox or apostate church is unequal, the advantage goes to the leaders. You do not have an equal say. You don't have equal authority or power. You are unequally disadvantaged.

In addition, whatever resistance you offer to the unfaithful leadership of the church puts you at odds with the biblical injunction to love, respect, honor and obey those who have authority over you. Resisting church leadership puts you in an untenable position, a position that will draw you further into unfaithfulness regardless of what you do, as long as you remain in the situation. To resist is to be disobedient to the lawful authorities over you, and not to resist is to sit under the unfaithfulness of the leadership, which will stunt your spiritual growth.

Where the gospel is being taught and preached in vain by church leaders it is more likely to be received in vain by church members. *So, said Paul, just leave.* Find a faithful church and use your time and resources there to support the genuine gospel by growing in the light of the truth of the gospel. There your efforts will not be wasted, but will be rewarded as they contribute to the furtherance of the gospel and not its retardation.

18. Promise of Comfort

Since we have these promises, beloved, let us cleanse ourselves from
every defilement of body and spirit, bringing holiness to completion in
the fear of God. Make room in your hearts for us. We have wronged no
one, we have corrupted no one, we have taken advantage of no one. I
do not say this to condemn you, for I said before that you are in our
hearts, to die together and to live together. I am acting with great
boldness toward you; I have great pride in you; I am filled with
comfort. In all our affliction, I am overflowing with joy.
                                                    —2 Corinthians 7:1-4

Paul began chapter seven by reminding the Corinthians of God's
promises. What promises was he referring to? The promises mentioned in the first chapter of this letter:

"As surely as God is faithful, our word to you has not been Yes and
No. For the Son of God, Jesus Christ, whom we proclaimed among you,
Silvanus and Timothy and I, was not Yes and No, but in him it is
always Yes. For all the promises of God find their Yes in him. That is
why it is through him that we utter our Amen to God for his glory.
And it is God who establishes us with you in Christ, and has anointed
us, and who has also put his seal on us and given us his Spirit in our
hearts as a guarantee"   *—2 Corinthians 1:18-22*

Paul referred to all of God's promises because all of God's promises
had been fulfilled in Jesus Christ. And part of those promises was the
establishment of Paul and the apostles with the Corinthians. Faithfulness was at the center of God's promises. God's faithfulness worked to
establish the faithfulness of His churches, which included the Corinthian church. God's faithfulness established the faithfulness of the
churches, and God had sent Paul to shore up the flagging faithfulness of
the Corinthians. Paul and the apostles had been anointed and sealed by

the power and presence of the Holy Spirit to establish the Corinthians in faithfulness. That was Paul's mission in Corinth.

PURGATION

On the firm basis of these promises—God's promises, said Paul, "let us cleanse ourselves from every defilement of body and spirit, bringing holiness to completion in the fear of God" (v. 1). They were to cleanse themselves *from* something and then cleanse themselves *by* something. To cleanse from means the removal or separation or expelling of something. The Greek word (*katharizō*) for cleanse can also be translated as *purge*. The root of the word is the English word *catharsis*. Medically, a laxative produces a catharsis. The point is that the first stage of the cleansing that Paul was talking about involved a purging of the body of Christ, as he mentioned in the final verses of the previous chapter.

The separation that Paul was talking about could take place in one of two ways. It could involve the faithful Corinthians leaving the main body of the church, as previously suggested, "go out from their midst, and be separate from them" (2 Corinthians 6:17). Or it could involve expelling the unfaithful from the main body, which is suggested here, "let us cleanse ourselves from every defilement of body and spirit" (v. 1). This idea is supported by the Greek word *apo*, which is a primary particle that means off, as in removing something away from something else—separating one thing from another.

Once the Corinthians had removed the contaminants from the body, had washed the dirt from the body, they were to cleanse themselves by something, by "bringing holiness to completion in the fear of God" (v. 1). The Authorized Version reads, "perfecting holiness in the fear of God." There is a lot in this little phrase. It essentially means holding together both the beginning and the end of a thing. How so?

The fear of the Lord is the beginning of both knowledge and wisdom (Proverbs 1:7, Psalm 111:10). The fear of the Lord is the proper starting place for faithfulness. The beginning of faithfulness issues from the fear of the Lord. The Greek word that the ESV translates as *bringing* and the Authorized Version translates as *perfect* (*epiteleō*) is used many times by Paul, and it is also translated as *perform, finish, make* and *accomplish*. It's an action word, a doing word. The word is composed of two parts: *epi*, a preposition that suggests that one thing is imposed upon another, and *teleō*, a form of *telos*, which suggests the final or ultimate purpose of a thing.

And what is the thing that we are to hold together by keeping in mind both the beginning and the end? *Hagiōsunē*—holiness, sacredness, set-apartness. Clearly Paul was talking about what is sacred—physically pure, morally blameless or religious, that which is also ceremonially consecrated. Let me suggest that what Paul had in mind here was worship, but not merely what we do on Sunday mornings—liturgy, and liturgy is important. Nonetheless, Paul had in mind the kind of worship that functions as the very heart and center of one's whole life, where worship informs one's attitude and approach to life, where worship is the basis for the art of living in Christ.

LIFE IS ART

The art of Christian living begins with the confession of Christ as Lord and Savior, and the commitment to live as a disciple (*mathētēs*) of Jesus Christ. Learning and practicing discipleship involves training and correction (*paideia*), which is usually (and unfortunately) translated as *chasten* or *chastisement*, but which Strong's Concordance defines as

> 1. *the whole training and education of children (which relates to the cultivation of mind and morals, and sometimes employs for this purpose, commands and admonitions, and at other times, reproof and punishment). It also includes the training and care of the body.*
> 2. *whatever in adults also cultivates the soul, especially by correcting mistakes and curbing passions; 2a. instruction which aims at increasing virtue, 2b. chastisement, chastening, (of the evils with which God visits upon men for their amendment).*

However, Paul was not recommending the ancient Greek practice of *paideia*. That form of Greek *paideia* sought the ideal of perfection, of excellence. The Greek mentality was to be preeminent in all things, to be at the top of one's class, the top of one's game, to win, to excel through superiority, to triumph over others. This idea is called *arete*—excellence, and was the central ideal of all Greek culture. To be Greek was to strive for excellence in all things.

In *The Iliad*, Homer portrayed the excellence of the physical characteristics and courage of the Greeks and Trojans. In *The Odyssey*, he accentuated the excellence of the mind, which was also necessary for winning. *Arete*—excellence—was a necessary ingredient for heroes and was necessary to win wars. The Greeks were conquerors. It is the ability to succeed or triumph over the competition, to conquer them. The Greeks were very competitive.

Consequently the Greeks kept only the best literature, the best art. The Olympic games were also products of this mentality of the preeminence of the superior over the inferior. *Arete*—the pursuit of superiority through excellence—was infused in everything the Greeks did.

But this was not what Paul had in mind, at least not in the way that the Greeks did it, nor did Paul have in mind the end that the Greeks pursued. To accomplish the Greek version of excellence, Greek children—boys—were separated from their families and raised in state sponsored institutions and trained for service to the state. Sparta, for instance, trained male citizens from the ages of seven through twenty-nine, teaching group conformity and the importance of the state over personal and/or family loyalty. All of this was part and parcel of what Paul objected to regarding Greek wisdom and culture.

NOT EXCELLENCE, BUT HOLINESS

Rather than pursuing personal excellence in order to win, Paul said that holiness was the goal. Rather than taking young boys out of their families to train them for state service, Paul suggested training them—and their brothers and sisters—within their own families for service to Christ, whose concern was for the wholeness and integrity of the entire society. Rather than seeking excellence through an abstract ideal of perfection, Paul taught Christians to seek holiness through the concrete reality of Jesus Christ through worship, with the understanding that the values and virtues practiced in worship on Sunday mornings should be practiced in everything we do.

Worship is not just what we do on Sunday mornings. Worship is what we do with our lives, how we live them. It involves the center around which our daily lives revolve, and God in Jesus Christ is to be that center. Paul will say in a few more chapters that we are to "take every thought captive to obey Christ" (2 Corinthians 10:5)—every thought, not just Sunday morning thoughts.

The idea that Paul has suggested in verse 1 is the imposition of the end or final purpose of God for humanity through the ordinary practice of faithfulness. That end purpose or goal is holiness, which means a worshipful life lived in response to the Holy Spirit through regeneration. Clearly this is an intentional action or conscious behavior—an attitude—that was incumbent upon the Corinthians—and upon all Christians everywhere at all times. It is our duty as a response to the grace of God to exercise personal and corporate faithfulness both in and as the body of Christ.

To be clear, this is not a function of works-righteousness because it cannot occur apart from the active leadership of the Holy Spirit through regeneration. It is through regeneration that the Holy Spirit takes the lead in providing the interest, the impetus, the strength and the perseverance of faithfulness. Yet, at the same time it is a conscious choice and a personal effort on the part of faithful individuals and of faithful churches. Where the Greeks sought excellence as a means of superiority, Paul taught Christians to seek holiness as an expression of humble service to the body of Christ. And, of course, as with all biblical concerns of the body, there are personal, corporate and spiritual elements involved.[14]

Accused

Paul continued, "Make room in your hearts for us. We have wronged no one, we have corrupted no one, we have taken advantage of no one" (v. 2). This is an interesting verse because it suggests that Paul was answering various charges that had been made against him. Apparently, some of the Corinthians had bad feelings about Paul, probably those who had sided with the corrupt leaders with whom he had differed. They had no room in their hearts for him. Some of them believed that Paul had wronged those with whom he disagreed, that he had corrupted those who sided with him, and that he had taken advantage of some of them. Paul was denying these various charges. There must have been quite a campaign against Paul by those who wanted to smear his good name.

Paul was a plain talker. He spoke his mind and made his point(s) without embellishment or regard for the personalities involved. To speak on behalf of the Lord, Paul had to have no concern for persons in the same way that the Lord had no concern for persons (Acts 10:34). That meant that Paul would not change what he had to say depending on who he was saying it to. He would not say one thing to one person and another thing to someone else. Rather, in the interest of justice and fairness he said what he had to say clearly, forthrightly and without adornment. And in doing so it appears that some people took offense. Toes were stepped on as Paul clarified the gospel.

So, in verse 3 he reminded them that, by saying what he said, he was not condemning them, not judging them. Rather, he was correcting them (*paideia*). It was a function of teaching, of making them understand. First, they had to be disabused of their false and wrong ideas about God and about Paul and about what he was doing. Then, once the wrong ideas were purged from their minds, they could better see what he was talking about. So, again, he was not judging them, as in writing them off as idiots or finding an excuse not to be friends with them. Rather, he said, "I do not speak this to condemn you, for I have said before that you are in our hearts for us to die together, and to live together" (v. 3).

Whether or not they agreed with him, whether or not they liked

---

14 For more on this see, *Arsy Varsy—Reclaiming the Gospel in First Corinthians*, Phillip A. Ross, Pilgrim Platform, 2008, p. 170, section "Three In One."

him, he said that he was committed to being in relationship with them no matter what. Paul's perspective was that they were in it together for the long run. He was willing to die with them and for them, and what is more, he was willing to live with them—to stay with them—as long as necessary, whether they liked him or not, whether they wanted him there or not. The fact that they were in Paul's heart meant that Paul had regard for them. He loved them and considered them to be his friends. He loved them so much that he would tell them the truth about Jesus Christ, even if they didn't want to hear it. Paul knew that the gospel was "the power of God for salvation to everyone who believes" (Romans 1:16). He couldn't keep it from them. He couldn't keep it from anyone.

Paul spoke and wrote with great boldness. He was without fear when he spoke to them. He held nothing back. He did not fear that they would reject what he said, nor that they would fail to understand him. He spoke as if they would understand exactly what he meant. Because he knew that they would—some of them, and eventually the whole extant world would understand. He knew that they would eventually understand what he was saying about the gospel of Jesus Christ because he knew that God would complete in them—and in the world—what He had begun. He knew that they would ultimately be faithful, so he gloried in them. He boasted to other people about them and their faithfulness.

This is interesting because he knew that by boasting about them word would get back to them through the grapevine about how delighted Paul was that they were being faithful by standing for the truth in the midst of difficulty and conflict. And when they heard through the grapevine that Paul was proud of them it would spur them to greater faithfulness as they would try all the more to live up to Paul's expectations for them.

COMFORT

Paul was filled with comfort (*paraklēsis*) regarding them. Jesus said, "And I will pray the Father, and He shall give you another Comforter (*paraklētos*), so that He may be with you forever, the Spirit of Truth, whom the world cannot receive because it does not see Him nor know Him. But you know Him, for He dwells with you and shall be in you" (John 14:16-17—Modern King James Bible [MKJB]). Here was Paul's comfort. Jesus had promised comfort to the disciples, that "the Comforter, the Holy Spirit whom the Father will send in My name, He shall teach you all things and bring all things to your remembrance, whatever I have said to you" (John 14:26—MKJB).

The truth of God in Christ is a great comfort to believers. "And when the Comforter has come, whom I will send to you from the Father, the Spirit of truth who proceeds from the Father, He shall testify of Me" (John 15:26—MKJB). Paul remembered that Jesus had said that He had to "go away; for if I do not go away, the Comforter will not come to you. But if I depart, I will send Him to you" (John 16:7—MKJB). Indeed, Paul had great comfort in Christ and because of Christ he also had comfort in the people of Christ, which included the faithful Corinthians.

As a result of Paul's comfort, he found that in all his affliction suffered in the service of the Lord, he was overflowing with joy (v. 3). He was joyful in the midst of affliction, joyful in the midst of *thlipsis*—anguish, burden, persecution, tribulation, trouble. He was joyful—*chara*, cheerful, calmly delighted, glad. But he was not merely full of joy, he overflowed with joy. He was not simply joyful as the result of his service to the Lord, but he was joyful precisely because he was actively engage in service (*ergon*) to the Lord, because the Lord had regenerated him, because the Lord had dispatched the Comforter to be with him. The presence of the Comforter trumped the pain and difficulty of the service. The comfort was so great that the anguish was simply forgotten. The joy buried the anguish.

This is the faithfulness that Paul taught, and it was not merely human faithfulness, but was the faithfulness of the Holy Spirit—the Comforter—who regenerates the people of God through His power and presence in their lives. The power and presence of the Holy Spirit through regeneration is so much greater than the human lives that are regenerated that it—He who is the joy of faithfulness—overflows the people inhabited. He is the center of the lives He regenerates.

19. Good Grief!

For even when we came into Macedonia, our bodies had no rest, but we were afflicted at every turn—fighting without and fear within. But God, who comforts the downcast, comforted us by the coming of Titus, and not only by his coming but also by the comfort with which he was comforted by you, as he told us of your longing, your mourning, your zeal for me, so that I rejoiced still more. For even if I made you grieve with my letter, I do not regret it--though I did regret it, for I see that that letter grieved you, though only for a while. As it is, I rejoice, not because you were grieved, but because you were grieved into repenting. For you felt a godly grief, so that you suffered no loss through us. For godly grief produces a repentance that leads to salvation without regret, whereas worldly grief produces death. For see what earnestness this godly grief has produced in you, but also what eagerness to clear yourselves, what indignation, what fear, what longing, what zeal, what punishment! At every point you have proved yourselves innocent in the matter. —2 Corinthians 7:5-11

A t verse 5 Paul began to provide an example of joy overflowing in the midst of affliction. Telling about himself and those he was traveling with, he said, "For even when we came into Macedonia, our bodies had no rest, but we were afflicted at every turn—fighting without and fear within" (v. 5). They were tired before they got to Corinth. They had trouble, conflict and affliction everywhere Paul preached.

He would remind them in a few chapters that he had been imprisoned, beaten—often near to death. Once he receive forty lashes at the hands of the Jews. He had been beaten with rods, stoned, shipwrecked, was often in "danger from rivers, danger from robbers, danger from my own people, danger from Gentiles, danger in the city, danger in the wilderness, danger at sea, danger from false brothers; in toil and hardship, through many a sleepless night, in hunger and thirst, often without food, in cold and exposure. And, apart from other things, there is the daily pressure on me of my anxiety for all the churches" (2 Corinthians 11:26-28). Paul's life was filled with trouble, affliction, conflict, pain and worry.

TITUS

But, said Paul, "God, who comforts the downcast, comforted us by the coming of Titus" (v. 6). In the midst of and in spite of all of this Paul found comfort. Paul knew what it was to be downcast (*tapeinos*)—depressed and humiliated. He knew these things all too well. And yet it was here in the midst of his depression and humiliation that he found comfort through Titus. Titus had come for a visit, and that visit provided Paul and company with great comfort. You and I would have been tempted to complain to Titus about all of the difficulty. We would likely have told him about our pain, and our anger and frustration, about how unfair it all was. But not Paul! Paul found comfort through Titus. How was this possible?

Well, it was "not only by his coming but also by the comfort with which he (Titus) was comforted by you (the Corinthians), as he told us of your longing, your mourning, your zeal for me, so that I rejoiced still more" (v. 7). Paul found comfort in the fact that the Corinthians had comforted Titus. Paul found comfort in the fact that the fellowship of the Holy Spirit was both genuine and functioning in the midst of the Corinthians. Not only did the Holy Spirit provide comfort for Paul's own aches and pains, but the fact that the Holy Spirit was providing comfort to others and through others in Corinth was an even greater comfort. The Comforter had in fact come. He was alive and well in the midst of the Corinthians. Everything that Jesus had told them was true!

Paul was also encouraged by the fact that the Corinthians were concerned about Paul's well-being. Titus told Paul how they longed for him, how they mourned his troubles, and how they had such zeal for Paul and Paul's teaching. The fact that the Corinthians felt so strongly about Paul, that they appreciated him and his ministry in spite of the charges against him, added to Paul's comfort and joy. Their love for Paul confirmed the truth and integrity of his ministry.

REGRET

Paul felt so good about the Corinthians that he began to regret the fact that he had been so hard on them in a previous letter, probably First Corinthians. "For even if I made you grieve with my letter, I do not regret it—though I did regret it, for I see that that letter grieved you, though only for a while" (v. 8). Paul went back and forth with his grief about the letter. He didn't want to make them feel bad, but he needed to tell them the truth because they would benefit greatly from hearing and accepting the truth. They would—and did—grow in the light of the truth of Jesus Christ, even though that truth stepped on their toes. Even though it humbled and sometimes humiliated them, it helped them. The hard edges of the truth cut us all to shreds, but the balm of comfort provided by the Holy Spirit in the process of sanctific-ation heals our wounds and makes us stronger, better, more godly, more humble, more loving, more sensitive, more empathetic, etc.

The point to notice about verse 8 is that Paul had mixed feelings about sharing God's truth with them. It was necessary and good for them, but Paul was also very aware that God's truth hurts and humbles sinners. That's exactly what it had done to Paul. That's how he knew what he knew about it. He didn't want to hurt them, but he wanted to help them grow in godliness. So, the pain was a necessary part of the joy of comfort that would be provided as the Holy Spirit mended their broken hearts.

REPENTANCE

Verse 9 provided the juice—the point, the punch. "As it is, I rejoice, not because you were grieved, but because you were grieved into repenting." As Paul shared the cutting edges of God's truth, the Corinthians were "cut to the heart" (Acts 2:37), as were the Jews when Peter preached to them that they had killed the Lord of Life. Peter's initial reception was no better. When Peter's audience heard the truth about themselves, "they were enraged and wanted to kill" (Acts 5:33) him.

This is the way that Christian evangelism works in the real world of sinners who hate the Lord! It is not merely that Jesus loves you and has a plan for your life to make you happy. Yes, Jesus has a plan for your life. And if you don't lovingly and willingly submit, He'll see that you burn in hell! Jesus is out to get you! He intends on ruining your life ... of sin! He's going to chase all of your unrepentant friends away! He'll replace them, of course—with godly nerds, people narrowly focused on pleasing Jesus in everything they do! Jesus wants to set you against your own family members, those who reject Him, who mock and deny His Lordship over their lives. He'll provide you with a new family, of course—more dweebs for Christ! Jesus wants to make you very unpop-ular ... with the godless and unrepentant sinners you so love and respect. He wants to take away many of the things that you love, your sins and bad habits.

This was Paul's central method of evangelism: speak the truth about God in Jesus Christ because the Holy Spirit inhabits God's truth and uses God's truth as a means of evangelism. God's truth then breaks our sinful hearts because it convicts us of our sin in the most personal ways possible. God's truth shows us our faults, our sins, which are all the more clearly exposed in the light of Christ. God's truth breaks our proud and defensive hearts.

But God doesn't leave us broken. He breaks our hearts in order to heal them, to set them right. God's cure cannot be pasted over a proud and unbroken, unrepentant heart. Unless our hearts are broken on the Rock of truth (Matthew 16:18), the Stone of stumbling, the Rock of offense (Romans 9:33), the Rock of ages, the Rock of Christ (1 Corinthians 10:4), they only become increasingly proud as we paste the pride of Christianity over our pride of life (1 John 2:16).

GRIEF

Paul said that the Corinthians had been "grieved into repenting" (v. 9). That is a beautiful phrase. How else are people moved to repentance? What, other than personal, painful grief, will lead a person to genuine repentance? Nothing. While I can be encouraged to repent, the feeling of being encouraged does not lead to repentance. Encouragement makes me feel better about myself, but what is needed for repentance is for me to feel worse about myself. I can be taught about repentance, about its benefits, about how it works and its necessity for faithfulness. But again, learning things does not lead to repentance, unless it involves learning that I'm a schmuck—a cad, a jerk, a blackguard, a schmo, a putz, a sinner. But whatever else happens in evangelism Christ must bring people to personal, powerful, intense grief, because apart from godly grief, repentance will simply not happen.

Clarifying what he meant, Paul continued, "For you felt a godly grief, so that you suffered no loss through us" (v. 9). The godly grief was not caused by Paul or by the apostles. Rather, it was a function of God's truth, of God's Holy Spirit. It was caused by the Spirit of God. Paul was not trying to personally offend anyone. Rather, he was preaching God's truth and applying it to the Corinthian situation, to the people in the Corinthian church.

If for some reason the Corinthians were unable or unwilling to see and feel God's grief for them, because of their sin, then Paul would go out of his way to point it out to them so they wouldn't miss it. Paul knew that they needed to see it and to feel it in order for them to be moved to repentance by the Spirit. Repentance was the goal of his preaching.

What he shared with them—God's truth in Christ—was not in any way detrimental or harmful to them, though it would break their hearts. It was necessary for their benefit, for their good. If the Holy Spirit was to manifest in their midst, repentance would come with Him. All Christians are repentant sinners, individually and corporately. Upon repentance and confession of sin and faith in Christ, the Holy Spirit pours out His comfort upon His people. At that point, they would be able to look back and thank Paul for his perseverance, for his tenacity, his unwillingness to let them slip by without confronting their sin and grief. When the Comforter poured His balm over their broken hearts, they would understand and rejoice with Paul—and they did! And the fact that they did brought great comfort to Paul.

This is so important, and so little understood. It was then and it still is today. So, Paul brought more clarity to the subject. "For godly grief produces a repentance that leads to salvation without regret, whereas worldly grief produces death" (v. 10). Not everyone in the Corinthian church appreciated Paul's efforts to grieve them. Not everyone experiences the grief that Paul shared in the same way. Responding to this issue, Paul enumerated two kinds of grief that result from preaching the gospel—godly grief, which he had been discussing, and worldly grief.

Two Kinds

Godly grief produces repentance and leads to salvation and life. But worldly grief, grief that issues from a heart that has been captured by the world, a heart that loves the world and its sin, produces the refusal to repent, which in turn leads to damnation and death.

The gospel divides. It always has. It doesn't necessarily separate the wheat and the tares physically. They both continue to grow together (Matthew 13:30) in physical proximity, but their separation—their difference—increases as they mature. The character of each becomes more clear over time. It becomes increasingly obvious that the wheat is wheat and the tares are tares. The wheat increasingly appreciates the wheat and eschews the tares, and visa versa. The lives of each increasingly conform to their different values as wheat conforms to the character of wheat and tares conform to the character of tares. Over time they are increasingly differentiated from each other.

But the gospel also unites. It separates believers from unbelievers in preparation for God's separation of the sheep and the goats. So, while it separates believers from unbelievers, it also unites believers with believers. I know that this may not seem to be true because there is much separation among churches and denominations. But, in spite of the apparent divisions, the gospel actually unites all believers. This most certainly does not mean that all believers agree about everything. Obviously, they don't. But believers do agree about Jesus Christ being Lord and Savior. Believers agree about the reality of the Trinity and the Holy Spirit, and about the necessity of regeneration, repentance and conversion—and other things.

And yet, in the midst of this unity, there is an amazing diversity of thoughts, opinions and ideas. While all of these thoughts about Christian unity are true, the only sense of unity and division that Paul has dealt with here pertains to his remarks on the different kinds of grief—godly grief versus worldly grief. Believers and unbelievers see and experience everything differently because they bring different presuppositions and expectations to their understanding and experience.

"For see what earnestness this godly grief has produced in you, but also what eagerness to clear yourselves, what indignation, what fear, what longing, what zeal, what punishment!" (v. 11). Here Paul lists several things that resulted from the godly grief experienced by the Corinthians: *apologia* (apologetics or the defense of the faith), *aganaktēsis* (indignation, irritation, vexation), *phobos* (phobia, fear, terror), *epipothēsis* (vehement desire or passion), *zēlos* (zeal, ardor, jealousy), *ekdikēsis* (punishment, vindication). This is a very interesting list.

APOLOGY

The first item on Paul's list is *apologia*. Godly grief produces the interest and ability to defend the Christian faith. How can this be? Because godly grief leads to repentance, and repentance expands the role of the Holy Spirit in the lives of believers. Then, as the Holy Spirit —the Comforter—plays a greater role in the lives of believers, we find ourselves not merely broken on the Rock of Jesus Christ, but we find that the healing that has come in the wake of the breaking has made us stronger, better, more loving, more sensitive, more of what we were created to be—more human. And because of all of this we understand and defend the process of conversion and sanctification provided by God through the Holy Spirit, who is in complete unity and harmony with Jesus Christ Himself. Godly grief leads to the defense of the gospel. We defend it because it is such a benefit to us!

INDIGNATION

Next is *aganaktēsis* (indignation, irritation, vexation). This is the emotional response of anger that has been aroused by something unjust, unworthy, or mean spirited. It is a kind of righteous anger. To be vexed is to be annoyed and irritated by a thing. Think of Jesus in the

Temple with the money changers.

Paul's use of this word is not negative, but he uses it as a positive result issuing out of godly grief. Conversion to Christ, the godly grief that breaks the hardened heart and brings the Comforter also brings godly vexation as believers find themselves wondering how they could have been so stupid and dense as not to have seen themselves as the Holy Spirit has revealed them to be. It's like catching yourself doing something stupid, and you become annoyed with yourself because you thought that you had already overcome that kind of immature stupidity.

At times this indignation spills over to other people, and believers find themselves vexed because other people don't seem to see their own stupidity and immaturity as they—the vexed believers—now see it through the eyes of the Holy Spirit. This is not necessarily a bad thing, but it often results in conflict because people come to realize that they see things quite differently than others see them, differently than unbelievers see things, which in turn increases the appreciation of believers for fellows believers.

FEAR

Phobos (phobia, fear, terror) follows. This is nothing other than the fear of the Lord, which leads to knowledge and wisdom. But it is still fear. Why fear? Because believers come to see the greatness and the power of God. Because believers come to understand to a greater degree the righteousness of God and the immensity of the separation between themselves as sinners from the God of righteousness that they so love—and that God's righteousness cannot countenance sin.

We come to better understand that God is out to destroy sin and unrighteousness, and that the destruction of such things is both necessary and good—good for God because it increases His glory, and good for humanity because it reduces our sin and increases our fellowship with God. Believers are not so much terrified by God Himself, but are terrified about the prospects for people we love, people who are not believers, people who face the wrath of God without Christ. Our hearts ache as we watch people live in ignorance and/or defiance of God, who wants nothing but the best for them, but who spit in His face because of their misplaced pride. We fear for them because they do not fear for themselves.

PASSION

What does Paul mean by *epipothēsis* (vehement desire or passion), the next term on his list? This is the same word that he used in verse 7, translated there as *earnest desire* and here as *longing*. It is simply the desire to fellowship with other Christians. It is the anticipation of the joy of shared values, shared experience, of finding someone who understands you. Godly grief leads to the desire to be with others who know godly grief and the comfort of the Holy Spirit.

ENTHUSIASM

Next is *zēlos* (zeal, ardor, jealousy). Zeal is a kind of enthusiastic devotion to a cause that results in tireless diligence in its advancement. Christians find their experience of regeneration so personally satisfying that they want to share it. Not necessarily to share all of the details of their own experience, but to share enough to encourage others to repent and come to know the comfort of Christ themselves, to become Christians themselves so they can enjoy fellowship together. Christians become vigilant in promoting and protecting the fellowship they love.

JUSTIFICATION

The last item on this list is *ekdikēsis*, translated by the ESV as *punishment*, but is better understood as vindication or justification. It involves the revisiting of the experience of godly grief and finding that while it was a difficult and painful experience, it was valuable. Having experienced the distress of godly grief and the joy of the resultant comfort, Christians seek vindication. They want to be cleared of any accusations, blame, suspicion, misunderstanding or doubt that may be negatively associated with the pain and discomfort of godly grief. Christians want to provide justification and support for the claim that godly grief and repentance are blessings.

Most people run from grief and the necessary struggles that produce maturity because the grief and struggles are painful. Spiritual growth and maturity don't come easy—nor should they! Good things are always harder, more difficult and more costly. That's what makes them more valuable.

Christians want to justify or prove the worth of Jesus Christ and the necessity of godly grief and repentance, especially in light of the reality and joy provided by the presence of the Comforter. Christians want to defend, maintain, and insist that the pain and struggles involved in godly grief, repentance and maturity in Christ are good, positive things that benefit people. Christians want to vindicate the gospel against those who misunderstand it and hate it.

Verse 11 provides a list of the benefits of godly grief that lead to repentance, and bring the assurance of the Comforter, the Holy Spirit, who inhabits His people to lead and guide them into sanctification and maturity in Christ, and who will see them—see us—through the difficulties to the completion of what God began. God's Word is the actual foundation of reality, and His decrees will not fail to bring His kingdom, "on earth as it is in heaven" (Matthew 6:10). Come, Lord Jesus!

20. In Earnest

So although I wrote to you, it was not for the sake of the one who did the wrong, nor for the sake of the one who suffered the wrong, but in order that your earnestness for us might be revealed to you in the sight of God. Therefore we are comforted. And besides our own comfort, we rejoiced still more at the joy of Titus, because his spirit has been refreshed by you all. For whatever boasts I made to him about you, I was not put to shame. But just as everything we said to you was true, so also our boasting before Titus has proved true. And his affection for you is even greater, as he remembers the obedience of you all, how you received him with fear and trembling. I rejoice, because I have perfect confidence in you.   *—2 Corinthians 7:12-16*

Verse 12 is problematic because there are differences in some of the ancient manuscripts. The Syriac, Arabic, and Ethiopian manuscripts, read *your care for us*, while the Textus Receptus reads *our care for you*. The difference can readily be seen in the ESV translation, "in order that your earnestness for us might be revealed to you in the sight of God," verses the Authorized Version, "that our care for you in the sight of God might appear unto you." They are the exact opposite, and the issue is not the translation of the Greek, but which Greek text is read.

Was Paul writing in order to show his care for the Corinthians, or to illicit their care for him? Speculation as to why or how these different texts arose is beyond our concern here. What we are concerned about here is whether Paul was teaching that church leaders should care for the church, or that the church should care for church leaders. Obviously, the answer is *yes*, there should be mutual care and concern between churches and their leaders. I believe that the Authorized Version is correct, and that Paul was leading by example by demonstrating his care and concern for the Corinthians. That has been his consistent ministry model.

Paul was not concerned merely about correcting those who had done wrong in Corinth, nor merely about those who had been wronged. Of course he was concerned about everyone involved, but his greater concern was not for the particular people involved. Rather, his greater concern was to demonstrate how the Holy Spirit worked in the midst of conflict for the sanctification and comfort of God's people. His intention was not to focus on the sinner, nor upon those who had been sinned against, but to focus upon the Holy Spirit who was working to heal the breach.

BEING EARNEST

The critical word in this verse is *spoudē* (earnestness). Paul had been working to reveal the *spoudē*, his for them and theirs for him. More important than the sin that had irrupted among the Corinthians was the earnestness, the care and diligent concern they had—not for their own justification in the face of wrong, or their insistence that an error be corrected, but their love, their earnest care for one another in the midst of sin. They were all sinners, and various sins would continue to haunt them. They could not eliminate sin in their midst. So, they had to deal with it. And the critical element involved in treating sin in the body of Christ is *spoudē*.

Yes, it means earnestness and haste, and it is reflexive in that it suggests a kind of self-earnestness or an earnest and honest concern for one's self. In this case it is a concern for one's own sanctification, whether for an individual Christian or for the whole body of Christ. It is the swift and immediate concern for the welfare of the body, the faithfulness of individual Christians and the faithfulness of the church body. It is a concern for the process of healing and sanctification that is required throughout the body, for each individual and for the whole of the church. Paul's concern from the beginning was to increase the faithfulness of the Corinthian church, not simply by healing the immediate situation, but by showing them how Christian healing works. He reminded them all that the lives they lived were lived "in the sight of God" (v. 12).

When people understand that they live in the sight of God, that God is always watching everything we do, our behavior improves. People tend to behave better when they know that they are being watched, when they know that there are witnesses. And knowing that God Himself stands as a witness to all human behavior, it tends to bring out the best in everyone. Conversely, it tends to keep the worst in us in check.

Paul wanted the Corinthians to know that their earnestness, their care and concern for one another and their care and concern for him were being witnessed by God. They needed to know that, so Paul was trying to reveal it to them.

"Therefore," said Paul, because of this "we are comforted. And besides our own comfort, we rejoiced still more at the joy of Titus, because his spirit has been refreshed by you all" (v. 13). Again, because Paul witnessed some of this happening among the Corinthians, he knew that God was among them, that the Holy Spirit, who brought them comfort, would continue to do so to the completion of God's plan to bring His people to perfection by the eradication of sin through the propitiation of Jesus Christ on the cross. Seeing the activity of the Comforter among them, Paul knew that the Lord was in their midst—and that brought Paul great comfort.

Repeating himself for clarity, he went on to say that his own comfort was not his main concern, but that his greater joy came because Titus had been comforted, refreshed, by them, by the Corinthians. God wasn't just comforting them, but was using them to comfort others. Nor was it simply that the church leaders were bringing comfort to the struggling Corinthians, but that the Corinthians were bringing comfort to their own church leaders, to Titus. This provided evidence that God was working in their midst, and it gladdened Paul's heart.

Setting The Bar

Apparently, Paul had been bragging about the faithfulness of the Corinthians to Titus, which, given his first letter to the Corinthians, is rather amazing. Paul brought some pretty serious criticism and chastisement to the Corinthian Church. And then, in spite of that criticism and chastisement, he told Titus that they had been faithful and were growing in grace. Paul was setting the bar of his expectations for them by telling Titus how much they were growing and how well they had been doing—how the Comforter had been ministering to them and through them.

And he had not been embarrassed by his claims of their faithfulness. It almost sounds as if he was surprised not to have been embarrassed, that he half expected that his claims about them had been at best premature. But everything he had said about them was true, which made his boasting about them to Titus true.

Titus' *splagchnon*, his spleen or deep-seated passion, his tender mercy for the Corinthians had increased (v. 15). The fact of that increase impressed Paul. Because he knew the extent of their difficulties, he knew the power of that which had overcome them and brought them to substitute the wisdom of the world for the wisdom of God. In thinking back on the situation, two things impressed Paul. First was their obedience (*hupakoē*), their intensity and their ability to listen. How did he know that they had been listening? How did he know that they were able to listen? By their obedience, by the way that they were able to submit to one another. And secondly, Paul was impressed by their fear and trembling, by their attitude of respect and honor that they accorded Titus. They had great respect for him and were eager to please him, to do as he suggested, to make the most of the wisdom that Titus had given them.

RECEPTION

They had received Titus warmly, and then continued in that warm reception by honoring the gospel that Titus had shared with them. They had received him, and then they received his teaching of the gospel. And Paul knew that they had received it because Paul had taught it to Titus, and then saw it reflected in the behavior of the Corinthians.

The circle of the gospel transmission had been completed as Paul witnessed the Corinthians, who were animated by the Holy Spirit, giving comfort to one another and to Titus. This filled Paul's heart with joy, which overflowed as he bragged to Titus about the power of the Holy Spirit in their midst. Then as he noticed that he was witnessing the fruit of the Spirit that he had planted among them with "much affliction and anguish of heart and with many tears" (2 Corinthians 2:4), he rejoiced all the more because the fruit had taken root —and that gave him confidence that the gospel had "taken" among them, that the Corinthian church had been successfully planted. He was like a grandfather rejoicing in his grandchildren—the family seed would continue.

21. Earnest Fruit

We want you to know, brothers, about the grace of God that has been given among the churches of Macedonia, for in a severe test of affliction, their abundance of joy and their extreme poverty have overflowed in a wealth of generosity on their part. For they gave according to their means, as I can testify, and beyond their means, of their own accord, begging us earnestly for the favor of taking part in the relief of the saints—and this, not as we expected, but they gave themselves first to the Lord and then by the will of God to us. Accordingly, we urged Titus that as he had started, so he should complete among you this act of grace.   —2 Corinthians 8:1-6

Paul had mentioned in 1 Corinthians 16 about the needs of the Jerusalem church. Christians had been under persecution at the time. Paul had been converted to Christianity from his position as the chief persecutor. However, we must realize that his conversion did not end the persecution, but heightened the efforts of the Jerusalem Temple authorities to stamp Christianity out. The center of that effort was Jerusalem, and the Jerusalem Christians had been under particular duress, as the Temple authorities persecuted the church, and the Roman authorities were preparing for a long siege against Jerusalem. Food and supplies for Christians were in very short supply.

Part of Paul's mission as he visited churches was to collect money for the relief of the Jerusalem church. He referred to this mission in chapter eight as he began a long section of this letter dealing with the topic of mutual care and concern. As a way of setting up the issues of Christian care and concern, of friendship and fellowship, he set the Corinthian church in its larger context as one of many new churches that had begun all over Macedonia. "We want you to know, brothers, about the grace of God that has been given among the churches of Macedonia, for in a severe test of affliction, their abundance of joy and their extreme poverty have overflowed in a wealth of generosity on their part" (vs. 1-2).

He wanted the Corinthians to know the situation of the other churches. There were probably two reasons for this. First, he wanted them to know about their affliction, about the persecution that they had suffered for the sake of preaching and promoting the gospel of Jesus Christ. And secondly, that the affliction that had driven them into poverty, also drove them into unparalleled generosity.

POOR IN SPIRIT

Unlike the Corinthians, who had built a successful, dynamic, influential and wealthy church in the seaport of Corinth by substituting worldly wisdom for God's wisdom, as we have discussed, the other churches, less tempted to make such a substitution, were also less well off. Most of the other churches felt the resistance of the unrepentant as they, along with the gospel, were sidelined, shunned and increasingly persecuted for their faithfulness.

Nonetheless, Paul had witnessed the same dynamic of faithfulness in them as he had now witnessed among the Corinthians. He knew it was the gospel at work among them, and as we have seen, he did not hesitate to tell them so. Now, however, he wanted the Corinthians to know that the Holy Spirit was widespread among the churches, and that the grace of God was on the move.

Verse 2 speaks of affliction producing joy, and of poverty producing generosity. Following Paul's teaching, the Corinthians should now be in a position to understand how trials and difficulties produce joy in the Lord. Paul had been talking about that for some time now, and showing how that same Spirit had been at work among them, among the Corinthians. They could resonate with that experience, and feel the common union of all Macedonian Christians. Paul was showing them what the Spirit had done in the other churches, and how the Lord was bringing the Corinthians out of their dilemma, their double-mindedness (James 1:8). The Corinthians could expect what the other faithful churches had experienced—joy in the midst of affliction and generosity in the midst of poverty.

No doubt Paul was hopeful that the wealth of the Corinthian church could bring much relief to the ailing Jerusalem church, and maybe to other churches as well. Because wealth has a way of accumulating among the stingy, Paul made a concerted effort to teach the Corinthians about the need, the opportunities and the joys of being generous.

The other churches gave as they were able, as they had the means, said Paul. And more than that, they gave "beyond their means" (v. 3). They gave more than they probably should have, trusting themselves all the more to the care of the Lord. And, as if to say that Paul and the Apostles had not pressed them with a heavy hand to give more than they should have, Paul added that they had given "of their own accord" (v. 3), of their own free will. No one had forced them to give so much. They did it willingly.

Be Careful

It sounds like Paul may have cautioned them to not give beyond their means. Surely Paul did not want them to find themselves in the same dire straights as the Jerusalem church. Paul had always been a very reasonable, rational and responsible person. But, he said, they were "begging us earnestly for the favor of taking part in the relief of the saints" (v. 4). The Authorized Version reads that they were "praying us with much intreaty" [sic]. *Paraklēsis*, translated here by the ESV as *earnestly* and by the Authorized Version as *with much entreaty*, is the same word that Paul had been using for several chapters and has usually been translated as *comfort* and *consolation*.

The people in the Macedonian churches, said Paul, were begging us to let them experience the comfort and consolation of taking part in the relief of the Jerusalem church. Their giving was not a burden, but a joy. They could not be refused the comfort of unity or the joy of fellowship that was part and parcel of sharing one another's burdens (Galatians 6:2). They were earnest about the comfort and joy of unity and fellowship.

To be earnest is to be characterized by a firm and humorless belief in the validity of your own opinions. It is to be undeterred by anything unrelated to a particular goal. Christians are here noted for their earnestness (*splagchnon*). The bowels (*splagchnon*) were regarded by the Greeks as the seat of the more intense passions, such as anger and love. But were regarded by the Hebrews as the seat of the more tender affections—kindness, benevolence, compassion, tender mercy. The Hebrews considered *splagchnon* to be more heart than guts, more a matter of sincerity, compassion and earnestness.

What makes something funny is an unexpected juxtaposition of divergent things. Something is funny when two or more unanticipated and unexpected things or perspectives are set side-by-side or related in an unexpected way.

Christians are known for their hope in Christ, for their assurance of being heaven bound. There is nothing funny about failing to anticipate heaven or having one's heavenly hopes unexpectedly dashed.

Christian hopefulness and faithfulness cannot be made into something funny or humorous. Christianity is not funny. It's not a joke. There is nothing funny about the comfort of Christ, and even less about the lack of it.

In Response

Things did not go as Paul had expected among the Macedonian churches. Paul admitted that things hadn't gone as they "expected, but they (the Macedonian Christians) gave themselves first to the Lord and then by the will of God to us" (v. 5). It sounds like Paul had gone to ask for money for the Jerusalem relief fund. But the money was only a small part of what had been received. In response to the Jerusalem need the Macedonian Christians gave themselves to the Lord.

That's interesting, and it seems to have surprised Paul, at least a little. Paul, too, had been growing in grace and sanctification. And this sounds like it may have been one of those experiences where the preacher is ministered to by those to whom he is preaching. It may have been that Paul asked for money and the Macedonian Christians were moved to greater commitment to Christ through the compassion, fellowship and unity of the church—and Paul also found himself instructed by the Spirit in their midst. Paul got more than he had asked for, and learned something important as he witnessed the body of Christ in action.

Furthermore, said Paul, they gave themselves "by the will of God to us" (v. 5). There were two things going on here. First, they gave themselves to Paul and the apostles. And secondly, it was by the will of God that they did so.

Yes, said Paul, they gave to the cause willingly, "of their own accord" (v. 4). But they also gave themselves to the unity of the church "by the will of God" (v. 5). So, was it God's will that drew them into unity, and then they gave generously of their own will? Or did they give of their own accord, and were thereby drawn into the unity of God's will for His people? Either way the two wills—God's will and their own—worked in harmony. And that was the point.

Finish It!

Then bringing it all full circle Paul said, "Accordingly, we urged Titus that as he had started, so he should complete among you this act of grace" (v. 6). As the Macedonians had entreated Paul and the apostles to be part of the Jerusalem mission, so Paul now prayed that the Corinthians would similarly entreat Titus to receive, not only their (*splagchnon*), their earnest unity and compassion—their tender mercy—

for their Jerusalem brothers in Christ, but their generosity, as well. If the Macedonian churches had given generously and beyond all expectations out of their poverty, Paul hoped that the Corinthians would follow suit and give generously out of their abundance.

May the *spoudē* (earnestness) and *splagchnon* (tender mercy) of the churches and those who inhabit them in our day increase. May we put our shoulders to this wheel for Christ's sake.

22. Moral Authority

But as you excel in everything—in faith, in speech, in knowledge, in all earnestness, and in our love for you—see that you excel in this act of grace also. I say this not as a command, but to prove by the earnestness of others that your love also is genuine. For you know the grace of our Lord Jesus Christ, that though he was rich, yet for your sake he became poor, so that you by his poverty might become rich. And in this matter I give my judgment: this benefits you, who a year ago started not only to do this work but also to desire to do it. So now finish doing it as well, so that your readiness in desiring it may be matched by your completing it out of what you have. For if the readiness is there, it is acceptable according to what a person has, not according to what he does not have. —2 Corinthians 8:7-12

Paul provides a mirror for the Corinthians so they can see themselves. Seeing one's self is not as simple as it might at first appear to be. Our eyes are pointed outward, so the only way that we can see our own faces is to see them in a mirror or reflection, which always involves a distortion. At the very least that distortion involves the reversal of right and left. We can never see ourselves as others see us, and one of the greatest services we can do for others is to help them see themselves as we see them. Honest self-assessment is the foundation for spiritual growth and maturity, but it cannot happen without the help of others. Paul here provides that help to the Corinthian church.

The most obvious thing to notice about the Corinthian church was that it had it all. It was one of the first things that Paul mentioned in First Corinthians, "I give thanks to my God always for you because of the grace of God that was given you in Christ Jesus, that in every way you were enriched in him in all speech and all knowledge—even as the testimony about Christ was confirmed among you—so that you are not lacking in any spiritual gift..." (1 Corinthians 1:4-7). The Corinthian church was large, rich, and influential. They really had it all, nothing was lacking. So, Paul reminded them of this fact.

EVERYTHING

They excelled (abounded) in everything—faith, speech, knowledge, earnestness and love. The first thing that Paul listed was faith (*pistis*), which is a kind of persuasion. To be faithful is to be persuaded that God is real and can be trusted, that God and His Son, Jesus Christ, have credence. Faith provides moral conviction, trusting in the truthfulness of God, and especially reliance upon Christ for salvation. Faith provides assurance, belief and fidelity.

The next thing that Paul mentioned was speech (*logos*). It's the same word used in the Prologue of John 1:1, "In the beginning was the Word...." *Logos* indicates something that has been said and includes the thought behind the words. By implication it indicates a topic or subject of discourse, and includes the reasoning or mental faculty that gives rise to the words spoken, and the motive for speaking. It includes the whole apparatus and the many complexities that are involved in speaking. Paul testified to the conclusion of John's Prologue, "And the Word became flesh and dwelt among us" (and was dwelling among the Corinthians), "and we have seen his glory, glory as of the only Son from the Father, full of grace and truth" (John 1:14).

Next on Paul's list was knowledge (*gnōsis*). The Corinthians were knowledgeable. They were smart, and much of their success as a church had been a function of their knowledge. Brains and worldly success often go together. Knowledge is not everything, but it is some-thing. It is important, though apart from the power and presence of the Holy Spirit through regeneration, it can easily lead people astray by causing them to trust in themselves and their own abilities. Scrip-ture repeatedly warns against trusting in our own judgment (Numbers 15:39, Deuteronomy 12:8, Judges 17:6, 21:25, Proverbs 3:5, 12:15, 16:2, 21:2, 26:5, 26:12, 26:16, 28:11, 30:12, Isaiah 5:21).

Earlier Paul had confessed the difficulties and struggles that had accompanied him and the apostles as they had proclaimed the gospel of Jesus Christ, and contrasted it with the experience of the Cor-inthians. "Indeed," said Paul, "we felt that we had received the sen-tence of death. But that was to make us rely not on ourselves but on God who raises the dead" (2 Corinthians 1:9). In contrast to the false leaders in the Corinthian church who had trusted in themselves and in the wisdom of the world, Paul and the apostles had not relied upon themselves, but upon Christ.

Yet, Paul was not saying that knowledge of the world was a bad thing. It was not a bad or evil thing. Knowledge is good, but it should not be used as a substitute for reliance upon the Holy Spirit, nor as a substitute for God's Word. The problem that the Corinthians had with knowledge was not that they had too much of it, but that they had elevated worldly wisdom above the wisdom of God in Christ Jesus. Here, Paul was simply acknowledging that the Corinthians were smart, and that God honors intelligence when it is properly used. Intelligence is a good thing, but it must be used in service to God. Whatever else intelligence serves becomes an idol.

Next on Paul's list was earnestness (*spoudē*, *diligence* in the Authorized Version). The word is sometimes translated as *haste* and *care*, as well. It indicates, not a rushing to judgment, but an eagerness to be of faithful service to God and His people. The Corinthians had an eager sincerity to live faithfully in the light of Christ.

Error Revisited

When we look at love (*agapē*), the last item on Paul's list, we find the same textual difficulties we noted earlier. The different Greek manuscripts say different things, and the consistency of the issue presented by this difference suggests that it was not accidental, that an ancient copyist intended to make a correction in the manuscript he was working on. That story is undoubtedly lost to history, and it really doesn't effect the integrity of the text.

The ESV reads, "in our love for you" (v. 7), where the Authorized Version reads, "in your love to us." Again, we see exact opposites. Was Paul talking about his love for them or about their love for him? And again, I will answer *yes*, because genuine love is always reciprocal. Christ calls all parties to love one another, and not to just love the people we like or the people who like us. And here Paul was saying that the Corinthians abounded in love for one another, in spite of the difficulties they were having. Paul knew that biblical love called people to love one another enough to treat one another earnestly, seriously, honestly. Real love requires us to tell each other the truth, and in particular, to tell one another about God's truth and our sin, about Christ's propitiation and God's forgiveness.

Therefore, said Paul, "as you excel in everything ... see that you excel in this act of grace also" (v. 7). What act of grace? The

> grace of God that has been given among the churches of Macedonia, for in a severe test of affliction, their abundance of joy and their extreme poverty have overflowed in a wealth of generosity on their part. For they gave according to their means, as I can testify, and beyond their means, of their own accord, begging us earnestly for

the favor of taking part in the relief of the saints" (vs. 1-4).

Paul was not calling for the Corinthians to match the gifts of the Macedonians dollar for dollar, so to speak, but to match them in the intensity of their generosity. Paul suggested that as the giving of the Macedonians provided a testimony of their faithfulness, so the giving of the Corinthians would also provide a testimony of their faithfulness. So, Paul called the Corinthians to be as faithful as the Macedonians had been.

Prove It!

But Paul knew that he could not command them or anyone to be faithful. "I say this not as a command, but to prove by the earnestness of others that your love also is genuine" (v. 8). God can command faithfulness, but Paul could not. Was Paul asking the Corinthians to prove their faithfulness to Christ? It was as if someone confessed, "Yes, I believe in Jesus." And Paul responded, "Okay, prove it!"

Wow. You don't hear much of that these days. When someone says, "Yes, I'm a Christian." If we follow Paul's example here, we need to respond by saying, "Great! Prove it. Show me your love for Christ in a practical, tangible way."

This is so different from our contemporary ideas about Christianity that it may be helpful to hear this verse in other translations:

I speak not by commandment, but by occasion of the forwardness of others, and to prove the sincerity of your love" (Authorized Version).

I do not speak according to command, but through the eagerness of others, and testing the trueness of your love" (MKJB).

John Gill said that Paul "did not speak in an imperious manner, extorting from them a collection, or laying his apostolical injunctions upon them to make one; he did not go about to force or oblige them to it, for men in such cases must act willingly, and what they do, must do of their own accord with cheerfulness, and not through constraint or grudgingly."[15]

This verse helps us understand the relationship of predestination and free will. Does God coerce His people into doing His will? Are people free to engage God's will or can they decline it? Paul taught that the Macedonians had been generous because they were faithful, and then called the Corinthians to demonstrate their faithfulness through their generosity to the same cause in the same way and to a similar

---

15 *John Gill's Exposition of the Entire Bible*, I Corinthians 8:8, public domain.

degree. So, were the Corinthians free to obey or disregard Paul's instructions as they saw fit? Or was Paul coercing them to prove their faithfulness by their generosity? Paul was teaching here that God *demanded* people to be faithful, and to do it of their *own free will*, to do it willingly. Can human willingness be commanded? Can people be commanded to act out of their own free will?

Yes, but only God can make such a command. We cannot command one another to act freely because we do not have any control over the free will of another. But God does. God can effect our free will and cause it to go one way or another, yet without disturbing its freeness. How? By causing us to want one thing over another. God hardens and changes hearts, which means that God is able to control—to harden or replace—hearts, human desires and inclinations, human preferences. Paul was simply saying to the Corinthians that if they were faithful, they would want to do what faithful people do. Was Paul coercing them? No, but he was pointing to God's coercion.

COERCION

God does in fact coerce people to do His will, He causes people to act in particular ways, through various kinds of pressure or necessity, and/or by physical, moral or intellectual means. God, through Scripture and His Holy Spirit, exerts moral persuasion that brings people into ultimate conformity with His will. God causes people to want to be faithful.

Like it or not, that's the reality, and that is what Scripture teaches here and elsewhere. If you are a Christian, you must prove that you are —prove it to God (though He already knows), prove it to the world and prove it to your brothers and sisters in Christ. You must establish the validity of your confession, provide evidence for the validity of your faith. But it is not a test. Rather, it is simply a matter of the living out of your faithfulness. It is not a matter of works-righteousness—trying to make yourself acceptable to God, but of works evidence—living out the faith that God has already graciously given.

The Corinthians already knew how God works, but Paul told them anyway. "For you know the grace of our Lord Jesus Christ, that though he was rich, yet for your sake he became poor, so that you by his poverty might become rich" (v. 9). Here Paul pointed to God's reversal of values. Christ was rich because as the Son of God, He owned everything, including "the cattle on a thousand hills" (Psalm 50:10). At his birth the wise men brought Him gifts to serve as a dowry for His care and education. But it wasn't that money wasn't a problem for the Lord. It was that it wasn't a decision making factor. Nonetheless, He came from heaven and all of its wealth to inhabit the son of a carpenter in a Podunk village in a backwater nation. He literally did go from wealth to poverty.

But He came to provide forgiveness and entry of His people into heaven. He came to take His people into the kingdom of God, to bring them from their poverty on earth to the riches of heaven. And no matter how wealthy a person is on earth, that wealth is meaningless in heaven. Christ came to provide a different kind of wealth.

Heavenly riches are not at all like earthly riches. Heavenly riches are more like the wealth of righteousness, which is the foundation of our human ability to earn an honest living. In Christ the foundation of truth and honesty, of love and service, provide the means for the acquisition of gold and silver—not for one's self, but for the mission of Christ's kingdom. Yoked to Christ, the power and presence of the Holy Spirit through regeneration provides the power of God to harness the resources of the world to accomplish God's will. There is no greater power for wealth than this.

But this doesn't happen all at once. It takes time. Paul made mention of the time involved in verses 11-12: "And in this matter I give my judgment: this benefits you, who a year ago started not only to do this work but also to desire to do it. So now finish doing it as well, so that your readiness in desiring it may be matched by your completing it out of what you have." They began collecting for the Jerusalem church a year earlier as Titus had come to them to tell them about the Jerusalem situation and their great need. Shortly thereafter, the Corinthians began to respond willingly. As they saw the need, they began to want to do everything they could to help.

Just Do It

So, now Paul called them to finish what they had begun with Titus, and to match their actual gifts with their *splagchnon*, with their tender mercy, their eager earnestness to be God's people and to fellowship with God's people. Paul was telling them that they could not give themselves into the poorhouse because the grace of God would provide for them—beyond their expectations. Paul was telling them to match the passion of their willingness to be Christians with the performance of their Christian duties, the duties of love, of fellowship, of care and concern for one another. Paul tied Christian being with Christian doing. He insisted that being a Christian was a matter of grace and faith, of course. But it also meant doing Christian things.

While genuine faith might mean giving large gifts, it didn't necessarily mean giving large gifts because it was the not the the size of the dog in the fight that was the key to understanding what Paul was talking about. Rather, it was the size of the fight in the dog. It wasn't the size of the gift of generosity, but the size of the generosity of the gift that Paul was after. People were not called to give what they did not have, rather Paul called them to give out of what they did have. "For if the readiness is there, it is acceptable according to what a person has, not according to what he does not have" (v. 12). If the readiness is there. What readiness?

READINESS

This phrase is sometimes translated as a willing mind. "For if there be first a willing mind, it is accepted according to that a man hath, and not according to that he hath not" (v. 12, Authorized Version). As you might suspect there are two parts of this: 1) the willingness and 2) the mindfulness. There is thoughtfulness involved, a thinking, an idea. Faithfulness does have a rational component. But this idea, the thoughtfulness of Christian love, is not so much imposed upon others, as it issues out of genuine care and concern.

So, while God imposes the moral obligations of love upon people by calling people to put their proverbial wallets where their mouths are, Paul does not so much impose the obligations of faithfulness as he elicits or draws out the willingness that resides in the hearts of God's people by grace, and suggests that the actual practice of Christianity ought to match the passion of their willingness.

The church, then, is the place to practice the willingness of faithfulness, the place to prove one's faith, not to prove it to other people (though others will observe it), but to prove it to one's self. We don't need to prove our faithfulness to God. If He gave it to us by grace, He already knows its there. And if He didn't give it, it isn't there, and He knows that, too.

As I've said before the lives of Christians are the proof for the existence of God. But it is not a matter of my proving something to your or of your proving something to me. Rather, it is a matter of my proving God's love and grace to myself, and of your proving it to yourself by actually living as the Christians we are called to be. The burden of proof is on you and on me to actually live the lives God has called us to live.

May it be so.

23. EARNESTNESS^3 (CUBED)

For I do not mean that others should be eased and you burdened, but
that as a matter of fairness your abundance at the present time
should supply their need, so that their abundance may supply your
need, that there may be fairness. As it is written, "Whoever gathered
much had nothing left over, and whoever gathered little had no lack."
But thanks be to God, who put into the heart of Titus the same earnest
care I have for you. For he not only accepted our appeal, but being
himself very earnest he is going to you of his own accord. With him we
are sending the brother who is famous among all the churches for his
preaching of the gospel. And not only that, but he has been appointed
by the churches to travel with us as we carry out this act of grace that
is being ministered by us, for the glory of the Lord himself and to
show our good will. We take this course so that no one should blame
us about this generous gift that is being administered by us, for we
aim at what is honorable not only in the Lord's sight but also in the
sight of man. And with them we are sending our brother whom we
have often tested and found earnest in many matters, but who is now
more earnest than ever because of his great confidence in you. As for
Titus, he is my partner and fellow worker for your benefit. And as for
our brothers, they are messengers of the churches, the glory of Christ.
So give proof before the churches of your love and of our boasting
about you to these men.   —2 Corinthians 8:13-24

aul pressed the same argument further by saying that it is a matter of fairness or equity that the Corinthians give generously
while they have an abundance of wealth and resources because
the time will come that the faithfulness of the Corinthians will lead
them into poverty and need, when other churches will then give generously to them. Paul was promoting a relationship of wider mutual care
and concern among the churches. It is important to note that Paul was

not suggesting that churches pour all of their resources into various rat holes of unbelief and sin—causes or organizations that did not then and do not now put Christ first. Rather, he was mandating the mutual care and concern of Christians for one another.

There would, of course, be an overflow of benefits that would spill out into the larger society as a result—and that would be a good thing for everyone. The benefit to unbelievers would be genuinely good for them, but that was not to be the main focus.

Social Gospel

That was the error of the Social Gospel Movement of the early Twentieth Century. The primary focus of the church must be on Christian faithfulness, not social service. We cannot exclude social service as a legitimate concern. Social service is a good thing. But it cannot be separated from the concern for and teaching of faithfulness to the God of Scripture. Social service must always be secondary to the proclamation of the gospel and the sanctification of the saints. Why? Because teaching the benefits of faithfulness is one of the church's primary means of evangelism. Understanding that Christians care for one another in an uncommon way provides an impetus for people to learn more about why that is and how it works. It attracts the right kind of people to the church. That is to say, it attracts people who have not merely been helped and who want to then help others in return. Rather, it attracts those who have responded to and are motivated by the gospel of Jesus Christ. It attracts the faithful and not just do-gooders.

Verse 14 refers to manna, God's provision for ancient Israel in the desert. The point he makes is that manna is given every day for the needs of that particular day, no more, no less. So, when you gather a lot of provision in a particular day, it is incumbent upon you to share with others so that on another day when you don't gather much others will be more inclined to share with you. Manna, God's provision is a share and share alike kind of deal. Paul appeals to self-interest in the same way that capitalism appeals to self-interest.

Paul then summed up his appeal by showing us how faithfulness works. "But thanks be to God, who put into the heart of Titus the same earnest care I have for you" (v. 16). Faithfulness works by the power of God to put it (faithfulness) into the hearts of believers. God put earnest care (*spoudē*) into Titus' heart just as He had put it into Paul's heart. And Paul could recognize the *spoudē* in Titus' heart because God had done the same thing to him. He saw in Titus what God had put into his own (Paul's) heart, proving the modern idiom that it takes one to know one. Christians recognize each other.

Paul continued to teach us how Christianity works. "For he not only accepted our appeal, but being himself very earnest he is going to you of his own accord" (v. 17). Two things happened. First, Paul and company appealed to Titus to go to Corinth to raise support for Jerusalem. They exhorted him, implored him, begged him. The Greek word (*paraklēsis*) suggests that moral obligations were imposed upon Titus, that they pressured him into it. But this is not the end of what Paul said about how Christian charity works because he also said that in spite of all of the pressure (or maybe because of it—it doesn't really matter because) Titus went to Corinth to raise funds for Jerusalem of his own accord (*authairetos*). He didn't go because he had been pressured, he went because he wanted to go.

PRESSURE

The pressure to go was undoubtedly composed of helping Titus understand Jerusalem's need, helping Titus understand God's love and concern for His people and helping Titus understand that God works through Christians, through those who give themselves to His service. The pressure was intense and complex. It also consisted of helping Titus understand that he himself (Titus) was in fact a Christian, and then helping him understand that it was his duty to serve God in practical, real, and tangible ways. And finally, it helped him to see that there was a window of opportunity for him to go to Corinth. As a result of seeing all of this, Titus actually wanted to go, to be of service to God, to respond to the opportunity before him. But make no mistake—Paul was pressuring him.

Here Paul gave us the outlines of a simple Christian education policy, a policy that does more than teach people how to parrot biblical facts. Here is a policy that integrates Christian education with Christian service. The two things should never be separated because God gives understanding in accordance with actual and immediate needs. God gives understanding in proportion to the service engaged.

Paul continued, showing us another important element of Christianity. "With him (Titus) we are sending the brother who is famous among all the churches for his preaching of the gospel" (v. 18). Tradition holds that the brother famous for preaching the gospel was Luke, who is thought to have been one of those who brought this letter to Corinth, that Titus and Luke went together to Corinth. This also means that Luke was probably one of the brothers who had helped teach Titus about Christian responsibility. So, Titus had been taught by the brother who was famous among all the churches for his preaching of the gospel. He had been taught right and he had learned well.

The important element that we need to see here is that Christians went out in mission in groups, not alone. They went in fellowship because Christian fellowship was very much a part of what they were teaching, and one of the best ways to teach it is to demonstrate it. So, they went in groups—twos or threes or more—so that they could enjoy the support and encouragement of fellowship, and so they could model it for new believers. Modeling the church was a key element of New Testament missions strategy. And the most natural means of engaging that strategy was/is to reach our nearest neighbors because they are in close proximity so they can witness the reality of the church in action. Our nearest neighbors can see God's love through us, they can see our earnestness, our care and concern for one another.

CONTAGIOUS EVANGELISM

This is the model of evangelism that has been lost and cannot be regained apart from the restoration of actual biblical practices, biblical procedures and the biblical authority/jurisdiction of local churches. New Testament evangelism naturally overflows the walls, borders and/or membership roles of the church into the surrounding community. God's love is contagious.

Paul then added another important detail. "And not only that, but he has been appointed by the churches to travel with us as we carry out this act of grace that is being ministered by us, for the glory of the Lord himself and to show our good will" (v. 19). Who had been appointed for this task? Either Luke or Titus, it isn't clear. But it doesn't matter to us because we can understand it to mean that there had been a commission of elders who had been charged and sent by the authority of other gathered Christians. There was a system of representative government among the churches that had authorized this mission.

This does not mean that all Christian mission efforts had been or needed to be formally authorized by such a body prior to engaging in missionary activity. But this one had been so authorized, and so Paul made reference to it in order to give it—the missionary contingent—weight (additional authority). Why would Paul do that? Because the problem in Corinth involved corrupt leadership. So, Paul consoled the Corinthians by showing them that they—the missionary contingent—had the authority and blessing of the wider church to do what it was doing in Corinth, which was correcting doctrine and collecting resources.

They were carrying out this grace, this charity (*charis*), which was being administered, managed (*diakoneō*) by the missionary contingent who had been given the authority to do so by the wider church in the service of God's glory and to demonstrate their own good will (*pro-*

thumia), their predisposition, their alacrity, their forwardness of mind, to demonstrate their readiness and willingness to serve.

The reason they did all of this was to protect the integrity of the mission, the integrity of the church, and the integrity of the gospel from accusation of financial mismanagement. They expected to receive from Corinth and take to Jerusalem a large gift, and large gifts invite attention. Large collections of cash invite temptation and corruption. So, they wanted the financial management of the mission to be transparent, to be above board, to avoid blame and any potential accusation of improprieties.

Why were they bothering with all of these administrative cautions? Verse 21 answers the question: "for we aim at what is honorable not only in the Lord's sight but also in the sight of man." Their intentions were honorable. They wanted to give honor to God by facilitating fellowship and cooperation among the churches. And to do that they needed to insure that honesty and honor would permeate the mission both publicly and privately, in the churches and out.

As if to say that there is safety in numbers, Paul added, "And with them we are sending our brother whom we have often tested and found earnest in many matters, but who is now more earnest than ever because of his great confidence in you" (v. 22). Yet another brother was added to the contingent who was particularly known for his earnestness, his *spoudē*, his diligence.

Note that this brother had been thoroughly tested and proved. The construction of the Greek here suggests additional or extra earnestness. This brother was very diligent. He was characterized by uncommon care and unusual perseverance in carrying out tasks, in staying on track, in being personally responsible. We don't know who this person was, and it doesn't matter to us. We are instructed by the fact that such a person was part of the missionary contingency. Having such a person involved insured the integrity of the mission.

And should anyone ask about Titus, Paul said, "he is my partner and fellow worker for your benefit" (v. 23). Titus was working with Paul. In all likelihood, Paul had been training Titus. Paul and Titus were tight, they were close. And they were working specifically for the benefit of the Corinthians, as if to say that their focus, their primary concern regarding the purpose of the mission was the benefit of Corinth, not merely Jerusalem. Their concern was to show that generosity was good for Christians, to show them how their own generosity would benefit their own sanctification, to insure that the Corinthians grew in maturity and sanctification as a result of the mission.

Paul continued, "And as for our brothers, they are messengers of the churches, the glory of Christ" (v. 23). The others were messengers of the churches, *apostolos* of the *ekklēsia*. *Ekklēsia* is composed of two words: *ek* (out) and *kaleo* (call or summon). They were messengers from or of the calling out. *Ekklēsia* was the common Greek word used to indicate a gathering of local neighborhood leaders, the building block of local government, Greek government. The point to note here is that the Greek word for church, used by the Christians, was the same word that was used for local governmental meetings, town hall meetings.

These brothers were not merely messengers of the churches, they were also the glory of Christ. He didn't mean that they were just doing a good job, but that they were actively engaged in work that was an actual, practical and local manifestation of Christ's glory. As faithful Christians they gave glory to the Lord in all that they did. They praised the Lord for His care and concern. Then they offered themselves to be servants of God's will, of God's glory, so that as they engaged the Lord in obedience, the glory of the Lord showed through them. They made the effort—and successfully so—to make themselves transparent to the glory of God in Jesus Christ through their service.

Paul then summed up his argument by repeating himself, "So give proof before the churches of your love and of our boasting about you to these men" (v. 24). In verse 8 Paul talked about Christians proving themselves to themselves by their earnestness, their *spoudē*, their diligence and eagerness to serve the Lord. Here Paul takes the proof that believers have given to themselves and tells them that through their service to the Lord, their *spoudē* will also be revealed to others, to the churches. People notice genuine Christian service. It's too rare. It stands out. We need to make it more common.

Can Christian service be abused? Of course it can, anything can be abused. Abuse in this case would turn our earnestness, our diligence and eagerness to serve into either a kind of works-righteousness or an expression of self-pride. Both are errors. Both are to be avoided. And only the Holy Spirit can avoid them. Only the Holy Spirit can insure that our service to Christ is rightly engaged. The Holy Spirit trumps works-righteousness by His presence in the life of the individual. The power and presence of the Holy Spirit through regeneration insures that service to Christ is engaged, not to attain salvation, but in response to the salvation that has already been given. The power and presence of the Holy Spirit dominates the ego through the inspiration of genuine love of God and the clarification of our identity in Christ, of our personal weakness, our inability and sinfulness before God's holiness—and of God's overwhelming love for His people. The result on the human psyche is genuine humility. Pride is humiliated.

But this humility in the face of God's Holy Spirit does not manifest as weakness. Of course it reveals and solidifies our understanding of our own personal weaknesses and insignificance in the midst of the reality in which we live. Atheists talk about this a lot. Our lives are revealed to be nothing more than "a mist that appears for a little time and then vanishes" (James 4:14). But that is not the end of the story.

The power of God in Jesus Christ is also revealed, and we find ourselves emboldened with unusual courage, clarity and strength to proclaim, celebrate and serve Christ who is the very power of God. We are weak and insignificant, but God is great and powerful. And God has sent Christ to us, to you and me, for our good, for our salvation and our sanctification through service. As we engage in service to Jesus Christ in the power and presence of the Holy Spirit through regeneration we find great strength and boldness.

Earlier Paul wrote, "Since we have such a hope, we are very bold, not like Moses, who would put a veil over his face so that the Israelites might not gaze at the outcome of what was being brought to an end. But their minds were hardened. For to this day, when they read the old covenant, that same veil remains unlifted, because only through Christ is it taken away. Yes, to this day whenever Moses is read a veil lies over their hearts. But when one turns to the Lord, the veil is removed." (2 Corinthians 3:12-15).

The removal of the veil that Paul mentioned is an allusion to the fact that the life and death of Jesus Christ clarifies the Scriptures. Christ is the unseen mystery of the Old Testament, not just for the Jews, but for the whole world. In Christ the veil is not merely lifted from the Jews, but it is lifted from everyone willing to engage the Old Testament in the light of Christ. Christ is the cornerstone of the Old Testament and the capstone of the New Testament. In Christ Scripture comes alive in such a way that service to Christ becomes the highest expression of freedom known to history.

Paul wrote the Romans, "For I consider that the sufferings of this present time are not worth comparing with the glory that is to be revealed to us. For the creation waits with eager longing for the revealing of the sons of God. For the creation was subjected to futility, not willingly, but because of him who subjected it, in hope that the creation itself will be set free from its bondage to corruption and obtain the freedom of the glory of the children of God. For we know that the whole creation has been groaning together in the pains of childbirth until now" (Romans 8:18-22), until the birth of Christ.

So, "when one turns to the Lord, the veil is removed. Now the Lord is the Spirit, and where the Spirit of the Lord is, there is freedom" (2 Corinthians 3:16-17). That freedom is our freedom, but it is not ours to keep. It is ours to share.

23. Doing Good

Now it is superfluous for me to write to you about the ministry for the saints, for I know your readiness, of which I boast about you to the people of Macedonia, saying that Achaia has been ready since last year. And your zeal has stirred up most of them. But I am sending the brothers so that our boasting about you may not prove empty in this matter, so that you may be ready, as I said you would be. Otherwise, if some Macedonians come with me and find that you are not ready, we would be humiliated—to say nothing of you—for being so confident. So I thought it necessary to urge the brothers to go on ahead to you and arrange in advance for the gift you have promised, so that it may be ready as a willing gift, not as an exaction. The point is this: whoever sows sparingly will also reap sparingly, and whoever sows bountifully will also reap bountifully. Each one must give as he has decided in his heart, not reluctantly or under compulsion, for God loves a cheerful giver. And God is able to make all grace abound to you, so that having all sufficiency in all things at all times, you may abound in every good work. —2 Corinthians 9:1-8*

What does Paul mean that it was superfluous for him to write to them about the ministry to the saints? He knew that they already knew what he was about to say. His writing to them about this was not necessary. He was not instructing them, nor admonishing them. And he was doing more than encouraging them. He was basking in the joy of fellowship with them. Paul found much joy in sharing the truth of Jesus Christ with the saints, with other believers. And he knew that other believers enjoyed gnawing on the bones of truth, as well. So, he was sharing more bones and enjoying the gnaw.

In particular, he was enjoying a fuller discussion of the joy of ministry (*diakonia*), the joy of serving the needs of believers. Christian service was a joy to Paul, and he wanted to communicate that joy to them as a way of increasing their joy and his own. He knew that they would share this joy because he was acquainted with their readiness (*prothumia*), their predisposition, their eagerness, their attitude. He knew their love of God and their love for the things of God. So, he knew that they would enjoy hearing what he had to say, even though they already knew it.

Paul knew them well, and had been boasting about them in Macedonia, sharing with others how they loved the Lord and about their faithfulness, eagerness and willingness to serve. It seems that he had been talking to the Acacians about them, and that his boasting about the Corinthians to the Acacians had helped get the Acacians ready. It served as a goad to their maturity. It is not entirely clear what Paul meant when he said that Acacia had been ready since last year. Ready for what?

READY

There are at least two possibilities. First, he may have meant that Acacia had been collecting gifts for Jerusalem since last year. Or second, he may have meant that his boasting about the Corinthians to the Acacians had helped them grow in faithfulness, eagerness and willingness to serve over the past year in the same way that the Corinthians had grown in faithfulness, eagerness and willingness to serve. Or both. He might have been referring to the actual gifts that were now ready to be collected and sent, or to the state of heart and mind that were willing to give that was now ready.

Paul boasted about the faith and commitment of the Corinthians to the Acacians, and the result was the stirring up of their zeal. Faith, seeing faith in action, is an encouragement to the faithful to become more faithful. It's the dynamic of faithful churches. It is the way that faithfulness is supposed to beget more faithfulness. Like produces like.

And because Paul's boasting of faithful Christians to other Christians helped encourage them to greater faithfulness, Paul sent a contingency to Corinth to do the same thing for them. He was sending them another round of encouragement so that they could hear about the growing faithfulness of other Christians and experience another wave of increased faithfulness in their own midst as a result. Paul was stirring up the troops so that they all would be ready, prepared.

Paul concerned that some Macedonians might come with him to Corinth, and he didn't want the Macedonians to be disappointed with the spiritual condition of the Corinthians. The Corinthians had been doing better, so he had boasted about them. But they were probably not on the same level of spiritual maturity as the Macedonians.

So, Paul wanted to give them another stirring in order to keep the Macedonians from being disappointed with the immaturity of the Corinthians. Paul had not lied or deceived anyone in his boasting. It was just that people do not grow and mature at the same rate or to the same level. So, while this additional encouragement was not necessary, it would be beneficial to all involved.

If the Macedonians found the Corinthians unprepared or were disappointed with the level or degree of their faithfulness, Paul would be embarrassed, and the faith of the Macedonians might be diminished as a result. It would not be a reflection on the Corinthians, but upon Paul, who did not want the Macedonians to be disappointed. The Corinthians had been growing and Paul relished in that fact. But Paul thought that they had fallen behind the Macedonians, probably as a result of the conflict and corrupt leadership that had plagued them of late. So, he sent them another dose of encouragement through the contingency that carried this letter to them. Paul had been pretty hard on them. He admitted that he had "grieved" (2 Corinthians 2:8) them, and may have been trying to make up for it.

This letter and the contingency who brought it were to help the Corinthians get back up to speed, to help them recover from their setback. Apparently, there had been a contingency that had gone around to various churches to collect help for Jerusalem. We can think of it as a caravan that picked up supplies and travelers at each stop. No doubt, the gifts and resources for Jerusalem were large because the need was great. So, as they went they also needed additional people to help with security, to keep the collection from being stolen. Paul may have wanted the Corinthians to be ready for the arrival of the caravan, so that the caravan would not have to stop for a protracted time while the Corinthians scrambled to get their corporate act together. So Paul sent this contingency ahead—to help prepare the Corinthians.

He also wanted everyone involved to know that all of the gifts gathered for Jerusalem were free will offerings and were not being extorted from the churches. There is a difference between encouraging Christians to be faithful and extorting them. The motive of extortion is fear, while the motive of faithfulness is love. Extortion exploits the fear of others, while faithfulness builds upon the love of God and of His people. While the fear of the Lord is the beginning of wisdom, love trumps fear in the long run.

Illustrating this idea, Paul said that, "whoever sows sparingly will also reap sparingly, and whoever sows bountifully will also reap bountifully" (v. 6), incorporating a common truth of farming that they would be familiar with. This was to be a guiding principle of faithfulness. Jesus had taught the same thing. "Everyone to whom much was given, of him much will be required" (Luke 12:48). Much had been given to the Corinthians. They had the means to sow bountifully, and the expectations regarding their faithfulness were high.

Finally, wrote Paul, "Each one must give as he has decided in his heart, not reluctantly or under compulsion, for God loves a cheerful giver" (v. 7). Christians should give as they perceive the need of those they give to. The greater the need, the greater the need for greater gifts. Here Paul teaches Christians to follow their hearts, to follow their empathy, their sympathy. But Paul did not want Christian giving to be based upon pity, feeling sorry for others, nor upon guilt regarding one's own situation. Pity and guilt were not to be the basis of Christian giving. Neither was compulsion, neither self-imposed or imposed by others. Christians were not to extort gifts, neither emotional extortion nor threats of violence or revenge. Rather, all Christian giving was to be of one's own accord, one's own willingness.

Sure, Christians were to understand the moral obligations of love for the brethren, and where such morality was not understood, it was incumbent upon other Christians to teach it, to share their love and understanding about how God's love works through other Christians, through the body of Christ. Mutual care and concern are fruits of Christianity. Such fruits were to be sown among the churches. Mutual care and concern were to be sown and planted in the churches so that there would be a rich harvest of mutual care and concern.

However, mutual care and concern were not to be a drudgery, but a joy. God loves cheerful giving, joyful giving, delight in contributing to the welfare of the saints, delight and satisfaction in contributing to the growth of the Christian mission, to the furtherance of the cause of Christ. There are several important lessons here, and surely one of them pertains to the recipients of the gifts. I mentioned earlier the importance of Christian missions being, first, Christian, and second, missions.

STRAIGHT THINKING

People enjoy giving to a winning cause, and they don't enjoy giving to a loosing cause. The implications of this idea have been abandoned by too many mission efforts in the modern world. Too many mission agencies separate social service from gospel teaching, rationalizing that people need to have food in their bellies before they can think straight. This would be good advice if the gospel was a matter of thinking straight—but it isn't! Of course thinking straight is important, but what thinking straight means from a gospel perspective is thinking God's thoughts after Him. It is thinking that is empowered by the presence of the Holy Spirit through regeneration. And that kind of thinking does not occur prior to regeneration, which means that unregenerate people cannot think straight from a gospel perspective.

Social services given to unregenerate people might contribute to Christ's cause in the world, and they might not, depending on whether such people become regenerate at some point in the future. Some will and some won't. So, it's a crap shoot from a human perspective because we do not know who is actually regenerate, and we know even less about those who might become regenerate in the future. But we do know that there is a higher occurrence of regeneration among those who claim to be regenerate, who claim to love the Lord, than among those who make no such claim. This means that Christ gets more bang for the proverbial buck when we support self-proclaimed regenerate Christians than when we support people who make no such claim.

In addition, our resources are limited and the needs are great. We cannot meet all of the social needs in the world. So, we must make some decisions and distinctions about who we as Christians support and what we as Christians do with our resources. Paul is here recommending by implication that we need to follow his example and sow mutual care and concern among Christians. Doing that, we will not separate social service from gospel preaching and teaching because Christians will be as hungry for God's Word as they are for food. The two things—social service and gospel teaching—go together in Scripture and we need to stop separating them. How do we do that? Those Christians who bring social services must also be regenerate and must bring the gospel message as part and parcel of all social services provided. They must also follow Paul's lead here and model Christian love and fellowship. It must be clear that these two things go together and that we will not separate what God has joined together, if I may mix metaphors.

I'm not saying that there are no Christian mission groups who do this today. Rather, I'm saying that the liberalization of Christianity over the centuries is the source of this separation, and that it needs to stop in order that the power of genuine Christian missions may again move the world. All missionary work, all church giving needs to issue from gospel joy and it must produce gospel joy, joy that is not and cannot be thwarted by the circumstances of the world, joy that issues out of our love for Jesus Christ, joy that increases through service to Jesus Christ.

Verse 8 shows us how God's grace unfolds and brings believers to greater maturity and effectiveness for Christ. First, it is God who is able to make all grace abound to believers. God is the source of this grace, this gift. In addition, it is God who makes it abound (*perisseuō*), who makes it abundant, plentiful.

Please understand that God's grace is not a thing, not a tangible substance that can be handled and passed around. The fact that the gospel is a gift given by God means that the gospel is something of substance. The good news of Jesus Christ is the story of an historical event that happened through an historical person. There is specific content to the story, and it needs to be told correctly or it fails to be the gospel. At one time in history Jesus Christ was an actual person who lived and could be handled and passed around as the apostles clearly and adequately testified.

The grace of God that sent Jesus to this sinful world is a characteristic of God. God is graceful, He is generous, loving and kind. And it was because of His grace that we have the gospel of Jesus Christ and the way of salvation. But this characteristic of God is not a tangible thing. It is a character quality that belongs to God. Of course, God wants us to have that quality, too. So, He sends it through His Holy Spirit to His people through regeneration. Christians then receive the Holy Spirit and share in the gracefulness of God. The Holy Spirit also brings gifts— talents, abilities and passions. These talents, abilities and passions then lead and guide us to accomplish God's purposes in hundreds of little ways in our lives, and in the lives of others. This is the primary way that God makes His grace abound.

Paul then tells us that the reason that God makes His grace abound is so that we—Christians, His people, His church—will be sufficient in all things. No one individual is sufficient in all things, nor even sufficient in everything that he or she does. Rather, Paul was talking to the church in her plurality, as a corporate body. God has distributed His gifts throughout the church(es). No one individual Christian or individual church has all of the gifts. Rather, they have been distributed in order to make the churches both sufficient and interdependent. God has distributed His gifts in order to make Christians dependent upon one another. That dependence, also called mutual care and concern, is an indispensable part of being faithful. And, Paul said here, that mutual care and concern in Christ is also our sufficiency. It will do the trick. It will complete the circuit, flip the switch, get the job done— pick your metaphor.

He went on to say in the last phrase of verse 8 that this grace is for *you*. If you are reading these words or hearing this message, it is for you. You are a near neighbor, and this is part of the overflow of God's love. But it is not for you to keep for yourself. It is for you so that you will abound in every good work. God blesses His people with an abundance of goodness, of talent and abilities, so that good works will abound. We are blessed so that we can be a blessing to others (Genesis

12:2).

We must not be so afraid of works-righteousness that we fail to engage in good works—in social service and the teaching of the gospel. While we must warn everyone that people cannot please God apart from their own actual regeneration—and that regeneration is a supernatural work of the Holy Spirit and not something that we can do for ourselves or cause to happen ourselves, but something that has already been done through Jesus Christ—we must also warn Christians that they cannot please God apart from doing good works. The primary good work that must be done, and the good work that must accompany all other good works is the preaching and teaching of the gospel of Jesus Christ. There is no work more good than this.

Of course, no one is saved by doing good works because "faith comes from hearing, and hearing through the word of Christ" (Romans 10:17). So, by harnessing the preaching and teaching the gospel to good works (social service) in such a way that it is clear that good works flow from the gospel of Jesus Christ as a consequence of the power and presence of the Holy Spirit through regeneration, the long standing confusion about works-righteousness may come to an end.

It is the morbid fear of works-righteousness that tends to separate belief and behavior, to separate faithfulness from obedience to God's Word. Too many Christians are afraid that obedience to God's Word is always a function of legalism, always a matter of works-righteousness, and so deny the necessary connection between faithfulness and obedience.

I'm not denying Christian freedom. Rather, I'm saying that in Christ we are free from sin and therefore free to engage in obedience to Christ. In Christ we are not free to deny God's law, God's Way. Rather, in Christ we are free to engage the Spirit of the law as it has been reformed by Jesus Christ and His apostles in the New Testament.

And so we must abandon the morbid fear of works-righteousness and take up the righteous works of God Himself, in whose Holy Spirit we have been regenerated through the propitiation of Jesus Christ, and before whose throne we will all appear for judgment.

And I saw the dead, great and small, standing before the throne, and books were opened. Then another book was opened, which is the book of life. And the dead were judged by what was written in the books, according to what they had done. —Revelation 20:12

24. Paul's Vision

As it is written, "He has distributed freely, he has given to the poor; his righteousness endures forever." He who supplies seed to the sower and bread for food will supply and multiply your seed for sowing and increase the harvest of your righteousness. You will be enriched in every way to be generous in every way, which through us will produce thanksgiving to God. For the ministry of this service is not only supplying the needs of the saints but is also overflowing in many thanksgivings to God. By their approval of this service, they will glorify God because of your submission flowing from your confession of the gospel of Christ, and the generosity of your contribution for them and for all others, while they long for you and pray for you, because of the surpassing grace of God upon you. Thanks be to God for his inexpressible gift! —*2 Corinthians 9:9-15*

Paul quoted Psalm 112:9 in order to show how God blesses obedience. Paul had been teaching the Corinthians about the nature of generosity, how generosity is a fruit of obedience, and how obedience and generosity work together to bless the faithful. The Psalmist wrote of the good and faithful person who has scattered (distributed freely or shared) his blessings, his seed, his wealth or resources among the community of saints. As a farmer plants his seed, not all in one place, nor randomly, but in carefully prepared soil in order to produce the maximum yield, so the faithful saints are to plant (share) their wealth, their gifts, their blessings with brothers and sisters in Christ according to the needs of the community and the ability of the giver. Note also that farmers plant their seed where they can tend and harvest it. They do not scatter it promiscuously hither and thither, or on land over which they have no control.

It is also important to scatter the seed, to distribute it where it will grow, and not to plant it all in one place. We can understand this prin-

172

ciple of sharing as diversification. The gifts that God gives us are intended to be seed, to reproduce. The gifts are not to simply be consumed by the needy, but are to be planted, invested, grown and harvested to provide an increase. Paul was teaching the Corinthians that the wealth of a community, its gifts, talents and resources are not fixed, but are renewable, expandable. God's blessings are not to be conceived of as a fixed quantity to be equally distributed among community members. Rather, God's blessings are to be conceived of as dynamic and capable of growth and expansion in order to meet the growing needs of God's growing people.

Abundance

God does not operate on the economics of scarcity, but on the economics of abundance. Wealth produces wealth. Generosity produces generosity. Economic diversification produces increased economic opportunities and increasingly refined divisions of labor, which in turn provide for increases in technological advancement and cultural development.

Supporting this process as both foundation and capstone (means and end) is righteousness. Biblical righteousness is the necessary ingredient or glue that makes the process work, that holds it together. And righteousness is also the social product that is produced. Righteousness (*dikaiosunē*) in this case means adherence to biblical moral principles. Such principles are to be adhered to both personally and socially, individually and corporately. And the glue of this adherence is the love of Jesus Christ. These principles are honesty, integrity, competency and purpose expressed as character qualities and as workplace values. While this is a high calling, it is intended to be the Christian norm, and not reserved for an elite few.

Of course, Christians know their own sin, their own flaws, their own failings. And rather than hide them, we are to confess them to God and to one another. We acknowledge them so that others can see our flaws and weaknesses, our blind spots, and help the community compensate through the love and righteousness of Christ expressed as differing gifts given to different saints and scattered throughout the community of believers.

One of the things to notice at this point is that the best way—the only way—to insure a good crop of righteousness is to plant righteousness. This may not seem very insightful in that if you want to grow corn you should plant corn—duh! God's ordinary way of growth is, well —growth, incremental growth, not revolution. God grows a thing by adding more of the same thing to it, not by tearing it down so that something else can grow. Righteousness grows by planting and tending righteousness, not by destroying or neglecting righteousness. May you have ears to hear this biblical principle in the midst of a culture bent on the opposite principle. Because Paul tells us that "righteousness endures forever" (v. 9), righteousness is the thing to focus on, the thing to build, the thing to plant, the thing to tend and the thing to harvest. Righteousness for Christ's sake!

CAPITAL DEVELOPMENT

This recipe for social success, for cultural development and technological advancement, is then clearly stated by Paul in verse 10, "He who supplies seed to the sower and bread for food will supply and multiply your seed for sowing and increase the harvest of your righteousness." While we are called to be laborers in God's vineyard, it is God who actually provides all of the tools and skills. God supplies the seed. God supplies the food. And God supplies the righteousness.

Verse 11 is an expression of the principle of capitalism, telling us that the good of the community can be furthered through self-interest. Being generous to others as Paul has instructed the Corinthians will enrich those who give generously because their gifts will increase the wealth and the righteousness of the whole community. It will raise the proverbial water level in the harbor and raise the level of all of the boats.

Paul added that giving "through us" as he has instructed, through the apostles, through the church rightly conceived and executed, "will produce thanksgiving to God" (v. 11). Why add this last clause? Because it is central to the process. Paul has been describing the way to do church—to plant, tend and harvest righteousness (Christ's righteousness, of course!) in the church as the engine of personal, social and cultural development.

The problem is that one sole righteous person in a community only gets laughed at by the self-centered, at best, and crucified, at worst. Righteousness needs a social foundation, common commitment, a place where growth, maturity and the cross pollenization of the division of labor can flourish. It needs a supporting community of like-minded righteous people in order to develop the cultural and technological tools that are required for the development of advanced specialization of labor. The knowledge, practices and procedures of righteousness require honesty, integrity, competency and purpose beyond the consciousness of self-interest.

So, self-interest is essential, as the shell (the seed coat or bran) is essential to the corn seed. The shell (self-interest in this analogy) holds the inner parts together and protects them from the elements. But the shell (self-interest) must be shed when the seed is planted in receptive soil in order that the seed of righteousness may take root and bloom into the flower of God's gifts, and the fruit of social prosperity may develop.

So, said Paul, engaging this process as he has described it will produce thanksgiving to God. That is, building Christ's righteousness into the social structures of the church in the light of Christ and by the power and presence of the Holy Spirit through regeneration within a faithful Christ worshiping church will produce thanksgiving to God. Those who engage this process will be thankful to God, not only for their own salvation, but for the righteousness of Christ that propels the community into increased fulfillment and prosperity. Faithfulness to Jesus Christ is a win-win proposition. Everyone benefits, even the ungodly who enjoy the benefits of increased community prosperity, even though they may not contribute to it.

WORSHIP

Paul could not contain his enthusiasm for this vision of the church of Jesus Christ rightly conceived and executed. "For the ministry of this service is not only supplying the needs of the saints but is also overflowing in many thanksgivings to God" (v. 12). Here Paul's focus is on the "ministry of this service" (ESV), "the administration of this service" (AV), the *diakonia* of this *leitourgia*—liturgy, the service of worship. This process is a function of worship!

The old English word for worship is *worthship*, and in the light of Scripture *worthship* conveyed the idea that the worship of God involved a kind of substitution or exchange of something between God and man. The Old Testament sacrifices substituted the death of an animal as a kind of substitutionary death of sin. Various animals were substituted for various sins. An exchange was made—the death of a valuable animal for God's forgiveness. A deal (agreement) or covenant was enacted with God. The greater the sin, the more valuable the animal needed to be in order to atone for the greater sin.

In the New Testament Christ is the ultimate sacrifice. Christ's life was exchanged for God's ultimate forgiveness. In true Christian worship our unworthiness is exchanged for Christ's worthiness. Our sin, our unworthiness is forgiven, but not just in a mental or spiritual way. It's not just that our sin is removed (though it is). Rather, it is that the unworthiness that is our sin is replaced by Christ's worthiness. It is a matter of bringing our worthlessness (sin) to God and exchanging it for Christ's worth, both His forgiveness and His gifts of the Spirit. The result of this worship exchange is that we trade our sin for forgiveness and Christ's gifts of the Holy Spirit—actual gifts, job producing skills that contribute to the building of Christ's spiritual church as "as living stones are built up a spiritual house, a holy priesthood, to offer up spiritual sacrifices acceptable to God through Jesus Christ" (1 Peter 2:5).

Of course, we have no worthiness of our own, all of our (human) worthiness is supplied by God. Christ is that supply. Christ is our righteousness. Christ is our worthiness. Worship is not simply going to church and listening to a sermon, though that's a good start. Worship is being filled with the Holy Spirit and engaging the gifts that have been given by God for the good of God's people in everything that we think, say and do. This worship is the work of the people (v. 9—*leitourgia*), the work of the community of saints.

It is primarily focused in the community of the saints, but it is not limited to that community. Paul tells us that it—this worship, this service, this *leitourgia*—overflows (*perisseuō*). It superabounds. It is excessive. It is extravagant, exuberant and superfluous in the sense of being more than is needed. The grace of God's love overflows the boundaries of the church into the wider community to provide the same kind of blessing provided for the people of God, only less for unbelievers because the godless do not appreciate it.

The enemies of God are threatened by it, threatened by our worship because they know (and rightly so!) that God requires their submission to His love and care, submission to the saints in the sense of the mutual care and concern shared by the saints (1 Peter 5:5). And so they see the love of God as an infringement upon their freedom, their self-determined freedom to love whoever they want, however they want. And more! They see it as a threat to their personal character, their personal identity, an identity that has been captured by the forces of sin and evil, an identity that prides itself on being apart from God, independent of God.

God's love overflows into this godlessness as a means of evangelism and conversion.

PRAYER

Paul was not finished. There was one more critical element to this process—prayer. Paul said that this process functions "by their prayer for you" (v. 14—AV). Prayer is involved. Prayer greases the wheels. Prayer points the way. The Greek phrase is *autos deēsis*, or self-petition, self-supplication. It's not that we pray to ourselves, but that we ourselves pray. It is individual petition, individual supplication, personal petition, personal supplication. This means, in part, that prayers are not inflicted upon us, that prayer is not imposed upon us by church leaders as a method of getting the goods from the saints. Nor that we engage in prayer of our own volition in order to get the goods from God.

The church is fueled by a kind of spiritual capitalism, wherein God provides the capital of Christ's righteousness for His people as the earnest or down payment regarding His promise to save the world. Prayer then is the dialog between God and His people where the specific needs for capital infusion (God's gifts) are requested and dispatched.

It's not that God doesn't already know what we need. He does! But we don't. So, through prayer we enter into communication with God to better understand the nature of His capital reserves and how we can make the best use of them. Our prayers begin in self-interest, but as we grow in grace and accumulate an excess of God's capital ourselves, our prayers increasingly become more community centered. As we mature in grace and sanctification the shell of our spiritual self-interest increasingly gives way (takes root) through self-sacrificial service (worship) to the needs of the community.

Nonetheless, our prayers must issue out of our own personal love of God, from our dedication and commitment to Jesus Christ. They must flow out of our love of the Lord. This outflow begins as prayer for others and becomes an outflow or overflow of service to the community. Our love of God overflows from us personally and from our churches in the form of service, which is a part of our worship. And it overflows into the lives of our nearest neighbors.

Of course we benefit from the goodness of God's grace, but we are not motivated by our own self-centered benefit. Rather, we are motivated by the benefit of others. We are to give ourselves away for the glory of God. We are to sacrifice our self-interests, our self-concerns for the glory of God, confidently knowing that God's glory is for the benefit of humanity. God will increasingly improve humanity and humanity will increasingly thank and glorify God.

So, why was Paul doing all of this? "because of the surpassing grace of God upon you" (v. 14). Because he had a vision of the abundance of God's grace, God's blessings that would accrue to faithful saints. He saw the sin of the world and the impending death and damnation that was a kind of waterfall over which humanity would tumble because it was adrift in the river of sin, that there was no escape apart from Jesus Christ.

REDEMPTION

Yet, he wasn't motivated by the fear of damnation, but by the love of God. He was motivated because God had given him a glimpse of the riches of His kingdom that awaited the redeemed in Christ. He saw the flowering of human culture in heretofore unknown and unknowable ways. And he saw the simplicity of Christ's cure for the evils of the world—God's grace, freely given. And he knew that the whole world, all of humanity would one day see the beauty and graciousness of Christ's cure, God's provision, because he knew the irresistibility of God's love.

God's love will one day completely overwhelm sin and evil. Destroying it, yes! But more like evaporating it in the light of Christ. One day it will just disappear. It will be no more, in the twinkling of an eye. Evil and sin will simply be abandoned for the superior love of God—one day.

Finally, Paul sighed with exhaustion and frustration from trying to describe this vision of God's grace. "Thanks be to God for his inexpressible gift!" (v. 15). He didn't mean that nothing could be said about God's grace, but that God's grace cannot be fully expressed. Our descriptions will always fall short of the reality, partly because of our human limitations, the myopia of our insight into the workings of God, and partly because of God's greatness, His eternalness and the infinitude of His measures.

But Paul did successfully provide a taste of God's grace. Paul's vision is sufficient for God's purpose. It is sufficient for us. The sufficiency of Paul's vision invites us into the sufficiency of God's grace. And in a similar way, the paucity of Paul's descriptions invite God's people into the myriad abundance, the multifaceted and multicolored cloak of God's grace (the robe of Christ's righteousness), to engage God's grace in ways inconceivable by Paul, ways that engage the multiplicity of God's gifts to His people and through which bring to flower the glory of His grace. This is the calling into which Christ calls all of humanity.

25. GOD'S WEAPONS

I, Paul, myself entreat you, by the meekness and gentleness of Christ—
I who am humble when face to face with you, but bold toward you
when I am away!—I beg of you that when I am present I may not have
to show boldness with such confidence as I count on showing against
some who suspect us of walking according to the flesh. For though we
walk in the flesh, we are not waging war according to the flesh. For
the weapons of our warfare are not of the flesh but have divine power
to destroy strongholds. We destroy arguments and every lofty opinion
raised against the knowledge of God, and take every thought captive
to obey Christ, being ready to punish every disobedience, when your
obedience is complete. —2 Corinthians 10:1-6

Having laid out his vision of the gospel and how the gospel will provide both foundation and direction for human culture under the influence of Christ, Paul now threatens to increase his boldness if they do not comply with his instructions before he arrives for another visit. This section is harsh to Postmodern ears. Not only does Paul not coddle them, but he threatens and manipulates them, not however to impose his own will upon them, but Christ's.

Entreat (*parakaleō*), also translated as *comfort, desire,* and *pray,* literally means to call near. He reminded them that when he had been with them before, he had been meek and gentle in his face to face dealings with them. Remember that meek does not mean mousy or timid, but simple, direct and humble. A good race horse is said to be meek to its rider, by which is meant that the horse is very sensitive to the commands and directions of the rider.

In contrast, Paul noted that his manner of writing these letters had been more bold. Perhaps he was making up for the lack of immediate interaction involved in letter writing because of the time and distance involved. He needed to be more clear in his writing, more firm in his letters to keep them from misreading his intentions. Letters don't communicate inflection or body language. Nor could he listen to their questions or observe their body language.

He described his demeanor as base (*tapeinos*—humble, lowly and poor in spirit) when he had been with them previously. I suspect that when he was with them he had been modeling Christian service, showing them what a Christian servant acted like. So, he kept his place. He deferred to them, watched his manners and didn't talk back to them. That way they could observe the ideal of Christian service. If they didn't see it in Paul and the apostles, they wouldn't see it any-where. So, Paul was base in the archaic sense of low birth or station, of being born to the servant class, as a way of modeling Christian service. Jesus had washed the disciples' feet to model Christian service, and that was Paul's model.

BOLD

But when Paul was not with them he didn't need to model that behavior, so he exhibited boldness in his letters. When he wrote to them he was not modeling behavior, but teaching them how to think biblically. So, he made the effort to be clear and forthright as he described the gospel and its function in society. He clearly demarcated the true gospel from the various false gospels he had encountered. Much of his boldness was a matter of the clarification between truth and opinion, separating the gospel truth of Christ's wisdom from the falsehoods of the Greek foolishness that masqueraded as academic (superior) wisdom.

In verse 2 Paul pleaded with them to understand his letters so that he would not be forced to speak to them with the same boldness with which he had written to them. He didn't want to go there because he knew that, in their current state of spiritual immaturity, they would perceive Paul's boldness in person as offensive. Boldness, which in this case is nothing more than the clear statement of God's truth, is often misperceived as anger and/or frustration—particularly when it is accompanied with emotional passion for truth.

God's truth is so different than what we naturally expect it to be that it jolts our sensitivities. This is why preachers are often thought to be angry when they preach. Apart from the ability to distinguish between anger and frustration, between anger and a personal commit-ment to moral principles in the sea of apathy and immorality, boldness is often misunderstood as anger.

But Paul was not mad at them. Yet he knew that in their state of immaturity the forcefulness and clarity of his thought in conjunction with the power and presence of the Holy Spirit would blow them away (if I may use a colloquialism.) They wouldn't be able to handle it. They'd react as if he was attacking them. They would take a defensive posture and would misunderstand his communications. They would mistake his clarity and courage to face the teachings of Christ squarely and honestly, without flinching in the face of God's anger and with the assurance of his own salvation, as pride and arrogance, rather than honesty and faithfulness.

But if they failed to understand, failed to to receive and respond to his message about generosity, about his vision of the gospel as the engine of cultural development, he would take it as a sign that he needed to ramp up his presentation because they were not getting it. So, he threatened to be as bold to their faces as he had been in his letters. He knew from personal experience that sometimes the presentation of the gospel needed to be delivered with enough force to shake the accumulated barnacles from the hulls of the listening souls. Sometimes the fields into which the gospel is to be planted are hard packed and bone dry—or overrun with weeds and underbrush. So, the soil has to be broken up and the weeds plowed under before the seed can find a receptive home.

Paul knew that he needed to press through the natural resistance to the gospel of Jesus Christ. He knew that there were two kinds of natural resistance to the gospel: 1) resistance unto death, and 2) resistance unto surrender. Some who resisted would never get it. They would simply drift in the river of sin over the proverbial waterfall. But others who resisted initially, would find their hearts suddenly and strangely warmed at some point, and change their minds. So, Paul promised here to press for the salvation of those whose resistance was not rock solid, those who would respond to additional persuasion.

Paul's threat was "to show boldness with such confidence as I count on showing against some who suspect us of walking according to the flesh" (v. 2). Apparently, some people thought that Paul and the apostles had been walking according to the flesh. They thought that Paul and the apostles were not sufficiently "spiritual," that their methods and sometimes their messages were a bit too body oriented, to physical and not sufficiently religious.

Those who are familiar with the categories of Greek philosophy and its bastard Gnostic children will understand that those who preferred to divide reality into the dualism of the physical and the spiritual had chastised Paul for failing to make a similar division. In fact, neither Paul nor Jesus so divided reality. Such a division was characteristically Greek, not Hebrew in origin. Paul and Jesus rejected dualism and labeled it as a heresy. Dualism was not a biblical teaching, and when Paul failed to teach it he was accused of "walking according to the flesh" (v. 2).

The problem was that the Greeks failed to comprehend God's reality, the reality in which the world and our human experience could not be neatly divided into the dualistic categories of physical and spiritual. Why not? Because God's world, God's reality is one. It is trinitarian in character, reflecting the character of the One who created it and the reflective character of the ones He created it for—one in three, three in one. Trinitarian reality notes distinctions of character and role, but not differences of substance.[16] And definitely not two substances or realms. Dualism is a Greek model, not a biblical model.

Paul then clarified his thinking, "For though we walk in the flesh, we are not waging war according to the flesh" (v. 3). He did not deny that we walk in the flesh. We have flesh and blood bodies, and our bodies are real. We cannot ignore them and should not deny them. Behind Paul's clarification here was not a better description or definition of dualism, but the denial of dualism. Paul was not clarifying the differences between physical reality and spiritual reality, nor was he suggesting that the Greek understanding of the spiritual realm was superior to the Greek understanding of the physical realm. Rather, he was saying that these dualistic, Greek divisions were themselves false.

"For the weapons of our warfare are not of the flesh but have divine power to destroy strongholds" (v. 4). Our weapons are not carnal (*sarkikos*), not *sarx*, but *soma*. Paul had in mind his earlier discussion about the body of Christ and the wider definition of body referred to there, the body of which we are "individually members" (1 Corinthians 12:27), the body in which we participate (1 Corinthians 10:16).[17] The context of that earlier discussion was the Lord's Supper, which represents the body and blood of Christ. Communion is the weapon that has divine power to destroy strongholds. Christ's covenant, that to which the Lord's Supper refers and represents, is the spiritual weapon that Paul had in mind.[18]

ALLIANCE

This is the weapon of alliance. Often when Kings went to war, their first action was to secure what alliances they could because there is strength in numbers. So also, said Paul, the Christians' first action should be the making an alliance with the most powerful force the world has ever known—Jesus Christ. This alliance brings God's arsenal

16 For more on the Trinity see Arsy Varsy—*Reclaiming The Gospel*, by Phillip A. Ross, Pilgrim Platform, 2008, chapter *Participation*, section *Three In One*, p.171.

17 Ibid, chapter *Body & Blood*, section *Body*, p. 211.

18 Ibid, chapter *Infection*, section *Communion*, p. 85.

on line, and God's arsenal has the divine power to destroy strongholds. Strongholds (*ochurōma*) or fortifications suggest both things and skills, raw materials and production—all of the things that are involved in the art and science of defense. Strongholds include things like supplies and the process of production and resupply, munitions, communications, training, etc.

In order to overcome such strongholds held by the enemies of God, the weapons of the Spirit include the same kinds of things, only marshaled by the Spirit and for the Spirit—the same things and skills like raw materials and production, supplies and the process of production and resupply, munitions, communications, training, etc. Paul did not mean that prayer can stop a spear or a bullet, at least not in the conventional sense. Rather, he meant that a society organized around God's covenant with Jesus Christ would mean that Christians would have control of the conventional strongholds and the weapons of conventional war. A society centered in Christ would have leaders centered in Christ.

We should also note that over time (throughout history) the weapons of conventional warfare have become less and less effective. In our own time, we most particularly note this fact about the current War on Terror.[19] This is a spiritual war, and it is long past time to engage God's arsenal of spiritual weapons—covenant and communion —as God's means of both defense and offense. Paul's point was that a society organized around Christ's covenant and the Lord's Supper will be actively engaged with God's weapons of spiritual warfare as the best method of keeping the peace. The best thing that we can do to protect ourselves against *al-Qaeda* is to claim the covenant and regularly participate in the Lord's Supper.

Paul then further clarified what he meant by destroying strongholds. "We destroy arguments and every lofty opinion raised against the knowledge of God, and take every thought captive to obey Christ, being ready to punish every disobedience, when your obedience is complete" (vs. 5-6). Hearing what Paul meant here will require careful attention because it is so counter to what it seems to mean when viewed through a Greek categorical lens. Our temptation is to spiritualize it into an abstraction so that it fits into an abstract Greek and pagan worldview. But that's not what Paul meant to do.

The targets against which Paul has aimed God's spiritual weapons are "arguments and every lofty opinion raised against God" (v. 5). Arguments (*logismos*), translated by the AV as imaginations, are computations of thought that we know as the process of reasoning. Paul has taken aim at the process of reasoning that the Greeks so loved, but

---

19 *God's War on Terror* by Walid Shoebat & Joel Richardson, 2008, ISBN: 978-0977102181.

that had led them astray through what we might call naked or abstract logic. Paul was not attacking the rules of logic or the value of logic, but the improper use of logic.

PAUL'S TARGETS

Logic in and of itself is the study of the principles of valid inference and demonstration. Contrary to popular opinion, logic is not able to prove a thing true or false. Rather, logic only testifies to the fact that the conclusion of an argument is a valid inference of its initial statement or assumption. For instance, if A = B and B = C, then A = C. So far so good. But note that the initial word in this logical argument is *if*. Logic says nothing about the nature or character of A or B, and it can't. It only says *if this, then that.*

So, if the initial assumption or statement is wrong, inadequate or incorrect, the inference may well be valid, but the argument would be no better than that initial statement or assumption. All of this is to say that logic in an of itself cannot be trusted to always reveal the truth. Logic is a tool, and if the tool is misused or misunderstood it is less than worthless because it will help solidify assumptions that may not be true. When logic is used in service (submission) to Scripture it is a powerful weapon for the truth. But when logic is not used in service to Scripture it is a powerful weapon against the truth.

The second thing that Paul was taking aim at was lofty opinions (*hupsōma*), translated in the AV as "every high thing." Because we are currently well into the 2008 Presidential campaign we have a ready suite of examples of lofty opinions at our fingertips. Take the acceptance speech of either candidate. We'll use Senator Obama's because it better exemplifies lofty opinions. To say that Senator Obama's opinions are lofty means that they are of high moral or intellectual content. His language is elevated, highfalutin, full of pie-in-the-sky promises that he cannot possibly keep. They may well be things that he wants to do, and would do if he could, but they are things that he cannot do because they are beyond his ability to accomplish, and/or beyond the powers and jurisdiction of the office he seeks. Political speech is often—and usually, if not always—full of exaggeration and embellishment. Or to say it more positively, political speeches are full of eloquence and ostentation. Political orators are accomplished rhetoricians.

These were Paul's targets—arguments and lofty opinions. But Paul further qualified them. He was after arguments and lofty opinions that were "raised against God" (v. 5). Paul was not saying that we should abandon all logic or high ideals, or that such things were not good tools to have. He was not saying that there was no place in our human experience for high ideals that wax eloquent and are well-decorated with flourishes of pomp and circumstance. Rightly used, these things are okay, but wrongly used they are worse than useless because they can fortify falsehoods and wrong opinions. Paul's argument was that these things need to be used in service to God.

Paul said that these things—arguments and opinions—needed to be taken "captive to obey Christ" (v. 5). And more than just these things, Paul said that we are to bring "into captivity every thought into the obedience of Christ" (AV—v. 5). Not just our opinions, high ideals and use of logic, but every thought. Not some thoughts, not just church thoughts or Sunday thoughts, but every thought. Even political thoughts.

Paul was not finished. He continued, "being ready to punish every disobedience, when your obedience is complete" (v. 6). This is not a matter of self-flagellation, so we need to look at the Greek. The AV translates it as *revenge* (*ekdikeō*), the ASV as *avenge*. The context suggests the idea of fixing the problem, so it is better understood as being ready to fix, repair or correct—even discipline—every disobedience, rather than to punish them (whatever that might mean). And how are we to do that? How are we to correct and discipline our thinking? By taking every thought captive to obey Christ, by submitting all our thinking to Scripture.

Okay, but what about that last phrase, "when your obedience is complete" (v. 6)? *Obedience* (*hupakoē*) literally means attentive hearkening, and by implication, it means compliance or submission. And the word *complete* (*plēroō*) conveys the sense of accomplishment. Putting it all together we get the idea that we are to make corrections in our thinking whenever we find ourselves not to be in full submission to Christ, to Scripture. And we are to do so until our obedience is complete. These corrections will involve a long, difficult and arduous process of sanctification. There will be many corrections to make, so we are to get right to it, and not think ourselves to be finished with it until our obedience is complete—not any time soon, and likely not in this life.

Completion—perfection—is a characteristic of glory, not of this world. This process of corrective thinking, of submitting all of our thoughts, our logic and our opinions—even our politics—to Jesus Christ through Scripture requires our immediate and prolonged attention. That's Paul's point. There is a battle to engage, and it is not winnable unless we engage it according to these instructions. We are to employ the weapons of the Lord, and we are to use them as we have been taught, in submission to Christ in everything.

This is our only security. This is our only freedom. Here and here alone do security and freedom overlap. Most of the time security and freedom are mutually exclusive. Pursuing one means destroying the other. But in Christ they overlap. By pursuing Christ in all things, by submitting all of our thinking to biblical categories in the light of Jesus Christ, can we be both free and secure—individually and as a society. May the Lord so bless us with Christ's freedom and security.

26. EYES OF FAITH

Look at what is before your eyes. If anyone is confident that he is Christ's, let him remind himself that just as he is Christ's, so also are we. For even if I boast a little too much of our authority, which the Lord gave for building you up and not for destroying you, I will not be ashamed. I do not want to appear to be frightening you with my letters. For they say, "His letters are weighty and strong, but his bodily presence is weak, and his speech of no account." Let such a person understand that what we say by letter when absent, we do when present. Not that we dare to classify or compare ourselves with some of those who are commending themselves. But when they measure themselves by one another and compare themselves with one another, they are without understanding. —2 Corinthians 10:7-12*

Please pay careful attention here. The variety of translations for verse 7 are astonishing. "Ye look at the things that are before your face" (American Standard Version). "Give attention to the things which are before you" (Basic Bible in English). "Do you look at things as they appear?" (English Majority Text Version). "Look at what is obvious" (Holman Christian Standard Bible). "Do you look on things after the outward appearance?" (AV).

Calvin said that the phrase "according to appearance" can be understood in either of two senses. One sense suggests the reality itself that is both visible and manifest—one's immediate perception. The other suggests that what is seen is a mask that deceives or hides the reality. In addition, this verse can be read either as a statement or as a question. The original Greek has no punctuation. Calvin understood Paul to have been chiding or rebuking his readers for their short-sightedness, for their failure to see the richer, deeper, fuller reality.

According to the outward appearance Paul looked like a loser. He was diminutive in stature, no doubt kind, quiet and well-mannered—the kind of person who gets taken advantage of a lot. He was poor because he was running for his life from the Romans and the Jews and had no regular employment. He couldn't stay in one place very long or his identity and whereabouts would be discovered by the authorities. He had been beaten, shipwrecked, etc. He was not much to behold. But he was aware of his own argument for Christ and of his ability to make that argument, and so he chided or cautioned his readers to take care to see God's reality and not simply our human circumstances.

Spiritual Eyes

He was encouraging people to look, not just at the immediate reality before them, but at the spiritual reality—the context, God's context, that is available to the eyes of faith. Knowing God involves seeing things differently. Paul himself had his vision taken away and then restored—renewed—by the risen Christ when he had been first converted. When he encountered the Lord on the Road to Damascus, he had been blinded by a flash of light. About the same time Ananias had a vision about Paul. Shortly thereafter, Ananias met with Paul and "something like scales fell from his (Paul's) eyes, and he regained his sight" (Acts 9:18). Paul's sight had not only been taken away and then restored, but it had been improved in that he now saw with the eyes of faith. When the scales fell from Paul's eyes he could see what he couldn't see before. He could see the role and purpose of Jesus Christ in the plan of God. It had always been there, but suddenly Paul saw it.

How are we to understand such a change as Paul underwent? One way might be to think in terms of proper context. To see a thing out of its context and to see it in its context can create strikingly different understandings or versions of the thing. To take a thing out of context is to imagine its relationship with reality. You might imagine the correct context and you might not, but whatever you imagine remains imaginary. But to see the thing in its actual context is to see it in its proper relationship with reality, to see it in relationship with the God of Scripture. When you are working on a puzzle, it is immensely helpful to have a picture of the finished product to help you arrange the pieces in their proper order. The picture of the completed puzzle shows the proper context of the various pieces. Such was Paul's vision.

Following Paul's conversion he was able to see the completed puzzle of Christ's role in God's purpose in his mind's eye. And because Paul was a highly trained biblical scholar to begin with, his vision of Christ's role in God's purpose suddenly fit hand in glove with all of the biblical data he had amassed as a Pharisee. He had been blinded by the light of Christ and then taken into the context of Christ, into the Christian community where he was healed of his blindness. The context of the church allowed Paul to see Christ in a new light.

Following his conversion, Paul's new eyes of faith cast a net of understanding or a presuppositional structure upon everything that he saw for the rest of his life. From that point forward Paul had an unyielding faith in Jesus Christ. In a sense, having faith in Christ is a matter of receiving Christ's faith and then projecting His faith upon all of the experiences that we encounter. It's a form of both exegesis and eisegesis.[20]

Having faith is not merely holding on to a set of beliefs, but is a matter of interpreting all of reality on the basis of those beliefs, on the basis of Christian presuppositions that are both seen to be inherent in reality and projected upon reality as a function of the will, of personal faithfulness. Having faith is a matter of seeing reality through the lens of God's purpose for Christ in history at the macro level, of course, but also at the micro level, seeing Christ as the foundation of one's own personal life and projecting Christ into all of one's experiences. Suddenly what was not clear becomes increasingly clear in the light of Christ. Faithfulness is both a perception and a projection.

ME TOO!

Paul continued, "If anyone is confident that he is Christ's, let him remind himself that just as he is Christ's, so also are we" (v. 7). Paul was saying more than, If you think you're a Christian, then so are we. Rather, he was saying that Christians know themselves to be Christians personally. They know how Christ has changed their own lives and the reality of their own changed lives provides the proof of God's reality and the proof of the reality of their own Christian character. So, Paul was saying, *Just as you know how Christ has changed your life, so we know that Christ has changed our lives.* And though we have not all been changed in exactly the same ways, we have all been changed in similar ways, ways that honor the character of Jesus Christ and the purpose of God.

Paul had been coming down pretty hard on them and thought that it was time to acknowledge that fact. "For even if I boast a little too much of our authority, which the Lord gave for building you up and not for destroying you, I will not be ashamed" (v. 8). Paul had been imposing the obligations of Christian love and faithfulness upon them regarding the needs of the Jerusalem church. He had been exercising his authority as an apostle—yes, but also as a Christian brother. He was not here apologizing for that.

There was no need for an apology because all Christians have the

---

20 See p. 67 on "The Light of Knowledge,"

responsibility to impose the obligations of Christian love and faithfulness upon other Christians. Doing so is a distinctive mark of faithfulness, and of the fellowship of faithfulness. That's partly what Christian fellowship is about. Paul expected more from fellow Christians than talk, as did James, who said, "My brothers, what profit is it if a man says he has faith and does not have works? Can faith save him? If a brother or sister is naked and destitute of daily food, and if one of you says to them, Go in peace, be warmed and filled, but you do not give them those things which are needful to the body, what good is it? Even so, if it does not have works, faith is dead, being by itself" (James 2:14-17).

Christians are free in Christ to be loving and generous and to expect love and generosity from other Christians. However, care must be taken not to abuse such freedom. The imposition of this expectation is a function of both responsibility and authority. The freedom Christians enjoy is the freedom provided by Christ, and so it must be exercised according to Christ's proscriptions and His authority. It is not to be used as a means of emotional or spiritual extortion—to get what you want or to fleece the sheep. Rather, it is to be used in the light of God's truth, God's reality—a reality that is only seen with the eyes of faith. It is to be used, not for our own purposes, but for God's purposes.

Paul reminded them that the authority of the Lord was for building them up (*oikodomē*)—for their edification, not for their destruction (*kathairesis*). Edification is more teaching than encouragement, more a matter of making people understand Christ, than making them feel comfortable about their relationship with Him. Paul understood himself to have been edifying them though the imposition of their God-given Christian responsibilities. He had been a bit stern with them, a bit authoritative with them—boasting in his own authority. But not to their detriment, rather to their benefit. So, he was not ashamed.

FRIGHTENING

He went on to admit that his letters may have seemed a little frightening to babes in Christ, "I do not want to appear to be frightening you with my letters" (v. 9). The AV and ASV translated it as *terrify* (*ekphobeō*)—"that I may not seem as if I would terrify you by my letters" (ASV). Here Paul recognized that he may have terrified some of the Corinthians with his authoritarian imposition of Christian responsibility regarding the Jerusalem church, and perhaps other things, as well. Paul had been goading them into faithfulness.

We should note that Paul's words sometimes struck terror in people's hearts and sometimes appeared a bit authoritarian because he emphasized the authority of God in Christ. Here we see that such tools of Christian edification are not off limits, though they need to be carefully used. If we take Paul's example, when we use them we should admit that we have used them after we use them, as Paul has done here.

Next, Paul acknowledged what people were saying about him. "For they say, 'His letters are weighty (*barus*) and strong (*ischuros*), but his bodily presence is weak, and his speech of no account'" (v. 10). Some people found Paul's writing to be burdensome—grave, serious, heavy, thick and powerful—forceful. Paul's letters were not easy to read. They were meaty and occasionally touched on the mysterious. No doubt, some people found them to be too philosophical, too theological, too complex and convoluted. Perhaps even erudite and academic because Paul had been endeavoring to explain the mysteries of God to people who had been mislead by academic speculation (Greek philosophy).

And Paul's letters provided a stark contrast to Paul's meek demeanor. In person, people found him weak and without account. The AV translated it as "his bodily presence is weak and his speech contemptible" (*exoutheneō*—v.10). No doubt, Paul had been humble and unassuming in person. To be held in contempt is to be charged with bucking the accepted authorities. And Paul had been countering the false teachers in Corinth and elsewhere, so he had been bucking the authority of the false teachers and demonstrating the authority of God's truth in contrast, the authority of God in Jesus Christ, an authority that the false teachers did not know and did not have.

God's authority is compelling because truth is compelling. To know something to be true is to yield to its reality. Human beings must adjust themselves to truth, truth does not adjust itself to human beings. And conversely, to fail to yield to the reality of a thing is to fail to understand it to be true.

Paul seemed to be responding to a particular person or group who had been saying things about him and his letters, accusing him of various things. He was taking aim at those who accused him of being weak in person and overly convoluted and harsh in this writing. This is the same person or group that Paul would soon charge with proclaiming "another Jesus than the one we proclaimed" (2 Corinthians 11:4). But we aren't there yet, so let's see how Paul set up this charge.

Substance vs. Style

"Let such a person understand that what we say by letter when absent, we do when present" (v. 11). Here Paul doesn't deal directly with the charges made against him, that he was weak in person and compelling and esoteric in his writing. Rather, he reshaped the terms of the argument so that it didn't concern his personal character traits, but was a matter of personal integrity, where integrity means that there is a correspondence between what a person says and what he does. Rather than talk about his personal presentation or writing styles, Paul shifted the argument to the content of his message.

Paul was saying, *Regardless of what you think of me or of the way I relate to people or the way that I write, you will find that I am who I say I am and I do what I say I will do because I know about the things of which I speak. You will find that my writing and my character have integrity. There is no distinction between what I say in my letters and what I do in your presence.* The issue was not a matter of style, but of substance.

"Not that we dare to classify or compare ourselves with some of those who are commending themselves. But when they measure themselves by one another and compare themselves with one another, they are without understanding" (v. 12). Obviously, Paul was contrasting himself and the apostles with the false teachers. He was showing how he was different from them. They commended themselves where Paul had been commended by other faithful Christians. It is true that Paul also commended himself because he knew himself to be true to Christ, but that was not what he was doing here. Here he was showing that they only commended themselves, that they were not in communion with the larger church, but were off doing their own thing.

Next, he showed that they used themselves or one another as the measure of faithfulness. They measured themselves by one another. Not so with Paul and the apostles. Paul used Christ as the measure, not other Christians. This is a critical issue. We cannot and must not measure or compare ourselves with other people. Doing so will result in either jealousy or depression, neither of which are to be associated with the gospel.

Rather, by using Jesus Christ as our measure two things result. First, we come face to face with our own sin. We can't hold a proverbial candle to Jesus Christ. And when we compare ourselves to Him, our obedience to His obedience, our faithfulness with His faithfulness, we always come up short. So short that we cannot ignore or deny our own sin in the face of a perfect God, Jesus Christ.

Second, we come face to face with Jesus Christ. That is to say that we are looking at Him. We are keeping our eyes on Him, and not on ourselves or on one another. Faithfulness can be defined as keeping our eyes on Jesus, keeping Him in mind at all times, of seeing Him in all things and of projecting Him—projecting His values, His character, His truthfulness—into all things.

Comparing ourselves with others, even with other godly people is not wise. It demonstrates a serious lack of gospel understanding. It might seem like a little thing to us, but it is not a little thing to God. It undermines two central concerns of faithfulness by minimalizing our sin and trivializing the activity of keeping Jesus in mind. It facilitates faithlessness by lowering the bar set by Jesus Christ. We have no right to reset the bar to make ourselves look good or feel good about ourselves. The bar was set by the Lord for a purpose—so that we cannot disregard or deny our sin. Human sin is the proper context for the salvation of Jesus Christ, and Jesus Christ cannot be properly understood apart from that context.

To deny, belittle, denigrate or obfuscate sin is to fail to understand the context of Jesus Christ, the history of the world in which we actually live. So Paul accused the Corinthian false teachers of being "without understanding" (v. 12). Because sin is the human reality, sin is the proper context in which to see Jesus Christ. But it is not that faithful Christians are to focus on sin—not at all! We are to focus on Christ, but we cannot see the Lord correctly, in His proper context, apart from human sin—our own sin. So, we cannot disregard, belittle or deny sin. Rather, we must see Christ through it, in the midst of it. We must see Christ's salvation through the eyes of our own sinfulness.

And when we do that we will see our need, our helplessness in the face of sin. This we see when we look at ourselves. We are not to ignore ourselves, our weakness. But neither are we to focus upon it. Rather, seeing our needs gives us the proper perspective for seeing God's power and Christ's role in our salvation. God has sent Christ to us in the midst of our need, in the circumstances of our weakness and help-lessness. And God has given Christ the power to save us, to change us, to make us whole, to make us human by filling the God-sized hole in our hearts with the love of Jesus Christ.

And yet we are not saved for our own sake. Rather, we are saved that we may be a blessing to the world, that we may become instru-ments of God, instruments of Christ's salvation through service to the cause of Christ and to the encouragement and enlargement of Christ's people.

May it be so in our lives and in our fellowship. Amen!

27. Outer Limits

But we will not boast beyond limits, but will boast only with regard to the area of influence God assigned to us, to reach even to you. For we are not overextending ourselves, as though we did not reach you. For we were the first to come all the way to you with the gospel of Christ. We do not boast beyond limit in the labors of others. But our hope is that as your faith increases, our area of influence among you may be greatly enlarged, so that we may preach the gospel in lands beyond you, without boasting of work already done in another's area of influence. "Let the one who boasts, boast in the Lord." For it is not the one who commends himself who is approved, but the one whom the Lord commends. —2 Corinthians 10:13-18

To measure or compare ourselves with others is to be without understanding, according to verse 12. Why? Because doing so ignores or misunderstands Christ, who provides the true measure of faithfulness. The false teachers under consideration here likely thought much of themselves because they exceeded other Corinthians in their various abilities and strength. Because they excelled among the Corinthian populace, they thought that they were something special. This is usually the case with those who excel in their field. People pride themselves on their relative measure. So, we can assume that the Corinthian leaders excelled among the Corinthians in various ways, and prided themselves on that basis.

Paul, on the other hand, was saying here that he and the apostles would "not boast beyond limits" (*ametros*—v.13). What limits? Their own. They would not boast in things or abilities that were beyond them, or beyond the limitations of their abilities. This is a reference to the false teachers who were boasting in their powers of philosophical speculation, as if they had some sort of special, even mystical, insight into the nature of reality. To understand this, requires familiarity with the ancient Greek philosophers. How could those philosophers possibly know the things they purported to know? The concern is epistemological.

The Greeks essentially worshiped reason, which seems to explain cause and effect in a logical manner, which is to say that they highly valued it, or over valued it in that reason is not divine. Reason involves the ability to think, to understand and draw conclusions in an abstract way, but in and of itself it does so without reference to God. It is usually understood to be objective or neutral with regard to the conclusions it draws, and is thus contrasted with emotionalism, which is thinking that is driven by desire, passion, or prejudice of one kind or another. The use of pure reason[21] is a conscious attempt to discover what is objectively true, right and/or best. Reason postulates a chain of cause and effect. The word *reason* can be a synonym for cause.

For the Greeks (and many others) reason functions as a god by providing causation and order in the universe, which are functions of the divine because apart from God there is no ultimate cause nor any ultimate order. And, in fact, the universe is orderly and reason (logic) is a very powerful tool. But reason requires a center or purpose around which to be ordered, and if it is not ordered by God (the God of Scripture), if it is not in service to God, then it is ordered and in service to something else—and becomes a tool of idolatry.

The Greeks speculated wildly about the nature of reality, about things that are beyond human ability to know, and their idolatry led them astray, into speculation and imagination (Genesis 6:5, 8:21; Luke 1:51; Acts 17:29). Paul was saying that he would not do that. He would not speculate without measure, without limits. Paul would ground all of his thinking, and especially his thinking about Jesus, upon Scripture.

Paul said here that he would not exceed the measure—the limits, provision, abilities, reach or influence—that God had given him. He would bloom where he had been planted, and would not attempt to reach beyond his ability to grasp, nor beyond what Scripture provided. The faithful apostles would "boast only with regard to the area of influence God assigned to" (v. 13) them. They would not speculate beyond their own abilities, on the one hand, nor beyond "the measure of the province which God apportioned to us (them) as a measure" (v. 13—ASV). They would remain within the limitations of the province or sphere of understanding and influence that God had given them. They would remain within their God-given, biblical, epistemological and intellectual proscriptions, and would concentrate or focus their efforts within the field of social influence that God had given them. That is,

---

21 This is an intentional allusion to *The Critique of Pure Reason* by Immanuel Kant, 1781, 1787, public domain, www.gutenberg.org/etext/4280.

they would not speculate beyond what God had given them to know, and they would share the knowledge they had with the people within their reach.

WITHIN REACH

The last phrase of verse 13, "to reach even to you" suggests that God had given the Corinthians to the apostles as a field of influence. Two things were communicated in this phrase: 1) that the message of the apostles was intended to reach the Corinthians, and 2) that God had assigned the task of reaching the Corinthians to Paul and the apostles. In essence Paul said, *Our message and teaching is for you Corinthians, and God has ordained it. God has given it to us to give to you.*

"For we are not overextending ourselves, as though we did not reach you. For we were the first to come all the way to you with the gospel of Christ" (v. 14). The language seems convoluted to us. Paul was saying that his message and teaching to the Corinthians was not an overextension of his abilities or his authority as an apostle. Rather, he had been sent by the Lord to deliver this message to them, and he had succeeded in doing so. He did reach them both physically and mentally. He had arrived in Corinth and his message had touched their hearts and changed their lives.

He also noted that his message to them had been the original message of the gospel of Jesus Christ. He had been the first to reach them with the gospel. The implication being that the false teachers in their midst had perverted the original gospel message that had been given to them. They had taken the gospel message beyond its limits and overextended themselves beyond what they could actually know, and certainly beyond any knowledge that God had given them. Metaphysical speculation is common among Gnostics, Mystics, and Eastern religions.[22]

"We do not boast beyond limit in the labors of others. But our hope is that as your faith increases, our area of influence among you may be greatly enlarged" (v. 15). There are limitations regarding the gospel message. There are limitations to our own understanding, and there are limitations to our use of the labors or work of others. Paul was saying that he would not speculate beyond the work of the Old Testament or the community of the apostles, that his boasting, his work, was within what we would call biblical limitations. He would not go beyond the parameters of Scripture, nor beyond the parameters of the community of the apostles, in that he and the apostles were in the

---

22 *The Shape of Ancient Thought: Comparative Studies in Greek and Indian Philosophies* by Thomas McEvilley, Allworth Press, NY, 2001.

process of writing the New Testament, of extending Scripture in the light of Christ. Paul was not so much expanding the Old Testament parameters to allow for Christ, as he was demonstrating how Christ Himself was—and had always been—the central organizing factor of the Old Testament.

In essence, Paul was saying that there was a body of acceptable knowledge, the Old Testament, to which he and the apostles, in the light of Christ, were adding the capstone—the New Testament. Paul was indicating his position in the community that produced the New Testament canon. Here is that phrase in the Authorized Version, "having hope, when your faith is increased, that we shall be enlarged by you according to our rule (*kanōn*) abundantly" (v. 15). Paul hoped that as the Corinthians grew in faithfulness and understanding, they would come to increasingly appreciate what Paul and the apostles had been doing, that the influence of the apostles and their work would grow as the Corinthians matured in the faith. And it did.

Evangelism As Overflow

Paul wanted them to understand that their acceptance of the gospel that Paul preached to them would greatly help in the expansion of the preaching of the gospel to others, to regions beyond Corinth. If they didn't understand Paul's corrections of the false teachers among them, then Paul and the apostles would have to spend more time and effort in Corinth straightening them out, dealing with false teachers, and that would impact their ability to go beyond Corinth to reach others with the message of the gospel.

Neither did Paul want the false gospel to go beyond Corinth because it would retard the preaching of the true gospel elsewhere. Paul wanted to preach the gospel (*euaggelizō*), to evangelize Corinth and beyond, and not to have to waste time dealing with false teachers (though in reality his interactions with false teachers have provided helpful clarifications of the gospel). Nor did he want to boast about his work in putting down the false teachers in Corinth. He wanted them to move through their leadership crisis so that he—and they—could get on with the work of preaching, teaching and reaching others for Christ.

Paul then said, "Let the one who boasts, boast in the Lord" (v. 17), paraphrasing Jeremiah 9:23-24: "Let not the wise man boast in his wisdom, let not the mighty man boast in his might, let not the rich man boast in his riches, but let him who boasts boast in this, that he understands and knows me, that I am the Lord who practices steadfast love, justice, and righteousness in the earth. For in these things I delight." Other versions use *glory* rather than *boast*. The meaning is not to be understood as a function of pride, but of trust, satisfaction and enjoyment. This kind of boasting was a zesty relishing in the knowledge of the goodness and trustworthiness of God.

This boasting or glorying of which Paul spoke here is more than knowledge, more than a reasonable endorsement. According to Jeremiah, it is nothing less than reliance on the Lord, who practices or exercises steadfast love, justice and righteousness. Steadfast love is translated as *lovingkindness* in the Authorized Version. It is the Hebrew word *chêsêd*, and is often translated as *mercy*, and understood as compassion. Paul was saying that Christians need to pride themselves or glory in God's lovingkindness, mercy and compassion. If you want to feel good about something, nothing will make you feel better than serving God, who manifests these qualities and is bringing them into human history.

Summing up these thoughts Paul wrote, "For it is not the one who commends himself who is approved, but the one whom the Lord commends" (v. 18). To commend (*sunistēmi*) literally means to stand in or by one's self. Such a person is self-sufficient, doesn't need other people —or thinks that he doesn't. The self-commending are self-centered, self-motivated and self-contained. Such a person provides a good definition of pride in the negative sense of overestimating one's own strength, abilities, talents, etc. Pride is both an overestimation of one's self and an underestimation of others.

In contrast to this Paul mentioned the one whom the Lord commends. Again, Paul was simply restating Jeremiah 9:23-24. We are not to boast, not to trust or relish in our own wisdom, power or riches. Why not? For several reasons. First, our own wisdom is the wisdom of the world (1 Corinthians 3:19) captivated by sin, against which Paul had been contending. We have no wisdom of our own. Our minds and experiences are very limited with regard to the vastness and complexity of the world.[23]

Soft Boundaries

So, for us to extrapolate about the nature of reality on the basis of our own knowledge, experience or reason would be much like the ant, floating down the river on a leaf, who hollers, "Raise the drawbridge!" To trust our own assessment of our knowledge, experience or reason is to overestimate our abilities and our objectivity. Our limited knowledge and experience are far too meager to provide significant information about the nature of reality, or the existence or veracity of God.

---

23 See *Fooled By Randomness—The Hidden Role of Chance*, by Nassim Nicholas Taleb, Random House, 2004.

There is much that we don't know and we can't know, and the sooner we own that truth the better off we will be.

That, however, does not mean that we have no information about reality or God. Quite the contrary! God has provided much information about Himself and about our reality, our limitations, in His Bible. There is, of course, a difficulty regarding that information—we cannot authenticate or prove it to anyone other than ourselves. I cannot prove God or the nature of His reality to you. In fact, the only way that I know that God is real myself is because He has broken into my world, my life, my ego. He has broken the pride of my own denial, my defenses, and utterly changed my perspective by giving me a piece of His perspective. We are called to faith not fact because it is our faith in God that makes the critical difference, not the facts about God—though we do not want to discount Godly facts.

The only way that you can know God is to know Him in a similar way. He must break into your world and humble your pride. And if you have followed this argument to this point, if you understand this, He has likely already done that. Just as God broke into human history in Jesus Christ, He breaks into our individual histories through the power and presence of His Holy Spirit through regeneration, and does so by the hearing of His Word. "He who has ears to hear, let him hear" (Matthew 11:15, Romans 10:17, see also Isaiah 30:20-22).

God is too immense and reality is too complex for us to get our puny minds around them—without help. Fortunately, God has not left us helpless. He has given us His Book—a big book. And through the presence and power of the Holy Spirit through regeneration, He has given us the means of understanding it—not completely or comprehensively, but adequately. And because our understanding of it is never complete, it continues to lead, guide and provide for us all of our lives, and all of human history, even through the end of time itself. It is a wonder of wonders, the depths of which are truly awesome.

In God's wisdom, He has provided Jesus Christ, who is our salvation. Why did God do this? Because He knows that we have no power to save ourselves. He knows that the power of sin and temptation are greater than our power to be good and to resist evil. We are not to trust in our power, in our ability. Our power, our strength (*gibbôr*) is inadequate to the task. It will fail. We don't have the ability to complete the circuit, to make the necessary connections. So, God intervened in history by sending Jesus Christ, and apart from His intervention we will fry ourselves on the griddle of reality. We cannot pull ourselves up to salvation by our own bootstraps. It just won't work. It can't happen. We are limited by our own subjectivity, trapped like rats in a maze.

So we boast in Jesus Christ. We trust in His power to do for us what we cannot do for ourselves, to provide purpose and meaning for us and for our world. We glory in Him! We must not be self-reliant, we must be Christ-reliant. We must lean on the everlasting arms of our Lord and Savior, lest we lean on our own broken crutches and fall again, and again.

MARKET APPLICATION

We must not boast in our riches. Riches and wealth are temporary accoutrements. Riches fail because financial systems fail because people are sinners. No intellectual or financial system (riches) is beyond the reach of sin because all such systems depend upon righteousness, honesty and integrity in order to be accurately measured and assessed.[24] For instance, it is not our trust in the market that keeps it going. Rather, it is the market's trustworthiness that makes it valuable.

The market is people, buyers and sellers. The market depends upon the righteousness—trustworthiness, honor and integrity—of the people in the market, such that the more market share a person or company has, the more righteous he must be. And that is the rub because market share brings power and power brings corruption. Markets work, not on credit as an abstract idea, but on the subjective righteousness of the players. Credit is nothing more than a promise to make payments on a loan. If we are faithful to that promise, our credit is good. Riches are good, but they are not trustworthy apart from Christ and His righteousness, for there is no other. Human beings have no subjective righteousness apart from what is given by Jesus Christ.

So, said Jeremiah, we must align ourselves with God, who practices steadfast love, justice, and righteousness. Paul was helping us understand what Jeremiah meant, that we must trust in and exercise God's lovingkindness, God's justice and Christ's righteousness. We have none of these things in or of ourselves, so if we are to engage them at all, we must engage God's.

So, God sent His Son, Jesus Christ, to provide for us what we cannot provide for ourselves. Christ is at the very center of our current financial crisis.[25] Christ is both the mediator and the means of our salvation, and the salvation of the world.

Quoting Isaiah just a few chapters back, Paul wrote, "'In a favorable time I listened to you, and in a day of salvation I have helped you.' Behold, now is the favorable time; behold, now is the day of salvation" (2 Corinthians 6:2). Now is the time that we need the righteousness of

---

24 See *The Demise of and Hope for American Capital,* by Phillip A. Ross, http://www.paross.com/wp/?p=58.

25 See *Global Financial Crisis of 2008,* http://en.wikipedia.org/wiki/Global_financial_crisis_of_2008

Christ. Lord, make it so.

28. CRAFTY

I wish you would bear with me in a little foolishness. Do bear with me!
For I feel a divine jealousy for you, since I betrothed you to one
husband, to present you as a pure virgin to Christ. But I am afraid
that as the serpent deceived Eve by his cunning, your thoughts will be
led astray from a sincere and pure devotion to Christ.
—2 Corinthians 11:1-3

The folly that Paul asks the Corinthians to excuse is a folly that he is not willing to abandon. It is not the foolishness that he has discussed before, but is different. He is not asking them to excuse him while he indulges in the foolishness of the world, the foolishness that he has been arguing against. No, this is a different word, a different kind of folly.

Paul's major thesis has been his argument against the wisdom of the world—humanism (though it had yet to emerge in history under that name), which he also calls foolishness. From the first chapter of First Corinthians Paul had been arguing that God has revealed that the wisdom of the world is utter foolishness (1 Corinthians 1:20), and we have seen that he had Greek philosophy, Greek culture, in mind as he made that accusation. Of course, Paul had in mind more than Greek philosophy and culture in a narrow sense. He lived in a Roman world that had absorbed the characteristics of the Greeks. That's what the Romans did. So, Roman philosophy and culture were included in Paul's category of foolishness, as are all of the philosophies, cultures and worldviews that are not based on the Bible in the light of Christ.

The Greek word that Paul had been using up to this point has mostly been a form of *mōria*, as expressed in 1 Corinthians 1:23, "but we preach Christ crucified, a stumbling block to Jews and folly (*mōria*) to Gentiles...." Paul used a different form of the same word two verses later, "For the foolishness (*mōros*) of God is wiser than men, and the weakness of God is stronger than men" (1 Corinthians 1:25). The word means foolishness, absurdity as in a idiot or blockhead who has nothing to say because he hasn't mastered language well enough to form his thoughts, much less communicate them.

EDUCATED FOOL

And yet, there is more to fixing the fool than teaching him language skills, more to the abandonment of the foolishness of the world than is provided by mere education. Indeed, to be educated meant then and still means today being versed in the wisdom of the world. Being educated means knowing how the world works. But an educated fool is more foolish than a dumb fool because he believes even more strongly that the wisdom of the world is actually wisdom and not foolishness as Paul has been teaching. No, education cannot cure the fool of his foolishness.

But this is not to say that education is a bad thing. It's only bad for fools because it tends to make them even more foolish by providing an intellectual justification for their foolishness. Education only makes fools more committed to their foolishness. It takes more than education to cure a fool of foolishness.

At the same time, there is nothing wrong with knowing how the world works. There is no problem with understanding the world, as long as you know the difference between the wisdom of the world and the wisdom of God. What I mean by this is that reason and logic must be in service to God and Scripture.

It's not enough that theology be the queen of the academy. Rather, *right* theology, *faithful* theology, *correct* theology must reign in the academy, lest academics serve the increase of foolishness in the world by trying to eliminate the difference between God's wisdom and worldly foolishness, between the wisdom of the Bible and philosophy—vain deceit, according to the tradition of men (Colossians 2:8). If academia denies the truth of Paul's teaching and embraces a false perspective like the false teaching that Paul found in Corinth or some other, it will only add respectability to worldly foolishness, and lead many people away from the truth of God in Scripture.

Paul was saying that the least intelligent aspect of God stands head and shoulders above the most intelligent aspect of humanity. As we have seen throughout our study of his letters to the Corinthians, Paul had been arguing that Greek philosophy and her like-minded children were/are speculative nonsense because they are based upon human imagination, and were all the more dangerous because they are clothed in reason.

Greek speculation has always been eminently reasonable. The rules of logic were followed, but the conclusions reached are only as good as the presuppositions they are based upon. And those presuppositions were godless and narrow minded, by which I mean that they were based upon the petty and short-sighted experiences and imaginations of men—mere mortals.

Paul was not arguing that logic and reason were not useful. They are! They are essential tools for life in the world. But they are tools and must be used correctly. And they have limits to their usefulness. In the area of physics their use is unparalleled, as the modern West has discovered, but in the area of metaphysics their usefulness is much more limited.

In opposition to this approach to understanding reality—physics, metaphysics and our role and relationship therein, Paul insisted upon the revelation of Scripture as the only reliable source. For him Scripture meant the Old Testament, but Paul's genius was seeing the Old Testament in the light of Christ. It was the light of Christ that revealed the real truth of the Old Testament. He had argued that apart from the light of Christ, God's purpose in the Old Testament had been veiled—hidden until the mission of Christ had been accomplished (2 Corinthians 3:13-16).

Paul's Foolishness

Here in chapter eleven Paul used a different word because he was describing a different kind of folly. Here Paul had his tongue planted firmly in his cheek, meaning that he was making fun of himself in order to make a point. Here he used the word *aphrosunē*, which also means foolishness. But this time he was asking them to bear with him, to tolerate him because what sounded like foolishness to them on his part would be cleared up as they came into fuller possession of his argument.

He was saying, *Grant me this for the moment because it will help you grasp the fullness of my argument, and then you will see that what you call wisdom God calls foolishness.* Paul was simply asking them to humor him in the short run so that he could put the fullness of his argument before them. He was asking them not to dismiss what he had to say before he had finished saying it.

In the second verse of this chapter Paul reminded them that they had already pledged themselves to Christ, to the Christ that Paul had first presented to them. Of course there are not actually two Christs. There is only one. Any others are imaginary in the same ways that Greek philosophy is imaginary. Paul reminded them that they were covenantally bound—betrothed, espoused, promised. And that their flirtations with the false teachers were not only philosophically wrong, but were immoral as well. They were in danger of apostasy and spiritual adultery.

Paul then reaffirmed his job, his responsibility for them. He was responsible for their betrothal to Christ. He had introduced them, helped them to get to know one another, suggested marriage—a covenant relationship with the Lord, and was committed "to present you (them) as a pure virgin to Christ" (v. 2). He was responsible for maintaining their purity, the purity of the church. Paul had been playing the role of a matchmaker. He had reached them as an evangelist and invited them into covenantal relationship with Christ and His church.

The responsibility of evangelism does not end with preaching. Preaching is a means of introducing people to Christ, but more than an introduction is needed. To think of evangelism as preaching or presenting the gospel is less than half of the job. Evangelists, according to Paul, are matchmakers for Christ. They work for Christ, for the intended Husband, and are working to procure bridal (covenantal) candidates. Paul was interested in more than tickling people's ears with the intricacies of God's trinitarian reality. He was interested in more than speculation, more than thinking about God or Jesus, more than reading the Bible, more than praying or going to church.

And yet the evangelists' responsibility is nothing more than presenting Christ. However, presenting Christ accurately takes more than preaching Christ or sharing Christ. The critical element here is that the presenter, the preacher and those who share Christ must insure that the Christ that is seen, known and understood—the Christ that is received—is the Christ of God's reality and not the christ of one's own imagination. For if you preach, teach or share the christ of your imagination, you have not preached, taught or shared the Christ of Scripture at all.

This is precisely what the false teachers in Corinth had been doing. They had been preaching, teaching and sharing their own speculations about Christ, speculations that made Christ into a false christ, a christ that existed only in the abstract realm of imagination. Such a christ was no Bridegroom.

Deceived

Paul continued, "But I am afraid that as the serpent deceived Eve by his cunning, your thoughts will be led astray from a sincere and pure devotion to Christ" (v. 3). This verse has abandoned all subtlety, for it is a gospel bomb targeted to destroy the root of unbelief. This verse is huge because it ties the errors of the false teachers at Corinth and elsewhere to the father of lies and false teaching, who is none other than Satan himself. Paul was throwing Jesus' own words at those who had been leading the Corinthians astray, saying that they were "of the Devil as father, and the lusts of your father you will do. He was a murderer from the beginning, and did not abide in the truth because there is no truth in him. When he speaks a lie, he speaks of his own, for he is a liar and the father of it" (John 8:44).

The false teachers in Corinth were making the same error that Adam and Eve made in the Garden. They trusted Satan, who had convinced them that they could trust themselves when it came to discerning good and evil, that they could know things as God knew things.[26] By eating the forbidden fruit, a kind of magic potion, they thought that they would become "as God, knowing good and evil" (Genesis 3:5). And when they ate the forbidden fruit their eyes were indeed opened, but they knew only "that they were naked" (Genesis 3:7), but not even whether it was good or evil to be naked.

Though their eyes had been opened, they did not know what God knew. So, God set about to share some of what He knew with them. He would do so in an orderly way, according to a plan that would unfold within the midst of human history. And He would keep track of His plan and its unfolding in a Book (the Bible).

Nonetheless, at that moment in the Garden fear came upon Adam and Eve and they sought to hide—to hide from God, to hide what they had done, to hide their nakedness. They did not know good and evil. They knew only sin and the shame of sin. From that day forward, they and all their progeny have sought to hide their sin, to hide it from each other, to hide it from themselves and to hide it from God.

That urge to hide sin is called blindness by the Lord (Isaiah 29:9, 42:17-19; John 3:3-5). Sin had blinded them to God's reality. That is the reality in which we still live. The blind will always fail to see reality as it is, fail to perceive it correctly, to understand it in its fullness, fail to see it through the eyes of Scripture, through the eyes of Christ. So Jesus spoke "in parables, because seeing they see not, and hearing they hear not; nor do they understand. And in them is fulfilled the prophecy of Isaiah which said, 'By hearing you shall hear and shall not understand; and seeing you shall see and shall not perceive; for this people's heart has become gross, and their ears are dull of hearing, and they have closed their eyes, lest at any time they should see with their eyes and hear with their ears and should understand with their heart,

---

26 This is a watershed issue in the history of the Bible (human history) and has been greatly clarified by the work of Cornelius Van Til, the father of Presuppositionalism, and whose books should be thoroughly studied.

and should be converted, and I should heal them'" (Matthew 13:13-15).

Isaiah's prophecy is mysterious only to the blind, to those who refuse to see God's truth. Those who see it correctly understand that in order to see Jesus for who He actually is, we must first see our own sin. We must stop hiding our sin from ourselves. Paul previously mentioned that the purpose of the Law was to reveal our own sin, so that we could then see Jesus rightly (2 Corinthians 3:13-16). As long as we continue to hide our own sin from ourselves, as long as we refuse to face the implications of God's law and our own culpability in sin, Jesus will remain hidden from us. Apart from the personal acknowledgment and confession of sin the purpose and power of Christ remain hidden.

CUNNING

Satan, the serpent "deceived (*exapataō*) Eve by his cunning (*panourgia*)" (v. 3). He beguiled her through his subtlety. He cheated her, tricked her, wholly seduced her in the sense of luring or enticing her away from her duty, her principles, and her proper conduct as a creature of God. Through cunning and adroit sophistry, he convinced her of something that was not true. Or more accurately and more effectively, he tricked her into convincing herself of something that was not true.

And what was this untruth that Satan peddled to poor, unsuspecting Eve? That God was not trustworthy, that He had not told her or Adam the whole truth, that He was hiding an important truth from them. And was God actually untrustworthy? No, He wasn't. Adam and Eve weren't ready or able to see the whole of God's truth. They could not bear it. We still aren't ready today. It's still too much for too many people. First, we must deal with our own sin, only then might we grow into readiness to hear more of God's revelation.

Was God hiding something? He was! He was hiding the ultimate purpose of the law, not just from Adam, but from Moses and all of the Old Testament saints who did not know Christ. The purpose of the law had been veiled from the Jews and others, until Christ could be revealed in His fullness. Even now there are too many people who are still hiding behind the veil of blindness, refusing to see their own culpability in sin, or twisting God's law to suit themselves.

Was God protecting Adam and Eve in the Garden? Of course He was. And they needed protection, as do we. Reality is too much, too strong, too harsh, too acidic for us. It will eat us alive, so to speak. We are mere lambs before it's slaughter. We must have a buffer to protect us, to protect our civilization from the destructive acids of sin and corruption. We are not able in and of ourselves to survive apart from

Christ, who mediates between us and reality, between us and God. Christ mediates God's judgment against sin, of which we are guilty as charged. And apart from Christ's mediation, we will all die from self-inflicted wounds, mortal wounds afflicted by humanity against humanity. We are all guilty. We are all in the same proverbial boat.

SUSTAINABLE DEVELOPMENT

God cannot let us pass into eternal life—or what we might also call sustainable development on earth as it is in heaven—because we are addicted to sin of one kind or another. It's not that we have to pass some kind of test so God can beam us into heaven. Rather, we must be weaned from our addiction to sin—to greed, graft, corruption, selfishness, slander and sleaze—because it is precisely those things, our sins, that make our cultural development unsustainable. The lies and deception make our measurements unreliable.

And we cannot achieve sustainable development ourselves. Why not? It's not within our power, partly because we have built on the sands of Greek and Roman culture, and partly because our whole system of life needs to be purged of sin, both individually and corporately. This purging needs to happen to each of us individually and to all of us collectively at pretty much the same time, "in the twinkling of an eye" (1 Corinthians 15:52). Otherwise, some of the sin will remain residual and grow to threaten us all again. On our own our "thoughts will be led astray from a sincere and pure devotion to Christ" (v. 3), like the compulsive drinker who can't stop drinking, the compulsive gambler who can't stop gambling, the compulsions that each of us cannot stop on our own.

And why can't we stop them? Because we don't want to. We love our compulsions. We find them very satisfying, in spite of the fact that they harm us, injure us and even kill us. We don't care! That's the problem that we can't solve on our own. An intervention is needed. So, God sent Jesus to intervene. God also intervened in Paul's life on the Road to Damascus when Paul was converted. Since his conversion Paul had been preaching Christ's intervention and revelation, showing how Christ fits into the eternal decrees of God found in the Old Testament.

And, as if Paul's job in Corinth was not difficult enough in and of itself, he found that his own people—Corinthian Christians—had been led astray by Satan, just as Eve had been led astray by Satan in the Garden. Though Satan has been ultimately defeated by Christ on the cross, his influence has not been eliminated, not then in Paul's day and not yet in our day either.

Satan's influence continued in the human drama that unfolded in ancient Corinth—as it continues in our own time to this very day. Satan has been defeated, but the echoes of his confusion, lies and distortions continue to sound in the empty minds and hearts of the faithless. In the hollow of an empty heart Satan's voice continues to call and confuse, to offer a false order (Luke 11:23-26), a false understanding of the character of God and the nature of reality, a false law, a false life, a false commitment to an understanding that leads away from Jesus Christ and into death and destruction.

Indeed, said Jesus, "Whoever is not with me is against me, and whoever does not gather with me scatters" (Luke 11:23). Everything depends upon Jesus Christ—literally, completely, absolutely.

May the Lord Jesus Christ fill the hearts and minds of people everywhere, and put an end to the hollow echo of Satan's confusion.

29. BURDEN OF LEADERSHIP

For if someone comes and proclaims another Jesus than the one we proclaimed, or if you receive a different spirit from the one you received, or if you accept a different gospel from the one you accepted, you put up with it readily enough. Indeed, I consider that I am not in the least inferior to these super-apostles. Even if I am unskilled in speaking, I am not so in knowledge; indeed, in every way we have made this plain to you in all things. Or did I commit a sin in humbling myself so that you might be exalted, because I preached God's gospel to you free of charge? I robbed other churches by accepting support from them in order to serve you. And when I was with you and was in need, I did not burden anyone, for the brothers who came from Macedonia supplied my need. So I refrained and will refrain from burdening you in any way.   *—2 Corinthians 11:4-9*

At verse 4 Paul put his finger on the sore spot. And because Paul was dealing with his central concern about the confusion of worldly wisdom with biblical wisdom regarding the Corinthians, it is not surprising that there is some translation confusion at this point. Paul's concern had not gone away since Paul first mentioned it back in First Corinthians. It continues to haunt Christians to this day. Just as the Corinthians didn't want to hear what Paul had been saying, neither do we. The accusation of apostasy that Paul brought to light in Corinth is so contrary to the Christian pride that inhabits Christian people that it is difficult for us to make sense of it because we do not want to hear it. It offends our pride. It can't be true. Surely, Paul was talking about something else.

The Greek does communicate a conditionality in the first clause, but it must be understood in a more definite sense than is usually attributed to it. "For if someone comes ..." said Paul, but he didn't mean to suggest that he was talking about some time in the distant future.

Rather, it is better translated as, "Therefore forasmuch as someone comes ...." He was not saying, "Maybe someday *if* someone comes ...," as if to speculate about some future possibility. Rather, he was drawing a conclusion about their actual situation at that time.

Because the content of this argument is at the very heart of Paul's concern about the difference between the wisdom of Christ and the wisdom of the world, we must understand that Paul was not pushing this possibility of a false Christ off into some unknown future. Rather, Paul was addressing their immediate situation.

Bringing this insight to this verse we can understand Paul to say, *Therefore, forasmuch as it appears that when someone preaches or has preached another Jesus than the one we proclaimed, or you receive a different spirit from the one you received, or you accept a different gospel from the one you accepted ....* The ESV is wrong to add the word *if* two more times in this verse because the word is in the Greek only once. The sense that the translators are trying to add is a sense of their own making, not the sense that is given in the Greek.

Listen to it in the AV, "For if (this *if* is there, but would be better translated as *forasmuch as*) he that cometh preacheth another Jesus, whom we have not preached, or if (here's that unauthorized *if*) ye receive another spirit, which ye have not received or another gospel, which ye have not accepted ..." To translate that *if* as *forasmuch as* is completely acceptable in the Greek. The word does suggest a conditionality, but it isn't as if the condition hasn't already happened. The condition had already been met in Corinth.

Paul's point in both this section and in this whole letter was that it had happened already to the Corinthians. Paul was pointing out that it had already happened to some of them, and if they weren't careful it would happen to more of them.

ANOTHER CHRIST

Paul's point was that another christ had been set loose in their midst, that the false teachers had already redefined Christ to suit their own understanding. They made the Christ of Scripture fit the categories of Greek philosophy, and thereby desecrated the trinitarian character of the Lord. Those parts of the Trinity that wouldn't fit into their own limited imaginations were omitted, ignored and/or denied. It wasn't that Paul was pointing out some future possibility. He wasn't worried that some day a thousand years down the road someone might come along preaching another gospel. His concern was what had already been happening at the Corinthian church for some time. Another christ had been preached, was being preached and Paul was pressing them to reject it. He both reminded them and suggested to them that they had not accepted or received the false christ that had been preached in opposition to the real Christ that he had preached, and which they had already received and accepted.

We are not finished with verse 4 yet! The last phrase is the difficult one. "... you put up with it readily enough." What does that mean? Paul said that they needed to take care not to believe the false apostles among them who had been preaching a false christ, and in this last phrase he suggested that they had been putting up with it—with the false teachers and their false message—readily enough. The phrase consists of two Greek words: *kalōs anechomai.* The meaning is that they had exercised kindness by putting up with it, insinuating that it was time to put an end to their overindulgent kindness.

Putting up with such a serious error is not kind at all. It leads to a deadly result—the rejection of Jesus Christ and eternal damnation. A little confrontation now would spare many people an eternity in hell. Paul had finally called it what it was—the false teachers were teaching a false christ.

At this point Paul began to be defensive, as if he were responding to various accusations that had been made against him. He simply refuted them. "Indeed, I consider that I am not in the least inferior to these super-apostles" (v. 5). Examining this response, we see that Paul had been accused of being inferior in comparison to the false apostles, which Paul called here super- (*huper*) or hyper-apostles. In what ways had Paul been accused of being inferior? The accusation seems to have been that he was both a poor speaker, unskilled in the Greek art of rhetoric or oratory, and ignorant about that of which he spoke.

Dim and Unlearnt

It is easy to see how his opponents came to this conclusion. From their perspective it was absolutely true—and Paul himself would not disagree that what they were saying was consistent with their perspective. From their perspective he was guilty as charged. He was not engaging in the art of rhetoric or oratory, nor was he defending the mysteries of Greek philosophy.

But Paul's argument against them was against their perspective, the perspective of Greek wisdom which highly valued both rhetoric and mystery. The Greek philosophers believed that their job was to explain the mysteries of the world, i.e., the Oracle of Delphi and the other mysteries of Gnosticism and Greek philosophy. Does this mean that we are to reject all of Greek philosophy? Not at all. But it does mean that we must put it in its proper context and reject any dominance it may claim over Scripture. Some of Greek philosophy is useful and some is nonsense.

Because the Greeks grounded their system of thinking upon human reason and experience, to the neglect of the God of Scripture, they were unable to tell truth from imagination. At best the Greeks subsumed Christianity—theology and Scripture—under reason. They applied reason to Scripture as a way of mining various truth nuggets from the Bible, nuggets that they could then fit into their own philosophical constructs. For the Greeks, human reason provided the standard by which to judge everything.

REASON & SCRIPTURE

In opposition to this Paul preached Christ as the standard bearer who alone would judge everything. Paul subsumed human reason under Christ, under Scripture, so that reason became a tool of Christ, rather than making Christ a tool of reason. This is an old debate between Roman Catholicism and the Protestant Reformers, where the Catholics through Aquinas and others fit Christ and Christianity into a Greek philosophical/theological system that was ordered by human reason. The Reformers on the other hand attempted to adapt their own rationality to the categories of Scripture so that Christ has sovereignty over human reason because that is what Scripture teaches.

It was precisely because of this issue, this difference between Paul and the false apostles, that led those who argued against Paul to over-value themselves and their own rational abilities. But it's not that someone with better rational abilities would be able to defeat Paul. Rather, the difference between them, between Paul and the Greeks, had to do with the role of reason in the explanation of reality.

Paul argued that Scripture could be trusted over human reason, and the false apostles, the Greeks, argued that human reason could be trusted over Scripture. When there was an apparent conflict between Scripture and reason, the Greeks would make reason explain Scripture, and Paul would make Scripture explain reason. For the Greeks reason was preeminent, for Paul Scripture was preeminent. It was precisely because the false apostles (Greeks) placed such a high value on human reason that they over-valued themselves and their own abilities.

Nonetheless, continued Paul, "Even if I am unskilled in speaking, I am not so in knowledge; indeed, in every way we have made this plain to you in all things" (v. 6). Notice that Paul admits to a lack of interest in rhetoric and oratory. Paul was not uneducated. He was a Pharisee of Pharisees. He was well-educated and fluent in Greek. So, it was not that he was ignorant of the Greek art of public speaking, but that he rejected it because the way that the Greeks framed it and used it was not biblical.

Rhetoric is the art of using language effectively to please or persuade people, particularly groups of people. Paul was unskilled in it because he wanted to be unskilled in it—because it was a form of psychological manipulation that he rejected because Scripture rejected it. Jesus was not doing psychological manipulation.

On the other hand, he challenged the accusation that he was unskilled in knowledge. He had been arguing since his first letter to the Corinthians that he had the upper hand regarding knowledge because he honored the wisdom of God. He had been arguing that they were in the inferior position because they honored the wisdom of the world, which Scripture called foolishness. (Proverbs is full of this concern.[27]) Paul was skilled in biblical knowledge, they were skilled in the art of human reason, philosophical speculation and rhetoric—the manipulation of feelings and opinions. Paul had been making his perspective plain to them in all things, everything that he had written and taught them.

WITHOUT CHARGE

He continued, "Or did I commit a sin in humbling myself so that you might be exalted, because I preached God's gospel to you free of charge?" (v. 7). It is common knowledge that things that are free tend to be thought of as being of little or no value. Why else would something be free? Paul wondered if he had made an error by working for his own keep and providing his gospel services without cost to the Corinthians. Of course, it is likely that the false apostles had control of the money at Corinth. And it's unlikely that they would have paid Paul to challenge their wisdom and authority as leaders of the church. So, he probably didn't have much of a choice at that point, but to work without remuneration to get them back on track.

While he had previously discussed his commitment to work with them without pay, that was not to be the norm for Christian ministry.[28] For Christianity to take its proper place in society, the ox that treads the grain should not be muzzled. Those who labor for Christ should share in the benefits of the gospel. As churches need to care for their buildings, so they need to care for their laborers, their pastors, missionaries and people—for all are called to labor for Christ in one way or another. Yet, not all labor is of the same value, nor should all care be

---

27 See *The Wisdom of Christ in the Book of Proverbs* by Phillip A. Ross, Pilgrim Platform, Marietta, OH, 2006.

28 See *Arsy Varsy—Reclaiming the Gospel in First Corinthians* by Phillip A. Ross, Pilgrim Platform, Marietta, OH, 2008, p. 151, "Ministry Model."

the same. Some things need more care than others and churches need to be free to direct their care (time, talent and treasure) as the Lord leads (1 Corinthians 9:14).

Because it is probable that those who opposed Paul had control of church finances, the Corinthian church would not have directed any finances in Paul's direction. This would have been a probable action of the false leaders at Corinth and would provide an example of false doctrine producing improper behavior. Paul, like anyone else, needed money to live. So withholding money from Paul was a way to attack him. Paul took a tent making job to help make ends meet, but it wasn't enough.

BORROWED

Paul explained, "I robbed other churches, taking wages from them to minister to you, and when I was present with you, and in need, I did not burden anyone; for the brothers who came from Macedonia supplied my need. And in everything I kept myself from being a burden to you, and so I will keep myself." (vs. 8-9).

Those who had opposed Paul would not have contributed to his livelihood while he ministered in Corinth. So, he robbed (*sulaō*) or took money that had come in from other churches and applied it to his personal needs while in Corinth. To say that he robbed other churches may be too strong a translation. The word (*sulaō*) literally means stripped or took. He likely borrowed from the money he had been collecting for Jerusalem, and was looking for the Corinthians to replace it, even to exceed it with their own gifts for Jerusalem. Perhaps this was one of the reasons that Paul had pressed the Corinthians so hard to contribute generously to the Jerusalem mission.

Regardless, Paul knew that while he was engaged in his conflict with the false leaders at Corinth he would not have access to any funds from them. But he could not allow that to derail his mission to reform the Corinthians. Paul was right. His version of the gospel was the correct version, and he needed to assert leadership in Corinth regardless of their willingness to fund his cause.

Here Paul modeled the level of commitment that was necessary to move the cause of Christ forward. Sometimes people willingly and readily received Christ and got with the program, as the Corinthians had initially done when Paul first ministered among them. But sometimes the gospel was repudiated by false believers and the ministers of Christ would need to move the gospel forward in opposition to resistance with whatever resources they could muster.

The lesson was that nothing could retard the forward movement of the gospel of Jesus Christ. Paul was committed to the service of Christ regardless of his reception or the response of those to whom he ministered. Yet, neither was Paul so bull-headed that he could not follow the leading of the Spirit. There were situations from which Paul walked away, such as Mars Hill.[29]

Paul was trying to not become a burden to those to whom he ministered. He didn't want to weigh them down or to allow them to think that he was in it for the money. The Lord had taught that we cannot serve two masters. "No one can serve two masters, for either he will hate the one and love the other, or he will be devoted to the one and despise the other. You cannot serve God and money" (Matthew 6:24).

At some point in everyone's lives there will come a conflict between God and money. Why is that? It is because God and money are vying for the same jurisdiction, the right of control. At some point in everyone's lives the value of money will supplant the value of God, or the value of God will trump the value of money. In times of crisis people will look to God or to money for salvation.

I'm not saying that God and money are always opposed. They can and usually do work together. But even as they work together, one will be more important than the other. One or the other will take the lead in everyone's life. And often personal and/or social crisis reveals the truth about our values. How people respond to crisis is always a measure of their true values.

Character is both revealed and forged in the midst of crisis, and the more severe the crisis, the deeper the revelation. Faith is always the human response to crisis. We cannot help but have faith in the midst of crisis. But the critical issue is faith in what? Faith in whom? In money or in God?

It's not that we have to choose between them. We don't have to choose one to the exclusion of the other. But we must choose which one will take preeminence, which will lead and which will follow, which is master and which is servant.

---

29 For more on Mars Hill, see *Acts of Faith—Kingdom Advancement* by Phillip A. Ross, Pilgrim Platform, Marietta, OH, 2006, p. 175-ff.

30. Listen Up

The truth of Christ is in me that this boasting shall not be silenced in me in the regions of Achaia. Why? Because I do not love you? God knows. But what I do, that I will do, so that I may cut off occasion from those who desire occasion; so that in the thing in which they boast, they may be found even as we. For such ones are false apostles, deceitful workers, transforming themselves into the apostles of Christ. Did not even Satan marvelously transform himself into an angel of light? Therefore it is no great thing if his ministers also transform themselves as ministers of righteousness, whose end shall be according to their works. Again I say, Let no one think me foolish. If otherwise, yet receive me as foolish, so that I may also boast a little. What I speak, I do not speak according to the Lord, but as in foolishness, in this boldness of boasting. Since many glory according to the flesh, I also will boast. For you gladly bear with fools, being wise. For you endure if anyone enslaves you, if anyone devours, if anyone takes from you, if anyone exalts himself, if anyone strikes you in the face. —2 Corinthians 11:10-20

Paul had been proclaiming Christ alone. And because the God of which Paul spoke is the only actual God, and God jealously insists that His people have "no other gods" (Exodus 20:3) before Him, this proclamation seemed like a boast. It seemed as if Paul had been speaking about God and about himself and his exclusive commitment to God in superlatives, as if he had been exaggerating. But the proclamation of salvation by grace through faith in Christ alone is not an exaggeration. And Paul had no intention of stopping, modifying or limiting his proclamation of Christ. If it was seen as a boast, then so be it. It was the truth of Christ and he would not be silenced in the regions of Acacia —Greece.

It is important to understand what Paul was doing here. He was communicating a profound and serious criticism of Greek philosophy and Greek culture. Paul was critical about the way that the Greeks understood reality, and he was voicing his criticism in Greece. Paul was not talking about the Greeks behind their backs. He was not stirring up gossip about the Greeks. He was correcting them directly by challenging their worldview. He didn't just undermine their beliefs and leave them to dangle in the wind. Rather, he challenged one system of thought with another. He didn't leave them with nothing. He left them with Christ as the key to unlock the mysteries of the Bible, the Old Testament. Many things in the Bible had been mysteries prior to the light of Christ, even to the Jews (2 Corinthians 3:14). But with the advent of Christ they were no longer mysteries. In the light of Christ the wisdom of the ages had been revealed for all who had eyes to see and ears to hear.

To those who clung to the categories of Greek philosophy and the practices of Greek culture, it seemed as if Paul was a dangerous revolutionary who was attacking the very foundations of Greek society. They asked why Paul was doing this. Why was he so intent on destroying Greek culture? Paul answered rhetorically, "And why? Because I do not love you? God knows I do!" (v. 11). Was Paul attacking Greek culture because he hated the Greeks? No, he loved them. He was doing what he was doing because he loved them. He was putting his life on the line for them, trying to break through the cultural habits that had accumulated over 600 years of what the Greeks understood to be their great cultural success. Greece had been a dominant world power.

The Greeks had done very well culturally. Like the Corinthian church Greece had been large, successful and influential. Though they had been defeated by the Roman Empire, the Romans had simply adapted what they thought to be the superior elements of Greek wisdom into Roman culture. Rome's defeat of Greece had been more of a corporate merger than the destruction of Greek culture. In Paul's day Rome was the dominant political and military force in the world and Greece provided the dominant philosophical foundation that under girded Greco-Roman civilization. Greek philosophy continues even today to provide the dominant foundation of Western culture and academics. Again, Whitehead's observation that the "safest general characterization of the European philosophical tradition is that it consists of a series of footnotes to Plato"[30] cannot be over emphasized.

Paul was intent on challenging, criticizing and replacing that foundation, which he called philosophical foolishness. Paul had been working to replace the Greco-Roman worldview with a biblical worldview, with biblical culture. But not with the then-existing Old Testa-

---

30 *Process and Reality*, Alfred North Whitehead, Free Press, 1979, p. 39.

ment culture of the Jews, which he knew had gotten diverted from its initial perspective and purpose. Rather, Christ Himself had provided Paul with a vision of the world in the light of Christ, the long-awaited Messiah of Old Testament prophecy.

REFORMATION NOT REVOLUTION

Contrary to their fears, Paul was not recommending a revolution against Rome or the Greek academy. Rather, he was recommending Christ. His intent was not to destroy Rome or Greece, but to save them from their own internal corruptions with the grace and wisdom of Christ. Paul's mission was not destructive, but was constructive in that he was applying the light of Christ to the foundations of reality. He was showing people a better way. Christ had come to change the world, not to destroy it.

But the old order, the old way of thinking and doing things would not easily release its grip on the hearts and minds of those who had embraced it. Old habits die hard. Right or wrong, there is emotional comfort in established habits and ways of thinking and being. Fundamental change comes hard to human beings.

Paul continued, "And what I do I will continue to do, in order to undermine the claim of those who would like to claim that in their boasted mission they work on the same terms as we do" (v. 12). Paul claimed to represent Christ, and was teaching a whole new way of thinking and living that was not only different from that which the Greeks had been teaching, but was opposed to the Greek categories of thought and use of logic at every point.

Paul was fighting a two-front intellectual and cultural war. On the one hand, he was critical of the Jewish establishment in which he had been a significant leader. With his conversion he became increasingly critical of the established Jewish way of interpreting and understanding the Old Testament. He had been given a new vision of the Old Testament in the light of Christ. He himself had been wrong, and the Lord had corrected him. Consequently, he was in conflict with the Old Testament worldview as the Jews had framed it at the time.

But he was also critical of the Greco-Roman worldview because his vision of Christ had shown it to be foolishness in comparison, as well. Paul's vision of Christ as the capstone of the Old Testament and the Messiah of the Gentiles put him at odds with both the Jews and the Greeks.

But that wasn't all. In Corinth and elsewhere a further difficulty had arisen in the form of false apostles, false teachers who masqueraded as representatives of Christ. These false apostles had been teaching the same old perspective(s) but dressed them in Christian garb. They talked about Christ and adapted some of Christ's truth into their various teachings. But they forced various elements of the Bible and Christianity into the old categories of Greek philosophy. They were trying to make sense of Christ by assimilating Christ into Greek philosophy (wisdom), by adapting Him to fit into the Greek philosophical categories that they thought accurately reflected and explained the truth of reality.

Arsy Varsy

They were looking at Christ through the categories of Greek culture, where Paul was looking at Greek culture through the categories of Scripture in the light of Christ. They valued the art of philosophical syncretism, without realizing that syncretism had itself been an ancient enemy of God. For instance, the ancient tradition of the Golden Calf was syncretistic (Exodus 32:1-ff). Syncretism has always been popular because it makes sense to sinful people. It appeals to their experience, intellect and feelings. But syncretism of any form is a violation of the First Commandment because it denigrates the uniqueness and exclusivity of God's claim on the hearts and minds of His people. Syncretism uses Scripture to prop up its own thoughts and ideas about God and reality. Whereas God's wisdom, biblical wisdom reveals the ultimate foolishness of all human thoughts and ideas about God and reality.

Consequently, Paul would continue doing what he had been doing, and undermined the syncretists at every point in order to destroy the foundation of their perspective, which was/is the pride of life—the over-estimation of human abilities, human knowledge and wisdom. He would reveal the false logic of the false apostles to the light of Christ at every opportunity. But he did not do this out of spite or anger, not because he hated them, not because he wanted to destroy them. But because he loved them and wanted them to see the truth of Christ. He did not want them to be dead and out of the way. Nor was he out to prove himself, but to prove Christ. He was not blindly committed to his own way. He was committed to Christ's way. He wanted them to become brothers in Christ. And nothing would dissuade him from this mission.

He was committed to what we would call a divisive mission—proving that the false apostles were unlike the real apostles at every point. He was committed to creating and maintaining a division between himself and the false apostles. He was committed to revealing their pride and their false ideas and assumptions every chance he could get. And from Paul's effort to divide the false from the true,

Christ's church grew. It thrived on the differences and divisions that Paul revealed. Paul did this "in order to undermine the claim of those who would like to claim that in their boasted mission they work on the same terms as we do" (v. 12).

No Offense

I am tempted to soften Paul's blow in the interest of not offending people. I am tempted to back peddle Paul's attack so as not to drive people away because of what may seem like excessive negativity on my part. But that is not what Paul did. Paul accented the divisions. "For such men are false apostles, deceitful workmen, disguising themselves as apostles of Christ. And no wonder, for even Satan disguises himself as an angel of light" (vs. 13-14). Paul buried the proverbial blade in the belly of his opponents and then twisted it. Paul did not think that good people—smart people, qualified people, faithful people—could differ on this matter.

Those who stuck to their guns—the Pharisees who sought to kill Paul, and the Greeks who thought his teaching to be nonsense—were bad enough. The Jews and the Greeks provided substantial difficulties for Paul's ministry. But worse than those who blatantly refused to conform to the light of Christ were those who disguised themselves as apostles of Christ, those who thought that they were helping the cause of Christianity by redefining it to fit into their own ill-conceived ideas. They usually tried to fit Christ into some veiled vision of the Old Testament (which led to Christian Kabbalah) or into the traditional understanding (categories) of Greek philosophy (which led to Gnosticism). Apparently, the errant Corinthian leaders had been involved in these kinds of creative adaptations of the gospel. As much as Jesus had opposed the Pharisees, Paul opposed the false apostles. Both were guilty of perverting the doctrines and wisdom of Scripture.

Such efforts to conform Christ to anything other than Paul's vision of Christ as the capstone and fulfillment of the Old Testament prophecy of the Messiah were deceitful in that they disguised and perverted the truth. They hid the truth, suppressed the truth in unrighteousness (Romans 1:18). And the particularly damnable thing about this effort was that they were doing it in the name of Christ! They twisted the teachings of Christ while posing as agents of Christ. In our own day this has become a highly developed art.

While Paul couldn't say that speaking in tongues was Satanic because he didn't understand what they were saying,[31] he knew what

---

31 *Arsy Varsy—Reclaiming the Gospel in First Corinthians* by Phillip A. Ross, Pilgrim Platform, Marietta, Ohio, 2008, p.278.

these false agents of Christ were saying. And he called them Satanic, "for even Satan disguises himself as an angel of light" (v. 14). The forces of Satan had set up shop in the church!

Before we think that this idea is impossible because it is so outrageous, we need to realize that this modus operandi is not at all unusual. Satan's methodology has always been to counterfeit the truth because he has no truth or light himself. Satan goes the extra mile to make his wisdom look like Christ's wisdom—and many people are fooled by it (Matthew 24:24, 2 John 1:7), "as the serpent deceived Eve by his cunning" (2 Corinthians 11:3). It's the same old same old, a different instance of the same thing.

"So it is no surprise if his (Satan's) servants, also, disguise themselves as servants of righteousness. Their end will correspond to their deeds" (v. 15). Pretending to be an apostle or representative of Christ is the most common method of Christian deceit. Too often the disguise is so good that people even fool themselves. They falsely believe themselves to actually be representatives of Christ. Jesus Himself acknowledged this tendency. "On that day many will say to me, 'Lord, Lord, did we not prophesy in your name, and cast out demons in your name, and do many mighty works in your name?'" Such people believe themselves to be faithful! "And then will I declare to them, 'I never knew you; depart from me, you workers of lawlessness'" (Matthew 7:22-23). They believed themselves to be faithful, but Jesus knew otherwise, and their end will match their deeds, their fruit.

Bear With Me

"I repeat, let no one think me foolish. But even if you do, accept me as a fool, so that I too may boast a little" (v. 16). Paul was not concerned about what they thought of him. They shouldn't think that he was foolish—stupid, but even if they did, he asked for their temporary acceptance so that he could complete his argument. Paul was taking a different tact, "What I am saying with this boastful confidence, I say not with the Lord's authority but as a fool. Since many boast according to the flesh, I too will boast. For you gladly bear with fools, being wise yourselves!" (vs. 17-19).

In verse 17 Paul said that they did not need to think of themselves as believers in order to understand what he was saying. They didn't need to accept God's authority, biblical authority, to understand his argument. He knew that he was speaking to both believers and unbelievers, true believers and false believers. He spoke with boastful confidence, complete confidence, not in himself, but in Christ, not in what he was saying, but in the vision that Christ had given to him.

Nonetheless, if they would simply allow him to put his whole argument on the table, he believed that he would be vindicated by the truth itself. He asked them to go ahead and consider him to be a fool if they must, but to hear him out anyway. He didn't mind that they thought him to be foolish because his argument was not about him. It was about Christ.

Pandering to their vanity, he suggested that they often had to bear with fools. Indeed, most of them thought that anyone who disagreed with them was a fool. And they often disagreed with each other! So, surely they could bear with Paul's foolishness. Surely they were used to putting up with a certain amount of foolishness—their being so wise and all.

Think me a fool. It's okay. But please indulge me. Allow me to finish, to put my whole argument before you so you can make an intelligent assessment of it. But don't dismiss it before you understand it. Bear with me. I'm not asking for any more courtesy than you give to the other fools who surround you all the time.

"For you bear it if someone makes slaves of you, or devours you, or takes advantage of you, or puts on airs, or strikes you in the face" (v. 10).

When someone makes a slave of you, you must put up with all sorts of foolishness because you are in an inferior social position. You can't afford to do otherwise. How might this happen? Paul listed various scenarios that could lead to slavery—poverty. A war could be lost that could result in the slavery of the defeated people. This was a common occurrence at the time. Or someone could fall into slavery by going into debt, another common occurrence. "The rich rules over the poor, and the borrower is the slave of the lender" (Proverbs 22:7).

How likely was it that someone could fall into poverty and/or debt —slavery. One way was to be devoured (*katesthiō*), literally to be eaten down. This simply means that you run out of money and resources. For whatever reasons—good or bad—you simply use up all of your money. It actually happens all the time. Suddenly you are poor and can no longer afford to not put up with the foolishness of others who might give you a job or lend you some money or provide some kind of help. You need to be "nice" to people and not offend them so that if they have an opportunity to help you, they might. At least so they won't think poorly of you, and simply write you off. If you make people mad by calling them fools, they will be less likely to help you. In this case, it's not that someone swindled you or tricked you out of your money.

But someone could swindle or trick you out of your money. Again, this happens all the time, too. Greedy, selfish scam artists are not new to the current age. So, if someone scams you out of your money, you're still poor and in the same boat.

Another way is to get taken advantage of. The Greek is one word (*lambanō*) and the AV translates it as, "If a man take of you" (v. 10). This still amounts to being swindled or tricked, but it's a nicer version of it. The culprit is more polite, has a better story. Perhaps it is a child or relative who takes advantage of you by suggesting that you have a moral responsibility for his or her care. And that care then depletes you of funds. Whatever the case, the result is the same—you end up in poverty.

Another way is to get taken in. Here the Greek (*epairō*) literally means to exalt one's self or to put on airs. This is a higher class swindle, perhaps an investment scam where someone poses as a rich person, convinces you of the success of some hair-brained venture, gets you to invest in the project, and leaves you high and dry. You've still been scammed and you still end up in poverty.

The last method on Paul's list is simple robbery. Someone knocks you out and takes your money. Same result.

Paul's point was that these kinds of things happen all the time to all kinds of people. So, people have to put up with different kinds of foolishness from all kinds of fools all the time. Therefore, they could put up with what seemed to them like foolishness from Paul. Why should they do that? Paul argued that they couldn't understand his position until they had the whole story in mind. Paul was certain that intelligent people would understand the wisdom of Christ if they would simply allow themselves to hear the whole argument.

THE WHOLE STORY

This is still the case, and for the most part those who reject Christ do so before they understand the whole story. Oh, they think they understand the whole story, but they don't. Not really. Few people are willing to study the issues long enough or hard enough to come to a realistic assessment. Most people today have been fed various false and godless thoughts and ideas about reality from so many sources— teachers, parents, media, movies, etc.—that any serious consideration of the actual biblical truth about Jesus Christ is rejected before it is even considered. The truth of Jesus Christ does not fit into the categories of the current Western worldview. Too many people don't ever hear anything about the actual biblical story because it is categorically rejected by their own presuppositions about reality before it gets on the table. That's where we are today, and that was exactly where Paul was at in Corinth.

To counter this tendency Paul wrote some letters to the Corinthian church and asked them to consider them carefully. That's what I've been doing here. And when we finish our consideration of Paul's Second letter to the Corinthians, we will then and only then have the whole of his argument before us for consideration. Until that time, until people have the whole argument before them, they should bear with it. Allow it to be put before them (before *you*).

If you want to think that I'm being foolish in this effort, that's fine. Go ahead and think it. It's okay. Just listen until I'm finished. Hear me out. That's what Paul said in these verses.

31. The Strength of Weakness

I speak according to dishonor, as though we have been weak. But in whatever anyone dares (I speak foolishly), I also dare. Are they Hebrews? I also! Are they Israelites? I also! Are they the seed of Abraham? I also! Are they ministers of Christ? (I speak as beside myself,) I am more! I have been in labors more abundantly, in stripes above measure, in prisons more, in deaths many times. Five times from the Jews I received forty stripes minus one. Three times I was beaten with rods, once I was stoned, three times I was shipwrecked. I have spent a night and a day in the deep. I have been in travels often; in dangers from waters; in dangers from robbers; in dangers from my race; in dangers from the heathen; in dangers in the city; in dangers in the wilderness; in dangers on the sea; in dangers among false brothers. I have been in hardship and toil; often in watchings; in hunger and thirst; often in fastings; in cold and nakedness; besides the things outside conspiring against me daily, the care of all the churches. Who is weak, and I am not weak? Who is caused to stumble, and I do not burn? If it is right to boast, I will boast of the things of my weakness.   *—2 Corinthians 11:21-30*

Paul was embarrassed by his own weakness. He was well aware of his own limitations and liabilities. He knew them in the light of Christ. He knew them because he knew Christ. In the light of Christ, Paul was weak, flawed and foolish. He knew that he had no ground upon which to boast of his own strength, intelligence or abilities. He had previously proven his own strength, intelligence and abilities by becoming a Christ-hating Pharisee. That's where his own strength, intelligence and abilities had brought him. It started without Christ and it ended without Christ.

But Christ had humbled him on the Road to Damascus. In the light of Christ he saw himself more clearly as weak, stupid (foolish) and lost.

Paul also knew that his humiliation in the light of Christ was not unique. All Christians are humbled by Christ in one way or another. The glory, power, authority and might of Jesus Christ, the very Son of God, humbles humanity. Humility in the light of Christ serves as a correction to human pride. All Christians see themselves for what they actually are and give up their pride in the light of Christ. We have no grounds upon which to boast.

But, said Paul, speaking foolishly (*atimia*), "whatever anyone else dares to boast of ... I also dare to boast of that" (v. 21). Paul knew that boasting at all was foolishness. Yet, in order to counter the boasting of the false apostles he needed to talk about his own strengths, his upbringing, his training, and his character because in every way Paul outshone the false apostles. Yet, he had no grounds upon which to boast. So, if he, who was superior to them in every way, had no grounds for boasting, then they had even less. So, he boasted foolishly and was ashamed of his boasting. But it was intended to serve the purpose of humbling those who were proud of their accomplishments.

THE BOASTING GAME

Though Paul had been humbled by Christ, if the false apostles wanted to play the boasting game, then Paul could play. Paul could compare himself with them, but not with Christ. In the light of Christ Paul's boasting was foolishness. But in comparison to the false apostles Paul could put his boast, his credentials, up against theirs. If they wanted to boast about their spiritual credentials, then Paul would boast in order to help them (all of the Corinthians) see that they had nothing to boast about. Their boasting about their wisdom and spiritual insights was foolishness in the light of Christ. If Paul, who was much more qualified in every way, was humbled in the light of Christ, then they, who could not hold a proverbial candle to Paul, should also be humbled in the light of Christ.

"Are they Hebrews? So am I. Are they Israelites? So am I. Are they offspring of Abraham? So am I" (v. 22). If genetics or heredity was the critical factor Paul had more of it than the false apostles. If Jewish culture or training was the critical factor Paul still had more of it than the false apostles.

"Are they servants of Christ? I am a better one" (v. 23), said Paul. If being a servant of Christ was the critical factor, Paul's service was greater. He had more experience than they did and he had a more difficult time of it. While the false apostles had been celebrating the success of the Corinthian church, Paul had been experiencing great difficulty and pain because of his service. Would the false apostles hold up under difficulty and pain as well as Paul? Would they maintain their faithfulness under pressure and difficulty? Or were they only willing to lead into success, wealth and influence? Were they servants of Christ only during good times? It is pressure and difficulty that reveal character. Anyone can do the easy stuff.

Paul suggested here that service to Christ, which always stands in opposition to the wisdom of the world and its false speculations and imaginations about Christ and His gospel of grace, doesn't lead to worldly success. Gospel success is not like worldly success. Where worldly success provides wealth, power and influence among the wealthy, powerful and influential, gospel success undermines pride "because all that is in the world, the lust of the flesh, and the lust of the eyes, and the pride of life, is not of the Father, but is of the world" (1 John 2:16).

It's not that the gospel leads to poverty, powerlessness and ineffectiveness, but that the gospel defines wealth, power and influence differently than the world does. The gospel is the power of God (Romans 1:6). Those who do not know the Scriptures cannot know the power of God (Matthew 22:29). The preaching of the cross is the power of God (1 Corinthians 1:18). God gives us the power to get wealth (Deuteronomy 8:18). God's riches include kindness, forbearance and longsuffering (Romans 2:3). The influence of the gospel leads to the fruits of the spirit—love, joy, peace, patience, kindness, goodness, faithfulness, gentleness, self-control (Galatians 5:23). The gospel does not lead to glitz, greed and glamor.

Suddenly Paul realized that he had been "talking like a madman." Nonetheless, he had experienced "far greater labors, far more imprisonments, (and) ... beatings" (v. 23) than any of the false apostles had— or all of them taken together! Paul understood that real faithfulness is perseverance, even perseverance against great odds.

The false apostles were living in the lap of luxury, as false apostles always do. Jesus, our Lord and Master, didn't spend any time in the lap of luxury. Oh, He was not afraid of wealth. He was not avoiding wealth, nor was He opposed to being rich. Rather, motivation is everything. Wealth in Jesus' name is to be used for Jesus' cause, not our own. Power in Jesus' name is to be used for the purposes of God's kingdom, not our own.

ALL TO ALL

Sure, Paul had "become all things to all people" (1 Corinthians 9:22) He became "as a Jew, in order to win Jews." He "became as one under the law ... that (he) might win those under the law" (1 Corinthians 9:20). He "became as one outside the law ... that (he) might win those outside the law" (1 Corinthians 9:21). Notice that Paul never said that he became rich to win the rich. It was not that Paul was opposed to wealth, only that amassing wealth is not the responsible use of wealth for the purposes of the kingdom. Nor did Paul become prideful in order to win the proud, nor hateful in order to win those who hate, nor stingy in order to win tightwads.

So, when Paul said that he became all things to all people he didn't mean *all* in the widest, most literal sense of the word. Rather, he said "all people" and then qualified what he meant. People too often rip one word of Scripture out of context and hammer it into whatever shape they want it to be in order to justify themselves, in order to conform Scripture to their own thinking rather than to conform their own thinking to Scripture. We must always limit ourselves to the context of the biblical narrative. Then whatever gems of wisdom come from that context, we are free to use for wider applications. But we are not free to force our own justification into Paul's words.

"To the weak (Paul) became weak, that (he) might win the weak" (1 Corinthians 9:22). Paul was simply identifying with various kinds of people in order to show them how the love, mercy and grace of God in Christ applied to them. God loves the poor in spirit, those who mourn, the meek, those who hunger and thirst for righteousness, the merciful, the pure in heart, and those who are persecuted for righteousness' sake. These are the people to whom Paul had been reaching out. These were the targets of Paul's evangelism. And note that these categories of people have nothing to do with money or wealth. Paul was not looking down on money and wealth, nor was he courting it. It simply didn't matter—unless it did.

It mattered to the Rich Young Ruler who had inquired about salvation and the kingdom of God, but who was disheartened by Jesus' response, and "went away sorrowful, for he had great possessions" (Mark 10:22). The Rich Young Ruler's wealth was in the way of the gospel. The Rich Young Ruler valued wealth more than Christ, and that was the problem. It wasn't the wealth, it was the wrong priorities that were his problem.

SERVICE RECORD

Paul then listed his service record. He had far greater labors, far more imprisonments, more beatings, and was often near death. Five times he received at the hands of the Jews forty lashes less one. Three times he was beaten with rods. Once he was stoned. Three times he was shipwrecked; a night and a day he was adrift at sea; on frequent journeys, in danger from rivers, in danger from robbers, in danger from his own people, in danger from Gentiles, in danger in the city, in danger in the wilderness, in danger at sea, in danger from false brothers; in toil and hardship, through many a sleepless night, in hunger and thirst, often without food, in cold and exposure (vs. 23-27). In spite of all of this Paul persevered in faithfulness.

The fruit of the Spirit is not worldly success, not wealth, power and worldly influence. The fruits of the spirit—the love, joy, peace, patience, kindness, goodness, faithfulness, gentleness, and self-control —are character qualities that are more often fired in the kilns of struggle and difficulty than grown in the lap of luxury. Luxury breeds laziness, pride and self-concern, which more often than not produces selfishness rather than selflessness.

Paul wrote to the Romans that he and the apostles had rejoiced in their sufferings, "knowing that suffering produces endurance, and endurance produces character, and character produces hope, and hope does not put us to shame, because God's love has been poured into our hearts through the Holy Spirit who has been given to us" (Romans 5:3-5). While Paul had been persevering the many difficulties that had come to him because of his commitment to Christ, the false apostles in Corinth had grown a large church, amassed much wealth, power and influence in the community, and had been engaged in sexual immorality all the while.

Clearly, Paul was comparing his faithfulness under pressure with their faithlessness in the midst of worldly luxury. They had appealed to a lot of people in order to grow their big church, but Paul identified their appeal as false teaching and faithlessness. They were not faithful to Christ. They were using Christ's name to feather their own nest, to support their own case, to justify their own speculations and to extend, not God's kingdom, but their own fiefdom. History is filled with this kind of thing.

WHEAT & TARES

It's like the wheat and the tares. Both have continued to grow since the wheat was first planted. Tares or *lolium temulentum*, typically known as darnel or cockle, is an annual plant that forms part of the Poaceae family and part of the Lolium genus. The plant stem can grow to be a meter tall, with a flowering in the ears and purple grain. It grows plentifully in Syria and Israel. It usually grows in the same production zones as wheat and is considered a weed. The similarity between these two plants is so extensive that in some regions cockle is referred to as "false wheat." It bears a close resemblance to wheat until the ear appears.

The ears on the real wheat are so heavy that they make the entire plant droop downward, but the "false wheat," whose ears are lighter, stands up straight. So, at harvest it is easy to tell the tare from the wheat. The tare stands up tall, where the wheat bows down from the weight of its grain (or fruit). In addition, Darnel (tares) should not be consumed because it poisons people with a kind of drunkenness.

Paul continued, "And, apart from other things, there is the daily pressure on me of my anxiety for all the churches" (v. 28). Add this anxiety (*merimna*) for the churches to all of the difficulties that Paul had. Other versions translate it as Paul's care for all the churches. And while anxiety is part of care, anxiety tends to limit the meaning to a mental or subjective activity, where care includes the planning, execution and evaluation related to the actual doing of things. Anxiety worries, where care does something about it. Paul's care for the churches involved much more than mere anxiety. He was in the field laboring for their growth. Paul had his very life on the line for them, all the time, twenty-four seven.

And after all of this, who would be weaker than Paul? Paul was weak when he began, he was a scholar and undoubtedly a nerd. Then he went through imprisonments, beatings, shipwrecks and more. Paul was tired, weak and wounded for Christ. Who among the successful Corinthians could possibly be weaker than Paul? The implication was that no one was as weak as Paul. Paul even excelled in weakness!

And who among them had been made to fall (*skandalizō*), had been scandalized, entrapped, or tripped up as much as Paul? Paul had been chased across the known world by angry Jews intent upon his death, and belittled by academicians and politicians (those who excelled in worldly wisdom and its application). He opposed false teachers and false successes built on false promises and faulty hopes at every turn. He preached "Christ crucified, a stumbling block to Jews and folly to Gentiles" (1 Corinthians 1:23) everywhere he went.

Previously, Paul had been boasting of his Jewish heritage and training, and was here boasting about his credentials regarding weakness and scandal. Perhaps the false apostles had tried arguing that they were weaker than Paul and that he had been picking on them (scandalizing or entrapping them). *Okay,* Paul said, *you want to talk about weakness? There is no one weaker than me. You want to talk about being picked on, being scandalized or entrapped?* No one was more picked on or scandalized than Paul.

BOASTING ABOUT WEAKNESS

Paul was convinced that if he had to boast, he would boast about the things that showed his weakness (v. 30). That's odd. Why would he boast about his weakness? Paul will soon share one of Christ's more important messages with the Corinthians. In the next chapter Paul will tell them that The Risen Christ had given a message to Paul: "My grace is sufficient for you, for my power is made perfect in weakness" (2 Corinthians 12:9). This was not a new message. The same idea had been communicated to Isaiah,

> *Have you not known? Have you not heard? The Lord is the everlasting God, the Creator of the ends of the earth. He does not faint or grow weary; his understanding is unsearchable. He gives power to the faint (the weak), and to him who has no might he increases strength. Even youths shall faint and be weary, and young men shall fall exhausted; but they who wait for the Lord shall renew their strength; they shall mount up with wings like eagles; they shall run and not be weary; they shall walk and not faint."*
> —*Isaiah 40:28-31*

God prefers the weak, the meek and humble because He doesn't have to overcome so much pride and/or so much commitment to one's own speculative errors. God communicated this message to Paul because Paul himself had been full of pride and full of the biblical speculations of the Pharisees. Paul had been a hard case. He had a lot to overcome when he came to the Lord.

Paul did finally overcome it, of course, and the record of his overcoming has been left to us as Paul's letters. He was able to write deeply and with an amazing assurance of faith. He was certain that he was right and the whole of the Greco-Roman and Pharisaic Jewish worlds were wrong! He knew that they were wrong because he himself had once believed exactly what they believed. And the Lord undid it all in Christ so that Paul could tell us how all those gargantuan and pervasive false beliefs are wrong and how they are undone in Christ.

Reading Paul's letters rekindles Paul's wisdom and experience. It shows us how Paul's experience and arguments defeated the Pharisees, the Gnostics, the Greek philosophers, the Stoics—and all who for the sake of some tradition or another have made void the word of God (Matthew 15:6).

Paul boasted about his own weakness because the Lord had worked very hard to drive Paul to confront his own weakness, to deal with it, to bring him to his knees in the light of Christ. Paul was praying that Christ's people would be weak before the Lord because the weaker they were, the less they would resist, and the easier their conversion to Christ would be.

As Christ's strength grows in us, as we increasingly rely upon Christ's strength, Christ's power, our own strength fades in the light of

Christ. As John The Baptist said, "He must increase, but I must decrease" (John 3:30).

32. DAMNABLE LIES

The God and Father of our Lord Jesus Christ, who is blessed forever,
knows that I do not lie.   *—2 Corinthians 11:31*

To say that God is the father of Jesus Christ suggests likeness in both character and image. There is a family resemblance in that children share genetic similarities with their parents, and there are behavioral similarities in that children tend to imitate the habits of their parents. This was more true in the period of history prior to the development of modern travel and communication simply because the experience of the children was dominated by parental factors.

But God's fatherhood of Jesus is not exactly like ordinary human fatherhood for a variety of reasons. God is Spirit, Jesus was flesh and blood that was unified with the Spirit of God. God and Jesus and the Holy Spirit are caught up together in the Trinity in a way that is both unique and authentic. The Trinity is individual, corporate, and eternal. No aspects of the Trinity are created, nor do they come into being as people do. There are similarities and differences between God's fatherhood and the fatherhood of human fathers, and Jesus' Sonship and the sonship of human sons.

Nonetheless, Paul's point is that Jesus shares the character of God. And the essential element of that shared character that Paul points out here is that God and Jesus are "forever blessed" (v. 31). The AV follows the word order of the Greek, "blessed for evermore." And the Greek is instructive. Blessed (*eulogētos*) is a combination of two words: *eu* which means good, and *logos*, which means word. John said, "In the beginning was the Word, and the Word was with God, and the Word (*logos*) was God" (John 1:1). John noted that there is a fundamental identity between God and God's Word, suggesting that the characteristics of God are also characteristics of God's Word.

Paul said that God, who is fundamentally identified with Jesus and with His own (God's own) Word is good (*eu*). The blessings of goodness that flow from God and from His Word also flow from Jesus and from His Word. But not only are they blessed, they (God, Jesus and His Word) are "blessed for evermore." The phrase *for evermore* is also composed of two Greek words. *Eis*, a primary preposition, suggests a point entered or a point reached in terms of time. It is often translated as *in* or *into*. The second word is *aiōn* and literally means age and implies a period of time in which the world exists. It could refer to a particular historical age or could include the entire age or period of existence of the earth itself.

Literally this phrase, *blessed for evermore,* could be translated *good Word into the earth,* or *good Word in our age or time.* The point is that God's Word is good because it is true. God does not lie. There is integrity between what God says and reality. God's Word accurately describes reality. There is a high correlation between what God says and what is actually true. Communication—words—are most useful when the words actually correspond to the reality of the situation described. Conversely, if the words spoken do not describe the reality of the situation, their usefulness and goodness are diminished.

Good Science

We see the goodness of this usefulness in science, in that scientific theories (words, thoughts, ideas—*logos*) must accurately describe the facts. And if the facts are found to contradict a particular theory, the theory is discarded. As new scientific facts are discovered old theories are often found to be wrong or inadequate, and are discarded or changed. Paul's point was that God's Word will never be found to be inadequate to the reality of this world. For as long as this world lasts, God's Word will always be found to provide an accurate description of the facts and have an appropriate application in the world. God's Word does not deceive us about the nature or character of the world. This is what it means for something to be true—and good. God's Word is true, and it will always be true, regardless of scientific developments. Furthermore, the truth of God's Word is good. It is a blessing. It is for our good.

So, Paul said here that God—who is the Father of Jesus Christ, and whose Word is eternally true and good—knew that Paul had not been lying in anything that he had said. Paul's words are true and trustworthy. This is why Paul's letters are included in the canon of Scripture. Paul was not lying (*pseudomai*), nor was he in error. The importance of this statement cannot be overstated.

LYING

Lying—deceit—is sinful. It is a form of corruption, error and inaccuracy. God cannot tolerate lying or deceit. Why not? Because God is truth, and lies and deception destroy truth. Let me suggest that lying may be the most serious sin that people can engage. More serious than murder? Yes. Why? Because murder is clearly understood to be wrong by all people, and is avoided by most. Even murderers know that murder is wrong.

But lying is perhaps the easiest sin to rationalize and dismiss. So, lying is undoubtedly the most popular sin. More people lie than commit any other sin. Lies and deception are used as the primary means of engaging in many other sins. One little lie may not seem to be very serious, but a lot of little lies can add up to a boatload of deceit and inaccuracies. One little lie may not seem to be very serious, but when other lies are built upon it the results can be multiplied or scaled to produce an exponential increase of inaccuracies.

It could even be argued that lying or deception is the original sin. After eating the forbidden fruit in the Garden, Adam and Eve, "hid themselves from the presence of the Lord God among the trees of the garden" (Genesis 3:8). They tried to deceive God regarding their whereabouts.

Satan had previously deceived them about God, convincing them that God had been deceiving them because He did not want them to become like Himself, "knowing good and evil" (Genesis 3:5). In essence, Satan accused God of deceiving Adam and Eve, of withholding the truth from them, of keeping them from the experience of enlightenment that would allow them, humanity, to know things as God knows things. Satan accused God of wanting to keep the truth about the nature of reality to Himself, to keep it from humanity.

But the real lie, Satan's lie, was that Adam and Eve could know things as God knows things, that such knowledge was possible, that they could become as God Himself was in this regard. Satan blurred the distinction between God and man, and encouraged humanity to believe the thoughts of their own hearts and minds more than God's Word.

In contrast, Paul was not lying. Paul had been accurately describing the relationship between God and man, between God and Jesus as Father and Son, and the reality of the Holy Spirit. Paul had been revealing the trinitarian reality of the relationship between God and man. Paul had been demonstrating that the truth about the relationship between God and humanity had been definitively demonstrated in, by and through Jesus Christ, the Son of God, who is the only mediator between God and man. And furthermore, that Jesus Christ had brought the dispensation or outpouring of the Holy Spirit upon humanity (John 20:22).

Outpouring

Paul had been showing the Corinthians how the prophecy of Joel had come to pass. Luke reminds us of that prophecy in Acts 2:17-18: "And in the last days it shall be, God declares, that I will pour out my Spirit on all flesh, and your sons and your daughters shall prophesy, and your young men shall see visions, and your old men shall dream dreams; even on my male servants and female servants in those days I will pour out my Spirit, and they shall prophesy."

God had not been hiding the truth of reality from humanity, but had been engaged in revealing that truth. But it is a big truth! And time was required for its full revelation to manifest in history. Apart from its full manifestation in Christ, it would be deceitful in that it would be incomplete. Even the partial truth—the truth of God's Old Testament law—falls short of the whole truth in the light of Christ. Thus, Paul said that the truth had been veiled from the Jews. "Yes, to this day whenever Moses is read a veil lies over their hearts" (2 Corinthians 3:15). It was not that God had been hiding the full truth, but that the full truth had to wait for the manifestation of Jesus Christ in bodily form. The truth of human existence is complex, but it is not an abstraction. Rather, it is trinitarian and exists in time—over time, through time.

There is a difference of intention or purpose regarding Satan and God. Satan uses deception to keep the fullness of God's truth—the truth of the reality of human existence and the trinitarian character of God—from people. And he does this by substituting a false truth for God's truth. Satan's understanding falls short of perfect or complete truth, where God's understanding plumbs the depths and reaches the heights of perfect truth.

Satan's methodology is to substitute an approximation for the reality, an abstract idea for the immediate meaning, imagination for actuality. Satan's approximation of the truth falls short of the eternal reality. And consequently, Satan's approximation is a function of death (or unsustainable cultural development), whereas God's perfect truth is the engine of eternal life (or sustainable cultural development). All forms of unsustainable cultural development always crash and burn at some point. That's what makes them unsustainable. Only human cultural development in the light of Christ—that is, in the full light of God's complete historical, trinitarian revelation—is capable of development that is sustainable through all of the various levels or degrees of so-called scientific discoveries, and the plethora of twists and turns of what we call nature and history.

The key to the development of sustainable culture is Jesus Christ. But not Christ as some kind of abstraction that is separated from the historical reality of God's complete biblical revelation. Rather, the history of God's revelation is to be, not simply the governing narrative of cultural development, but is itself the engine of such development. The reason for this is that God's intent is to instill His own character into humanity, to instill those communicable character qualities that are the expression of God's absolute goodness, both individually and corporately. This is the outworking of the fact that we are created in God's image (Genesis 1:26).

Prevarication[32]

Now perhaps we can see the importance of deceit and lying. We have—humanity has—developed such an extensive justification about lying that we all believe that some lies are harmless. Such a belief is at the very heart of our fallen nature. We have invented a category of insignificant lies that we call white lies, which are also called prevarication. Lying (deception) is a complex subject, both philosophically and biblically. And at the same time is it absolutely simple. Isn't it?

We all know the difference between the truth and a lie. Don't we? In fact, we don't—but we think we do! And that is at the heart of the effectiveness of the deception of lies. Lies are effective! They work because we believe the deception and accept the lie (or what is less than the complete truth) as being true, at least for a while.

This is intimately involved with the issue of knowing things as God knows them. Do we—can we know things as God knows them? Cornelius Van Til said *no*. Gordon Clark said *yes*.[33] A more complete answer might be that we will know things as God knows them in the fullness of time (in heaven, in glory, in the future), but not until then. In other words, yes, but not yet. Not until the unity of the Godhead is fully manifest in human culture.

John of Patmos glimpsed this reality and wrote that he had seen, "the holy city, new Jerusalem, coming down out of heaven from God, prepared as a bride adorned for her husband" (Revelation 21:2). The holy city or New Jerusalem represents sustainable or eternal human cultural development (life, city life, corporate life) that is established, built and founded upon the complete historical revelation of Jesus Christ the Son of God as the very source of eternal life, of sustainable development.

---

32 *Prevaricate*: To stray from or evade the truth; equivocate; to be deliberately
    ambiguous or unclear in order to mislead or withhold information.
33 *The Clark-Van Til Controversy*, by Herman Hoeksema, Trinity Foundation (May 1995).

UNITY

At the heart of this revelation, following the proclamation of Jesus Christ as the Savior of the whole world, is the manifestation of the unity of the saints, the unity of the church—a unity that will ultimately include every existing, living and extant person. But not an administrative superstructure that spans the globe. Rather, Christian unity is the reality of a common understanding and commitment to Christ as the foundation stone of the economy[34] of God.

Such unity does not make people all alike, but is rather the actual source of individual uniqueness. It is the source of our differences. In the same way that unity with Christ enhances individual human character and personality by making individuals more unique than any individual could ever be apart from Christ, unity in Christ provides for an infinite diversity regarding human personality and is the source of the division of labor that is itself the engine of economic development. And more than the cold development of the mere economic sustainability of human culture, unity in Christ actually provides the infinite diversity of human personality such that human love, friendship, fellowship and interaction provide for the satisfaction of our most basic need for companionship in ways that are infinitely diverse and interesting.

Consequently, unity in Christ (on earth or in heaven) is not boring or monodimensional. The goodness of God is not boring at all, but is the most interesting thing available to humanity. In reality it is our bondage to sin that requires an excessive and habitual repetition of base gratification that is revealed in the light of Christ to be the real source of boredom and monotony. Sin keeps us eternally scratching the same itch, trying to satisfy the same desires without end. The itch is never fully relieved. The desire is never fully satisfied apart from Christ. Apart from Christ people are bound to their sin, like a tether or leash binds a dog to a stake.

Sin is the actual source of boredom, whereas the journey into perfection in Christ requires the breaking of our tether to sin so that we can make real progress on the path of life in the unity of Christ

---

34 In the New Testament the word *economy*, an anglicized form of the Greek word *oikonomia*, is strongly used. For instance, this word is used in Ephesians 3, a chapter which reveals that the riches of Christ are preached to the nations so that the church can come into being. Verse 9 speaks of "the economy of the mystery." *Oikonomia* is composed of two Greek words: *oikos*, meaning house, and *nomos*, meaning law. Hence, an *oikonomia* is a house law, a family administration. Some versions translate *oikonomia* as "administration," and others as "arrangement" or "plan." God's economy is His plan, His administration, His arrangement. (from *The Satanic Chaos in the Old Creation and the Divine Economy for the New Creation*, by Witness Lee, p.13.)

through the dispensation of the gifts of the Spirit. Hell is actually the place of eternal torment, where the itch finds no relief, "where their worm does not die and the fire is not quenched" (Mark 9:48), where the tether is not broken.

This is simply to say that such vistas will open to each of us as we live in the light of Christ, who is the revelation and manifestation of God's truth. The key to this journey in truth is to abandon lies and deception. Lies and deception cannot lead to the truth. Love cannot countenance lies and deception. The sustainable development of a financial economy cannot be built upon lies and deception. Science and technology cannot develop apart from the reliability of the truth and integrity of the reporting of the observations and insights of which science is composed. Accuracy requires honesty, truth and integrity.

Paul said, "God ... knows that I am not lying" (v. 31). This is ground-zero of God's invasion into human history. God's purpose is to eradicate sin, to eradicate lying and deception, and to bolster love, patience and perseverance with integrity while the totality of God's truth in Christ unfolds in human history. God's temporary purpose is to eradicate the culture of frustration and death, the culture of lies and deception that are short of God's perfect truth in Christ. God's purpose is to eliminate the culture of sin and death. Why? Because God's eternal purpose is the establishment of the eternal sustainability of human culture on earth as it is in heaven, to sustain a culture of life and satisfaction in Christ, to include the fullness of all that is implied in God's Word about eternal life in Christ. It is to this eternal purpose that God calls His people. And Paul was laboring in the service of this purpose.

HONEST LYING

I wish that I could argue that all lying and deception always go against God's purposes, but life is not that simple. Abram lied about Sarai, his wife, being his sister (Genesis 12:13). While it is true that she was his half-sister, Abram's lie to Pharaoh stands. And he did it again after his regeneration and subsequent name change (Genesis 20:3). The best we can do with this is to say that Abraham lied to people outside of God's covenant and that the lie served God's purpose. Consequently, there is some justification for lying to God's enemies while engaged in the service of God's purpose.

Rahab lied to the soldiers who were looking for the Jewish spies in order to protect them—and herself (Hebrews 11:31). Here deception was used as a defensive strategy to protect God's people. Can we generalize from this? Perhaps, but such situations are rare and do not establish precedents.

CONSEQUENCES

In contrast stands God's treatment of Ananias and Sapphira in Acts 5. God killed Ananias and Sapphira for lying to the church, to God's people. The story is stark and shocking to our sensitivities. Therefore, we must assume that its purpose is to provide a shock to our sensitivities. Their sin doesn't seem to be very great. Ananias and Sapphira had been accepted by the church and were engaged in good deeds, selling some of their property in order to donate money to the church.

Two stories come in rapid succession. Barnabas sold some property and laid the proceeds at the apostle's feet (Acts 4:34-37). Then Ananias sold some property, kept some of the proceeds for himself and his wife, and laid what was left at the apostle's feet. There was a discrepancy between the actual price of the sale and the reported price of the sale. Peter asked Ananias,

> why has Satan filled your heart to lie to the Holy Spirit and to keep back for yourself part of the proceeds of the land? While it remained unsold, did it not remain your own? And after it was sold, was it not at your disposal? Why is it that you have contrived this deed in your heart? You have not lied to men but to God   —Acts 5:3-4

Apparently, the church needed money. Barnabas set the pattern, and Ananias followed—with the exception that he kept some of the proceeds for himself and his wife. Where is the crime in that? It was their money, wasn't it?

The story is sketchy, but the point is Peter's accusation that Ananias lied about something. What he lied about is difficult for us to see. The church at that time had instituted a policy of having all things in common, of pooling their assets. It was a temporary policy mutually agreed upon and enacted for whatever reasons, Scripture doesn't say, and it isn't relevant to the story. Rather the point is that Ananias conspired to hide some of his assets from the common pool—for whatever reasons. It again doesn't matter to the story. The moral is that he died as the result of his deception, and the story is repeated as Sapphira recounted the same deception to the apostles. Both Ananias and Sapphira simply fell over dead, apparently as a result of their deceit.

The only point that can be drawn from this story is that God will not countenance lying or deceit among the people of God. While there might be a rare occasion to lie to God's enemies while specifically engaged in the accomplishment of God's purposes, lying to God's people is here strictly forbidden, with death as the consequence. The triviality of the lie emphasizes the importance of the issue.

The fact that lying results in death is important for reasons that I have been discussing. Ananias and Sapphira died, not because of the severity of their sin, but as an example to the church about the importance of not lying to each other. The point is that while their sin may have been small, the consequences of lying are great.[35]

The Lord constructed the story to clearly show us the connection between lying and death—regardless of the size of the lie. Lying serves the purposes of death. Even when we lie to God's enemies, the purpose is their death and destruction.

Again, Christians cannot (should not) lie to one another. The kingdom of God cannot be built with lies. Lies of any kind or any size are incompatible with God's kingdom, except inasmuch as they serve to destroy sin and evil. Whatever employs lies and deceit among God's people cannot contribute to the kingdom of God. Lies and deception corrupt the data and inhibit science and technology, upon which modern culture depends. The importance of this truth with regard to sustainable cultural and economic development cannot be overemphasized.

Christ's truth is the bedrock of salvation!

---

35 I'm not suggesting that liars receive the death penalty. God is gracious and merciful in Christ. I'm simply suggesting that we should not lie to one another. Nonetheless, the widespread habit of lying in a culture will keep it from good science and sustainable development, and could result in cultural death if it goes uncorrected.

33. The Basket Case

At Damascus, the governor under King Aretas was guarding the city of Damascus in order to seize me, but I was let down in a basket through a window in the wall and escaped his hands.

—2 Corinthians 11:32-33

These last two verses of chapter eleven are quite different from the surrounding text. They appear as a kind of parenthetical comment, as if Paul suddenly remembered something that was related somehow, and yet was a bit tangential to the subject he had been discussing. So, we need to remind ourselves of the context of these verses.

Chapter eleven contains Paul's account of his credentials. He had been boasting about his qualifications as a Christian leader, demonstrating the superiority of his credentials over those of the false apostles. Paul was a theologian, but not an armchair theologian. Having been trained in biblical scholarship as a Pharisee, he was uniquely qualified as a Christian to put Christ into the proper biblical context, to see Christ as the fulfillment of God's plan. Furthermore, Paul's preaching and teaching of Christ had put him in many kinds of difficult situations and personal dangers. Paul's point in boasting was that neither personal difficulty nor danger had dissuaded him from his commitment to Christ. Rather, it was his commitment to Christ that had put him into personal dangers and difficult situations. Clearly, Paul was not in it for himself, not for his own personal gain—other than the heavenly rewards of earthly obedience.

Then in the midst of this boasting, Paul remembered the time in Damascus when he had barely escaped the authorities who sought to kill him. He had been trapped—cornered—in Damascus and, were it not for some faithful friends, he would have been captured and killed.

King Aretas had been after him. Paul mentioned Aretas by name.

Here we see that it wasn't the Jews alone who sought Paul, but the Jews had convinced the Damascus authorities to help. And who were these Damascus authorities? They were Nabateans, dessert people of ancient Edomite ancestry. The Jews and the Edomites had a long history of antagonism. The Edomites were ancient enemies of Israel.

Roots

Josephus mentioned Aretas as king of the Arabians, whose royal seat was at Petra, the ancient city that had been carved into the cliffs in the area we now call Jordan. The name Aretas or Al-Hareth signifies the lion, and the lion was a symbol of royalty and dominion, probably in reference to King David, the lion of Judah. It may also be of significance that Ali, the son-in-law of Mohammad, was called by the Arabs and Persians the lion of God, no doubt pretending to be an heir of the throne of David, and suggesting some sort of Islamic Edomite heritage. The point is that King Aretas and the city of Damascus had long-established roots on the Arabian side of the historic conflict between Israel and her neighbors.

The religious systems of the Arabs prior to the birth of Mohammad involved the ancient doctrines of the Magians and Sabaeans, children of the Edomites, who had succumbed to idolatry and polytheism. Ancient astrology had become the basis of their religion, and the stars which represented deities to whom prayers were made, became objects of worship. And graven images were made in honor of them.

Among the Arabs each tribe worshiped a particular star, and included the setting up of star idols, such that Pagan polytheism became the religion of the ancient Arabs. The object of greatest veneration was the celebrated Black Stone, at Mecca, fabled to have fallen from heaven at the beginning of time with Adam. Over this stone was built the Kaabah, a small oblong stone building. And around that was later built a great mosque. That mosque was then decorated with three hundred and sixty idols (one for each ancient day). And to it ancient Arab pilgrims would bring precious offerings.

It was like the shrine at Delphi in ancient Greece,[36] in that it was a source of religious mystery, teaching and profit for the priests who tended it. Of course there were other religions in the area of ancient Jordan, and many Jews at Medina. Later a corrupted form of Christianity came into being there, no doubt having mixed with and adapted to the existing religions in the area. In addition, the various

---

36 See *Arsy Varsy—Reclaiming the Gospel in First Corinthians*, by Phillip A. Ross, Pilgrim Platform, Marietta, Ohio, p. 233.

religions and sects in the area had been balkanized, and were mutually hostile. Arabians are famous for religious and sectarian wrangling.

ISLAMIC FRUIT

Into this mix came Mohammad, who accommodated his fasts and feasts and holidays and pilgrimages to fit the ancient customs of the people. Doing so he was able to teach lessons of worldly wisdom that drew from those ancient beliefs and religious cultures. For instance, Astarte, the old goddess of Sabaean idolatry, was worshiped on Friday, and this day was then made the Islamic Sabbath. Also, the month of Rhamadan, from ancient times had been set apart for fasting and pilgrimage. Declaring that he had received his first revelations during Rhamadan, this festival was also adapted by Mohammad. Pilgrimages to the Black Stone in Mecca, which continue to this day, were adapted to honor Mohammad and his revelation. Worldly success always involves an appeal to popular beliefs and practices.

After Mohammad's famous flight to Medina he further adapted Islamic doctrine to the ancient pagan customs of the area, blending biblical truth with pernicious error. He adapted his religion to the passions (feelings) and habits of the people in order to make it more acceptable. Tapping into the existing beliefs and customs, to popular culture is a tried and true method of religious advancement or church growth.

Of course, Mohammad would not show up for another six hundred years beyond Paul's Damascus experience, but the seeds of Islam were already there. Of course, Paul did not encounter the organized doctrines of Islam in Damascus, but he did encounter the pagan practices and culture that would become the building blocks of Islam.

So, here we find that it was not just the Jews who sought to kill Paul, but the Arabs were also involved. To this day Islamic Arabs group Jews and Christians together and fight against them as if they represent the same threat. It is not insignificant that Paul reminisced about his near capture at Damascus—and that it was not just the Jewish Pharisees who sought him, but also the Arabs.

Nor is it insignificant that in our own day—during the current War on Terror, a world-wide war against Islamic terrorists who are intent upon the destruction of the Western, Judeo-Christian culture—that the guiding light of Islam is the Koran, which explicitly teaches the use of murder, lying and deceit against those who do not believe or accept Allah, the god of Islam. Indeed, wherever lies, deception, intimidation and murder are used among people to accomplish any purposes whatsoever, Islamic terrorism finds common ground and is able to forge strategic alliances, both formal and informal.

Sin clusters. That is to say that all deceit, deception, lies, intimidation and murder flow from and flow into the ultimate purposes of Satan, the father of lies (John 8:44). It is also significant that Islamic terrorism uses the tools and serves the purposes of Satan. Satan's ancient and contemporary purpose is the undermining and destruction of the kingdom of God by any and every means, including but not limited to deceit, deception, lies, intimidation and murder. Thus the kingdom of God and the kingdom of Satan are antithetical, opposite of one another in every way.

OUROBOROS

Sin clusters. Where one sin is found others will be near because sin feeds off itself. Sin is cannibalistic. Sin is a parasite that kills its host, and once the host is dead it turns on itself. Sin is the Ouroboros, the Greek mythological tail-devouring snake. The Ouroboros comes from the imagination of Plato, who described (in his Timaeus) a self-eating, circular being as the first living thing in the universe—an immortal, perfectly constructed creature. Indeed, the Ouroboros is Plato's god, the source and destiny of all Greek philosophy and culture.

The Ouroboros has a long and diverse history. It is mentioned in the disparate traditions of Gnosticism and Norse mythology. In Alchemy it is the symbol of the eternal unity of all things, the cycle of birth and death from which the alchemist sought release and liberation. As such, it has philosophical similarities to Buddhism and Hinduism, which themselves have philosophical similarities to Platonism. There are also similar snake stories in the traditions of ancient African religions and the Aztecs of South America. Indeed, the Ouroboros seems to be everywhere in the world and is consistently identified with the self-destructive spirit of the world—death.

Paul, who had been boasting about his qualifications as a true apostolic leader of the Christian church, who had committed his life to Christ, and who had that commitment fired in the kilns of preaching Christ among people who did not know Christ, suddenly glimpsed the ultimate struggle between Christ and the world, between Christ and sin, between Christ and the Ouroboros, between Christ and Satan, between eternal life in Christ and the cycle of death and destruction that is built on lies, deception, intimidation and murder. Suddenly Paul remembered how King Aretas had sought to kill him, and the time that he had been cornered in Damascus. Paul's preaching of Christ crucified was not only a stumbling block to Jews and folly to Gentiles (1 Corinthians 1:23), but it would in time become heresy to Muslims.

Twice Saved

But Paul had been saved by those who loved him, saved by those who knew Christ, saved by those who like Paul had been regenerated by the power and presence of the Holy Spirit, saved by the Christian community. Paul had not only been saved on the Road to Damascus by the Risen Christ who had called him out, blinded him and put him in the dust. But Paul had also been saved by the people of God, by his fellow Christians who had "let (him) down in a basket through a window in the wall" (v. 33) at Damascus. Paul had been twice saved— saved by both the Risen Christ Himself, and then by the community of the Risen Christ.

There is a great lesson in these two verses about Christian fellow-ship, about the mutual care and concern that Christians have for one another. It is a lesson about the dangers of true Christian leadership, and about the dependence that leaders have upon their people. Not only do Christian leaders care for and serve the well-being of the Christian community, but the Christian community cares for and serves the well-being of its leaders.

Indeed, this event of Paul's rescue from King Aretas was another reason that Paul could boast. This was another important qualification of his Christian leadership. Paul's people loved him and protected him from danger. Not only did Paul love and serve the fellowship of Christ, but the fellowship of Christ loved and served him, as well. Their love was mutual. Their service was mutual. While Paul had been arguing against false apostles and false Christians in Corinth, trying to reestab-lish the doctrines of Christian truth and the bonds of Christian com-munity, he remembered the unity of the saints that he had experi-enced in Damascus.

While these verses seem at first to be out of context, they are not. The story of Paul's Damascus rescue was simply another of Paul's boasts. The false apostles in Corinth had not been running for their lives. They had not been fleeing those who sought to kill them because of the message they preached. Not at all! Rather, the false apostles in Corinth had appealed to the popular ideas of Greek philosophy and culture, and built the Corinthian church on an amalgam of Greek and Hebrew ideas, a synthesis of Christ's wisdom with the ancient wisdom of the world, wisdom that is found in the various religions and cultures of the world. But this was an error. Christ alone stands opposed to it all!

As such, the theology of the false apostles at Corinth appealed to false believers, to Gnostics and syncretists of every sort—and there were (and still are) a bunch of them. Gnosticism and syncretism have always been popular. They have always appealed to the natural mind, always built upon human imagination. They are always concocted in the hazy shadows of ignorance and superstition. And the church at Corinth grew large, rich and influential while Paul, who preached Christ crucified and risen, had been chased around the known world by the enemies of God who sought to kill him. Paul shone the light of Christ into the dark corners of human creativity, and people hated him for it.

This was part and parcel of Paul's boast. This fact of Paul's commitment to Christ and to Christ alone in fulfillment of the First Commandment of Moses was the point of mentioning the story of his escape from Damascus. Paul boasted in Christ's watch-care of him in the midst of difficulty and danger. Paul was God's man.

Paul boasted in Christ alone, and Christ alone stands as a threat to ignorance and superstition—ancient and contemporary. Christ alone is able to break the bonds of sin, and free humanity for service to God's purpose, God's real glory. That was true in Paul's day, and it has been true ever since. There is nothing else in which to boast, nor need there be. For Christ alone is both necessary and sufficient.

34. Caught Up

I must go on boasting. Though there is nothing to be gained by it, I will go on to visions and revelations of the Lord. I know a man in Christ who fourteen years ago was caught up to the third heaven—whether in the body or out of the body I do not know, God knows. And I know that this man was caught up into paradise—whether in the body or out of the body I do not know, God knows—and he heard things that cannot be told, which man may not utter.
—2 Corinthians 12:1-4

To this point Paul had been boasting about his upbringing, education, training, and experience as an apostle. His focus had been on the kinds of things that people put in their resumes, respectable things, common things. He had not yet spoken of his spiritual experiences, of his conversion encounter with the resurrected Christ on the Road to Damascus some fourteen years earlier. There Paul had seen and heard the Risen Christ, been blinded by the light of Christ and healed by the love of Christ. In the midst of that experience—whatever it was—Paul had been given a vision of Christ, an insight about Christ, a perspective from which to understand Christ as the long-awaited Messiah predicted by the Old Testament.

That vision, insight, perspective—whatever it was—changed everything for Paul. His life and his understanding of Christ, of the world, of Scripture, of everything. He would never be the same. Paul spent the rest of his life explaining the vision that had come to him, explaining what happened to him, what he came to understand in that flash of blinding light.

It was a mysterious experience, but not mystical in the sense of the pagan, Greek or Edomite mysteries. Paul had not talked about it because it was not to be confused with the kind of pagan mysteries that he had been arguing against. He had not mentioned it for fear that people would be too quick to categorize it with the other kinds of mysteries they knew about, the kind of mysteries that Paul had been arguing against. He hadn't wanted to talk about it because it could too easily become a source of confusion and misrepresentation.

UNTIL NOW

And besides, Paul didn't really understand it either. It just happened. It is interesting to note that Paul had not spoken about it, and did not want to speak about this kind of very personal spiritual experience of Christ. He had avoided speaking about it until now. And yet, this is the very thing that contemporary Christians want to speak about. This kind of mystical, spiritual, emotional experience is the stuff of contemporary testimonials. It's practically mandatory today, and people make a wreck of it. People today love to speak about and to hear about these kinds of mystical, "spiritual" experiences, to exaggerate and embellish them—and then to speculate about them, no doubt just as they did in Corinth.

Paul had been wary of talking about his personal experience, but he had thought about it a lot over the past fourteen years. Paul was afraid that such an experience would be misunderstood to be mystical or spiritual in a pagan sense, and would lead people to think of Christ in mystical, pagan ways—much as had been done in Corinth by the false apostles.

Though the time had come for him to say something about his own mysterious experience on the Road to Damascus, he found himself hesitant to speak about it. "I must go on boasting. Though there is nothing to be gained by it, I will go on to visions and revelations of the Lord" (v. 1).

Calvin thought that the sense of this verse was, "I should have preferred to be silent, I should have preferred to keep the whole matter suppressed within my own mind, but those ambitious, obstinate persons will not allow me. I shall mention it, therefore, as it were in a stammering way, that it may be seen that I speak through constraint."[37] It may have been that the false apostles had charged Paul with inconsistency and confusion because on the one hand he argued against mysteries and yet on the other he himself had a mysterious experience. So, Paul needed to clarify this concern. But the clarification of mystery is not an easy thing to do.

Nonetheless, the time had come for Paul to explain himself, to explain in more detail the personal experience that had so changed

---

37 *Calvin's Commentaries*, Volume XX, Baker Book House, 1993, p. 367.

him and provided the foundation and impetus of his many letters and teachings.

The Man

Commentators are agreed that when Paul said that he knew "a man in Christ who fourteen years ago was caught up to the third heaven" (v. 1) he was referring to himself, to his Damascus Road experience. It is less clear why Paul did not speak in the first person. Perhaps the Greek provided a colloquialism or some commonly understood way of speaking at the time that has been lost in the translation over the centuries. Nonetheless, based upon the personal, subjective nature of what Paul revealed we understand him to have been speaking about himself.

Fourteen years ago Paul had been "caught up to the third heaven" (v. 2). The ASV, keeping with the Greek word order reads, "I know a man in Christ, fourteen years ago (whether in the body, I know not; or whether out of the body, I know not; God knoweth), such a one caught up even to the third heaven." Paul prefaced his mention of the third heaven with the proviso that he wasn't sure if it had been a bodily experience or some kind of spiritual experience. He wasn't sure if he had been dreaming or not because the experience had been so real, and yet it was not like any other regular bodily experience he had ever had.

At the heart of what we understand as Christian mystery is the trinitarian nature of God and the reflected trinitarian nature of man, who was created in the image of God. It is significant that Paul mentioned some personal confusion regarding his understanding and experience of his body.

Remember back to First Corinthians where Paul had discussed the trinitarian nature of the body of Christ, the different uses of *sarx* and *soma*, two Greek words, both meaning body, used to distinguish between fleshy body and spiritual body or individual body and corporate body. Remember back to Paul's discussion of the body of Christ as an element of the Lord's Supper, and the mingling of the Lord's body with our individual bodies and with the body of the church through the sacrament. The bread represents the body of Christ and at the same time the representation conveys (communicates, transmits, legitimates) the body of Christ.[38]

Consider now that the "place" that Paul had been "caught up to" was "the third heaven." The fact that it was the *third* heaven and not

---

38 For more on this see the sections, "Communion," p. 85, "Three In One," p. 171, "Body," p. 211,. in *Arsy Varsy—Reclaiming the Gospel in First Corinthians*, by Phillip A. Ross, Pilgrim Platform, 2008.

the second or the fourth is significant. Because the Trinity is at the heart of Christian mystery, Paul's allusion to the third heaven was a reference to the Trinity. Christian mystery is intimately related to the unique and individual—yet overlapping—characteristics of the Father, Son and Holy Spirit, and the reflective character of humanity having been created in the image of this trinitarian God. Paul was suggesting that the vision of Christ that had been given to him was trinitarian in that it had elements that seemed to stretch the boundaries of his body, as if there had been an overlapping of 1) his individual body (*sarx*), 2) the corporate body (*soma*) of the church as an element of humanity and 3) a spiritual or eternal body (*soma*).

It is confusing, confusing to experience, and much more confusing to try to communicate. But much of the confusion comes from our attempt to understand it from a natural perspective, a perspective that has been soaked in centuries of worldly wisdom, centuries of thinking in terms of Greek and pagan categories. The difficulty of under-standing Paul is the difficulty of divesting ourselves of our old habits of unredeemed forms of thinking. We are creatures of habit, and too many of our habits are worldly and godless.

Caught Up In The Light Of Christ

Paul's experience of Christ on the Damascus Road had to do with Christ's role in his own life, with Christ's role in the life of humanity, and with Christ's role in heaven, in eternity with God, as God—Father, Son and Holy Spirit. Christ had manifest Himself to Paul on the Dam-ascus Road and the light had been so bright as to blind him. He could see nothing but the light of Christ. It had been as if he was looking at the sun. Over time and through prayer Paul's worldly sight returned, but from that day forward he retained the spiritual insight that he had been given.

He saw Christ in everything. Christ had become dominant in Paul's life, and he spent the rest of his life trying to explain himself, explaining how Christ is literally at the center of everything. Paul worked from that day forward to explain Christ's role in conversion, Christ's role in history and Christ's role in eternity. Paul had been caught up in Christ, "whether in the body or out of the body I do not know," said Paul, "God knows" (v. 2).

He continued, "And I know that this man was caught up into para-dise—whether in the body or out of the body I do not know, God knows —and he heard things that cannot be told, which man may not utter" (vs. 3-4). He repeated himself about being in the body or out of the body, he didn't know, God knew and that was enough. Biblical repeti-tion is a function of importance. And here was another important point, though equally difficult to explain. Paul equated paradise (*para-deisos*) with the third heaven (*tritos ouranos*) by using them as equivalent expressions. To be caught up in one was to be caught up in the other.

When Paul said that he had heard things that cannot be told and which may not be uttered he meant that such things were beyond the limitations or constraints of language (Romans 8:23-26).[39] The AV reads, "heard unspeakable words, which it is not lawful for a man to utter." The phrase "not lawful" is composed of two Greek words: *exesti ou*. The second word (*ou*) puts the first word in the negative.

ECSTATIC

Exesti, is itself a compound of two words: *ek* and *eimi*, and literally means *out of the source of one's own existence*. This word suggests something that issues out of the source and/or context of one's own existence. Remember that the word following puts it in the negative. So, Paul was saying that this mysterious experience of Christ that had come to him on the Road to Damascus did not issue out of himself. It was an experience of the Other, as some theologians refer to God's utter otherness or transcendence.[40]

Clearly, Paul suggested that the use of the ideas of heaven and paradise in Scripture were related to the trinitarian character of God, of God's reality and of humanity as the image or reflection of God. God is immanent and transcendent at the same time. Yet, this dual aspect of God is neither an antinomy nor a paradox because it is not a contradiction, nor does it involve a contradiction. In Christ, God is both flesh and Spirit, both immanent and transcendent, one yet three—Father, Son and Holy Spirit, but not two, not dualistic.

Christ Himself is an uncreated, unified and eternal whole—eternally present in, through and as the Father, Son and Holy Spirit. Christ Himself is both divine and human, but is not a synthesis or mixture of these things. The experience of Christ through the power and presence of the Holy Spirit in regeneration is synthetic, meaning that it is not of natural origin. Regeneration does not well up from within us, but is imposed upon us from without. Through Christ the eternal has broken into the temporal.

---

39 For more on this see section: "Various Kinds of Tongues," p. 255, in *Arsy Varsy—Reclaiming the Gospel in First Corinthians*, by Phillip A. Ross, Pilgrim Platform, 2008.

40 For instance, *The Otherness of God (Studies in Religion and Culture)* by Orrin F. Summerell, University of Virginia Press, 1998. But keep in mind that it is an error to think of God's otherness in Platonic or classically mystical (Pagan or Greek) categories because in Christ believers are in trinitarian unity with God's otherness.

Union

Yet that experience or encounter culminates in union with Christ, some would say that it is a mystical union, and in many ways it is. It is a mystery because it is beyond us, ultimately beyond our ability to fully understand it. And yet we are called to understand it, drawn into its understanding. We can know Christ and we do know Christ, but as in a mirror dimly and only in part. Someday, of course, we will know fully even as we have been fully known (1 Corinthians 13:12)—but not now, not yet.

Nonetheless, our union with Christ begins in regeneration, in the new birth. Just because it is not yet fully complete does not mean that it is anything less than genuine union. It is a real union, though not a completed union, because God completes what He begins. Similarly, a newborn baby is fully human, but not fully grown. Our union in Christ takes us beyond our limited, human bodily definition or understanding and expands our personal identity. This is simply to say that in Christ we are Christian. Our union in Christ expands the boundaries of who we understand ourselves to be—here and there, little by little, two steps forward and one step back, in fits and starts. In Christ, in union with Christ we are even now at the beginning of our union more than we were apart from Christ, and less than we will be in the fullness of Christ.

And yet, we do not become Christ. We remain who we have always been, but with the healing and reconciliation of Christ, with the promise of sin forgiven and ultimately destroyed. Then, with our relationship with God restored, we are infinitely more than we could ever be apart from Christ. In Christ we are becoming, developing, growing into the person—the people—who God created us to be. In Christ we are individually and corporately a more complex whole, an assemblage of individual parts that are regarded as a single entity—Christ's church (informal and formal, militant and triumphant, historical and eschatological—one yet many).

Christ's church is the people of God, people who have been redeemed by the blood of Christ, people who have been born again, who have been regenerated, people who have been invaded by the Holy Spirit—waylaid, captured, captivated, caught up in the Spirit of Christ for the salvation of the world, and in the service of the salvation of the world.

In Or Out

While Paul was not certain whether his vision of Christ, his experience of Christ, had been in the body or out of the body, he was certain that he had been called into the body of Christ for service to the body of Christ in this world. Christ had broken into this world, and into Paul's life. Christ has come into this world, and into our lives. To this world Christ's kingdom has come. And Christ's people were being prepared there in Corinth and here and now, not for escape from this world, but for service to this world, to change this world by being who and what God has called them/us to be in Christ.

This is the mystery of Christ, the mystery of life in Christ that is between the already and the almost, in the body yet beyond the body, in these individual bodies yet unified in the body of Christ. The mystery of Christ is the reality of the church of Christ. Christ is in these individual bodies—in me and in you. Yet, Christ is also in us, with us and through us all together as His church, the body of Christ.[41] It is a wonder of wonders, yet completely ordinary—common. Christ is what we have in common. Christ is our common union, our communion. Praise be to God in Christ!

---

41 For more on the church as the body of Christ see *Arsy Varsy—Reclaiming the Gospel in First Corinthians*, by Phillip A. Ross, Pilgrim Platform, 2008, p. 169, "Participation."

35. Thorn of Weakness

I will boast about this person, but not about myself, except of my weaknesses. For if I want to boast, I will not be a fool, because I will be telling the truth. But I will spare you, so that no one can credit me with something beyond what he sees in me or hears from me, especially because of the extraordinary revelations. Therefore, so that I would not exalt myself, a thorn in the flesh was given to me, a messenger of Satan to torment me so I would not exalt myself. Concerning this, I pleaded with the Lord three times to take it away from me. But He said to me, "My grace is sufficient for you, for power is perfected in weakness." Therefore, I will most gladly boast all the more about my weaknesses, so that Christ's power may reside in me. So because of Christ, I am pleased in weaknesses, in insults, in catastrophes, in persecutions, and in pressures. For when I am weak, then I am strong.   *—2 Corinthians 12:5-10*

The idea of priding himself in reference to his spiritual gifts or his abilities as a church leader disgusted Paul. He wanted nothing to do with such a frivolous game. And yet it seems as if a gauntlet had been thrown down and he had to respond to the attacks and challenges of the false apostles. To say nothing would further the false impression they made by boasting about themselves. Their shallow and false boasts required a reply, but Paul was convinced that his reply must honor Christ over himself. Yet, verse 5 speaks again of "this man," the man who had been caught up into the third heaven.

"On behalf of this man I will boast, but on my own behalf I will not boast, except of my weaknesses" (v. 5). Clearly, Paul has made a sharp distinction between himself and this man who had been caught up into heaven. Yet, we understand Paul to have been speaking about himself. This distinction, then, must refer to the old man (self) and the new man that Paul discussed in Ephesians 4:22-24: "to put off your old self, which belongs to your former manner of life and is corrupt through deceitful desires, and to be renewed in the spirit of your minds, and to put on the new self, created after the likeness of God in true righteousness and holiness." This new self or new man was the product of Paul's regeneration and was so different than his former self as to be a completely different person. Saul became Paul. This new man is the man about whom Paul referred.

In addition, Paul attributed this change to Christ. Everything that this new person was, whatever skills, abilities, talents, gifts, graces, etc. that he had, belonged more to Christ than to Paul. It was Christ in Paul or through Paul who deserved the glory. Paul was very aware of his own weaknesses and infirmities in relationship to his service to Christ. Whatever good that would come from Paul's ministry was attributable to Christ alone and not to Paul. Paul would boast on behalf of this man—his regenerated self—Paul, not Saul. This man, Christ in or through Paul, was the source of his strength and the object of his boast.

And yet Paul was aware of his considerable skills, abilities and training as a Pharisee. Paul got the job of chief persecutor of Christians because of his superior skills and abilities with regard to the other Pharisees. Saul had been at the head of his class. He had been an excellent Pharisee. He couldn't deny that. But all those Pharisaical skills and abilities that he had acquired meant nothing in comparison to what he had become in Christ. Yet, in Christ those skills and abilities did not disappear or fall into disuse. Rather, they found a higher purpose. The Lord didn't retool Saul, he renewed and redirected him, redirected the tools he already had. Paul's previous training didn't become useless in Christ. Rather, it found its true purpose. In Christ Paul used the same skills that he had as a Pharisee—his leadership and biblical training. But in Christ he used them for a different purpose. From this point forward, they would serve the glory of God in Christ.

ON THE CUSP

Paul was caught between two historical epochs. The Old Testament establishment was passing away, but not gone, and the New Testament kingdom had begun, but yet barely. Consequently, Paul understood himself to be not unlike John The Baptist, of whom Jesus said, "Among those who are born of woman there is not a greater prophet than John the Baptist. But he who is least in the kingdom of God is greater than he" (Luke 7:28). Paul lived on the cusp, between the old age and the new age. John was the greatest of the old prophets, when compared to the old prophets. But when compared to those in the kingdom of God, he was the least. Similarly, Saul had been a great

Pharisee, but when he found himself in the kingdom through regeneration in the light of Christ, he was humbled by his own insignificance, particularly in comparison to Christ.

So, while Paul could boast of himself, especially in comparison to the false apostles, and his boasting would be true and would show his superiority over them, he would keep his boasting to a minimum so that he wouldn't exceed what the Corinthians knew of him. Though he could boast about things that people didn't know about him, things that were true, skills and abilities he had that people didn't know about, such boasting could lead people to think that he was exaggerating and consider him a blow hard. So, rather than overemphasize skills and abilities that people were not familiar with, he would limit himself to boast about only what the Corinthians knew of him. That way there would be no question about the truth of his statements. And he would not be charged with exaggeration. Paul relied on the value of understatement.

Because Paul had been given such a grand vision of Christ, and because Paul was able to demonstrate that Christ was indeed the actual, historic fulfillment of the Old Testament hopes and predictions regarding the Messiah, Paul was given a thorn (*skolops*) in the flesh to keep him humble, to remind him of his humanity and his limitations. Because Paul had been caught up into the third heaven and may have wanted to remain there, he was given an annoyance—a pain—that would regularly remind him of his own fleshly existence. He called it a "messenger of Satan to harass me (him), to keep me (him) from becoming conceited" (v. 7).

Because Paul was an excellent biblical scholar we would be amiss not to look to the Old Testament to understand this comment, to look for allusions to thorns because it would be very much in keeping with Paul's character to make such an allusion. And we know that Scripture interprets Scripture. Does the Bible refer to thorns or thorns in the flesh anywhere else? This is the only New Testament reference to Paul's thorn and it is sufficiently vague in and of itself that we should immediately turn to the Old Testament to understand what Paul meant by it.

THORNS IN THE OLD TESTAMENT

Thorns and thistles were part of the Curse (Genesis 3:18) and their purpose is to make like more difficult. But the most likely reference to Paul's comment is tucked away in Numbers 33:55, "if you will not drive out the people of the land from before you, then it will be, those of them whom you let remain shall be goads in your eyes and thorns in your sides, and they shall trouble you in the land in which you live."

This troubling of the people of God is a major theme of the Bible, Old Testament and New.[42] Thorns represent people who are ruled by corruption, disobedience and unfaithfulness. This problem has also continued down the corridors of history in that it is the source of the West's continuing conflict with Islam, our War On Terror.

The major Old Testament story regarding this problem is found in Samuel's treatment of Agag, King of Amelek. Samuel, prophesying before King Saul, said, "Thus says the Lord of hosts, 'I have noted what Amalek did to Israel in opposing them on the way when they came up out of Egypt. Now go and strike Amalek and devote to destruction all that they have. Do not spare them, but kill both man and woman, child and infant, ox and sheep, camel and donkey'" (1 Samuel 15:2-3). This is one of those horrendous verses that gives contemporary Christians a great deal of trouble. We find it to be excessively cruel on God's part to issue such an order. But issue it He did.

Saul also found it to be a bit over the top, so "Saul and the people spared Agag and the best of the sheep and of the oxen and of the fattened calves and the lambs, and all that was good, and would not utterly destroy them. All that was despised and worthless they devoted to destruction" (1 Samuel 15:9). This story is conspicuously absent from most Sunday School curriculum because it is not a pretty story. It causes Sunday School teachers to squirm, little testosterone filled boys to go nuts with sword envy and little girls to squeam over the blood.

The gist of the story is that God told Saul to utterly destroy the Amelekites. Saul understood the order, went to battle and afterward reported to Samuel that he had done what God told him to do. But when Samuel came to visit Saul he found King Agag alive, along with much of the booty that God had explicitly said to destroy. Saul said that he did what God said, but he hadn't actually done what God said. Samuel then took Saul's sword and hacked Agag to death in Saul's court as an object lesson. "And the Lord regretted that he had made Saul king over Israel" (1 Samuel 15:35). This failure on Saul's part to obey God has become a major driver of the engine of human history and the source of human conflict.

This is the thorn in the side of humanity (the failure of the gospel to produce spiritual fruit among various people, the failure to produce obedience to God) and is the most likely explanation of Paul's thorn. Paul's thorn (skolops) in the flesh (sarx), which he described as a messenger of Satan who opposes God at every turn, was a painful irritation that opposed Paul everywhere he went, everywhere he preached. Paul's thorn regularly harassed (kolaphizō) him. The Greek word liter-

---

42 See also Joshua 23:13; Judges 2:3, 8:7, 8:16; Proverbs 15:19, 22:5; Jeremiah 4:3; Ezekiel 28:24, Micah 7:3-4; Matthew 13:7, 13:22; Mark 4:18; Luke 8:14.

ally means to rap with the fist. It is an allusion to the many beatings that Paul had suffered, and which had caused him much pain in the flesh.

And yet such beatings and difficulties did not dissuade him from his mission. He even found a blessing in them. They were given to keep him from becoming conceited (v. 7). They served his sanctification in Christ by keeping him humble in the Lord. Rather than becoming depressed and morose because of all the trouble that followed him, Paul used the pain and difficulties for his own good. He put them to work for Christ.

Lingering Injury

It is also possible that some lingering injury from one of his beatings haunted Paul. What makes me think this? The fact that Paul said, "Three times I pleaded with the Lord about this, that it should leave me" (v. 8). It seems to have been an enduring problem. Maybe he sustained some kidney damage or some other trauma that wouldn't or didn't heal, or didn't heal correctly. The reference to his thorn in the flesh could have referred to some particular injury, and at the same time to the situation and/or people who caused the injury. Paul probably meant it as an allusion to this biblical theme of antagonism toward the people of God. God's people have always been harassed by unbelievers—always.

Finally, in the midst of one of Paul's pleas for this problem to leave him—to be healed, to be gone, the Lord spoke to him, "My grace is sufficient for you, for my power is made perfect in weakness" (v. 9). This is a very important and far reaching idea that sums up Paul's life and ministry, and certainly his boast to the Corinthians. In spite of any problems or difficulties that Paul had—and he had a bunch!—the grace of Jesus Christ was sufficient (arkeō). God's grace had preserved him at every turn—always.

Again the Greek is instructive. Arkeō (sufficient) suggests the idea of raising a barrier to ward something off. God's grace protected Paul from the dire consequences associated with the curse of thorns, thistles and troubles, associated with Satan and his messengers. God's grace kept Satan at bay. Good thing, too! Paul could not defend himself against Satan on his own. He was too weak, and Satan too strong. Satan would overpower him. But in his weakness Paul clung to Christ, who was his strength. Christ could defeat Satan—and did! Paul's life was a testimony to the sufficiency of Christ in the midst of life, in the midst of difficulties, of thorns and thistles, in the midst of a world saturated in sin.

In addition, not only is the power of Christ made perfect in weakness, but it is perfectly made for weakness. The fact that it is perfect does not mean that Christ's power comes to people without any flaws or foibles. Rather, the perfection (*teleioō*) of Christ's power suggests the accomplishment and/or consummation of God's power in the sense that God will see it through to the end. God will finish what He has begun. Christians don't need to be strong because Christ is strong—good thing too! Because we aren't strong. We are weak, flawed and broken—just the way God wants us.

BROKEN TO BE HEALED

I'm not saying that God's purpose is to keep His people weak, flawed and broken. Not at all! Rather, in Christ God's power becomes ours. In Christ our flaws will be overcome, "so that he (Christ) might present the church to himself in splendor, without spot or wrinkle or any such thing, that she might be holy and without blemish" (Ephesians 5:27). In Christ we are broken in order to be healed, like an improperly set bone needs to be rebroken and properly set in order to heal correctly.

Why do people need to be broken? The primary stumbling stone that people have regarding Jesus Christ is their own pride. Many people would rather die than receive charity (grace). People want to be righteous in and of themselves. People don't want to be wrong and resent it when they are shown to be wrong—and that is precisely what the Lord does! He shows us our sin, our wrongness. Not so that we can wallow in it, but so that He can forgive it in Christ. Think of being broken by Christ as a horse is broken in or domesticated.[43]

The Old Testament Jews and Pharisees thought that they were beyond sin. They thought that they could work it out for themselves, or that their rounds of sacrifices would atone for their sin. "Why?" asked Paul in Romans 9:32-33. "Because they did not pursue it by faith, but as if it were based on works. They have stumbled over the stumbling stone, as it is written, 'Behold, I am laying in Zion a stone of stumbling, and a rock of offense; and whoever believes in him will not be put to shame.'"

Odd idea, this. That belief in One who is the stone of stumbling for many will keep others from shame. Put positively: people are saved only when they put aside their own pride and agree with God about their sin. Only then will people receive the forgiveness of Jesus Christ.

---

43 Contemporary people have an aversion to the idea of being domesticated. Popular culture (sin) touts the thrills of the "wild life." But human domestication in Christ is a consistent theme of Scripture. For most people being domesticated is an allusion to marriage, where people come under a covenant.

From our humility comes Christ's glory. From our weakness comes Christ's strength. Paul summed up this argument, "Therefore I will boast all the more gladly of my weaknesses, so that the power of Christ may rest upon me." (v. 9). Paul would boast, but he would boast only in Christ alone through his own weakness. It's not that Christ's power depends on our weakness, but that it is best shown through our weakness. Paul understood that his own weaknesses became the means of Christ's glory.

"For the sake of Christ, then, I am content with weaknesses, insults, hardships, persecutions, and calamities. For when I am weak, then I am strong" (v. 10). These irritations brought real pain to Paul's flesh. They weren't just psychological difficulties. They hurt Paul. They damaged him. Paul went through the proverbial mill for Christ, and he did it gladly, willingly, because it glorified Christ and Christ was his strength. So, what gave Christ glory made Paul stronger. And the fact that it made Paul stronger gave Christ more glory.

My Old Man would like to pray that we don't need to learn this lesson, that Paul or Jesus endured suffering and difficulty so that we wouldn't have to. But that's not the case. Paul is our model in this matter, as Jesus was his model. We are to imitate him. My New Man knows better. My New Man looks to the future with great optimism because he knows that God's people are weak. God's churches are weak. But our weakness is—and will be—a measure of Christ's glory. Come, Lord Jesus. Have mercy.

36. Spending Projections

I have become a fool; you forced it on me. I ought to have been recommended by you, since I am in no way inferior to the "super-apostles," even though I am nothing. The signs of an apostle were performed among you in all endurance—not only signs but also wonders and miracles. So in what way were you treated worse than the other churches, except that I personally did not burden you? Forgive me this wrong! Look! I am ready to come to you this third time. I will not burden you, for I am not seeking what is yours, but you. For children are not obligated to save up for their parents, but parents for their children. I will most gladly spend and be spent for you. If I love you more, am I to be loved less? Now granted, I have not burdened you; yet sly as I am, I took you in by deceit!

—2 Corinthians 12:11-16

At verse 11 Paul changed tactics. Rather than selling himself to them by boasting of his superiority over the false apostles, he began to upbraid them for their failure to be responsible followers of Christ. He began this tact by calling attention to his failure to acknowledge their failure. Perhaps he had expected them to be more mature than they were. "I have been a fool!" (v. 11), he cried. He wanted so much to believe that they could understand what he had been telling them about the Lord, about Christ's trinitarian nature and His role as the long-awaited Messiah—and how His presence is both immanent and transcendent.

But it was not for the simple joy of theology that Paul shared the vision the Lord had given him, though he undoubtedly enjoyed it. Paul was not engaged in abstract speculation, but was providing the theological foundation for a practical way of life in Christ that avoided the speculative justification of ungodliness and overcame the sin problem. The immanent and transcendent presence of God through Christ provided both an engine for cultural development, and a governor that would keep the engine from blowing itself apart. The reality of God in Christ—the trinitarian nature of God—is much more than mere cognitive abstraction. Just as actions and decisions have consequences, so the way in which people think of God or don't think of Him—theology —has very real consequences, as well.

Perhaps Paul had expected too much of the Corinthians. They had not been caught up in the third heaven, he had. They hadn't seen Christ on the Road to Damascus, he had. Though he had tried to explain himself and his vision of the Lord as best he could, and though it sometimes seemed as if they understood what he had been talking about, maybe they didn't. Maybe they couldn't understand it yet. Maybe he had been imposing his regenerate views upon them prematurely. Maybe he had given them more than they could take in. Maybe he had been the fool for expecting too much of them too soon.

Forced His Hand

But they—the Corinthians leaders and those who took the false apostles seriously—had forced Paul to show his hand, to explain himself as clearly and as fully as possible. They had forced him to defend himself because they had not defended him. "You forced me to it, for I ought to have been commended by you" (v. 11). Perhaps Paul had erred by telling them everything he knew because it made him look like he was proud of his accomplishments, like he had been boasting in himself, in his own knowledge and understanding.

Had things gone right, it would have been the faithful Corinthians who had championed Paul as an elder of the first order in the Corinthian church. There should have been no leadership dispute in Corinth. The right order of things should have been that the followers commended Paul's vision and skills, not that he had to take his attention off the gospel in order to commend himself to his own followers. Self-commendation is not the way of the gospel of Jesus Christ. Nowhere does Jesus tell His disciples that they must defend or promote themselves as the rightful heirs of the kingdom of God.[44] Rather, Christ declared that His people would inherit the kingdom of God (Matthew 19:29, 25:34), and that should be sufficient.

The heirs of the kingdom are not those who win an intramural debate among those vying "with one another about who was (is) the greatest" (Mark 9:34). The way of the Lord is service not position or personal advancement. Jesus had taught them that "he who is least

---

44 The proper way for Christians to defend their kingdom inheritance rights is to proclaim the gospel. The gospel itself is our defense.

among you all is the one who is great" (Luke 9:48). The kingdom of God is built upon a reversal of worldly values. Perhaps Paul's defense of his own leadership credentials had been the wrong way to go. Perhaps Paul had been lured into prideful boasting as a defense against the prideful boasting of the false apostles, and he should have been above that fray.

But had no one said anything in his defense, the false apostles may have furthered their own cause and led even more of the Corinthians down their false path. The faithful Corinthians should have honored and commended Paul in the first place, then he would not have had to defend himself. After all, Paul, "was not at all inferior to these super-apostles, even though (he was) nothing" (v. 11). As we have seen, Paul's credentials were superior to the other Corinthian leaders. No one in Corinth or anywhere else had better Christian credentials than Paul. But somehow some of the Corinthians had been beguiled.

MIRACLES

They should have known better. After all, the signs of true apostle-ship had been performed among them "with utmost patience, with signs and wonders and mighty works" (v. 12). Here Paul confirmed that miracles had not been performed for the sake of their recipients, but as signs to provide apostolic verification. And this was not new! It was the Old Testament practice of prophetic verification. Miracles had always provided authenticity for the prophet who performed them.

Nonetheless, too many people had come to Jesus seeking miracles for themselves. They wanted the Lord to work magic to make their lives more pleasant, but that was not the reason that the Lord worked miracles.[45] The miracles were not for the recipients of the miracles, but for the community of faith. They were signs of godly leadership. They established the authority of prophetic and apostolic leadership. Confusion about the nature and purpose of miracles has proven to be an enduring problem, as has church authority generally.

Nonetheless, the Corinthians, who had witnessed such miracles, should have come to Paul's defense. They should have testified to Paul's leadership credentials so that Paul didn't have to. Their testimony of Paul's abilities would not be misunderstood as pride and self-promotion, as it might be when Paul was forced to defend himself. And this was not a difficult task for them to do because Paul's credentials and experience were in fact superior to the super-apostles.

So, why hadn't they done that? Paul wondered. Why hadn't they

---

45 See *Marking God's Word—Understanding Jesus*, by Phillip A. Ross, Pilgrim Platform, Marietta, OH, 2006.

come to his defense? What was wrong with them that they hadn't done so? "For in what were you less favored than the rest of the churches, except that I myself did not burden you?" (v. 13).

The one thing that set the Corinthian church apart from the other churches was that Paul had not burdened them. What did he mean? The reference goes back to 2 Corinthians 8 (and elsewhere), where Paul had been talking about raising money for the Jerusalem church, and how he did not want to give the impression that he was after their money. The Corinthian church had been large, wealthy and influential, which meant that they were money conscious.

FREE SERVICE

Paul had supported himself while engaged in ministry with them. In order to demonstrate his commitment to the gospel Paul did not ask them for any personal support. Perhaps he should have. Perhaps by providing his services for free he made it appear that those services were worthless. There is no "buy in" for something that is free. Perhaps Paul's effort to demonstrate his own commitment had been misunderstood. After all, misunderstanding was rampant in Corinth. That was the only difference between the Corinthians and the other churches that Paul had served. On reflection, Paul considered that that may have been an error. And if it had been an error, Paul begged their forgiveness. "Forgive me this wrong!" (v. 13).

Again, they should have known what they had in Paul. They should have recognized Paul's service, his integrity and the importance of his teaching. But they didn't—too many of them didn't. Joni Mitchell was right, "You don't know what you've got, 'till its gone." In one sense Paul had been aware of this phenomena. He knew that he had been "untimely born," as he described it in 1 Corinthians 15:8. Whether this comment referred to his physical birth or his spiritual birth is immaterial. It equally applied to both because it meant that Paul was out of step with his contemporaries.

He was so far ahead of many of them that he seemed not to be one of them. To many people he must have seemed to be the enemy, though he labored for their benefit. Some had even thought he had lost his mind, that his many letters had turned him to insanity. Festus, the Roman governor of Judea certainly thought this, and accused him of it (Acts 26:24). And Festus would have represented the most respectable of the worldly opinions of his day. To disagree with the governor would have been an act of self-denunciation—foolishness—in the eyes of the community.

But Paul would not back off or rescind his position. He was committed to Christ, come what may. Nor would he give up on the Corinthians. He had planted the gospel seed among them and would do whatever he could to bring it to fruition. "Behold," he said, "a third time I am ready to come to you. And I will not burden you, for I do not seek your things, but you" (v. 14). He was not after their money, he was after their hearts. He would accept nothing less than their conversion.

He had ministered among them twice before and would come again if it was necessary. Nor would he burden them for their financial support of his ministry among them. Mistake or not, that was the pattern of his ministry there. Besides, those who have money tend to be hypersensitive when it comes to money, overly concerned about it. So, for that reason he would pay his own way—so they wouldn't think that he was after their money.

As their spiritual father, he was also duty bound to care for them. "For the children ought not to lay up treasure for the parents, but the parents for the children" (v. 14). He was not looking for them to take care of him. Rather, he was looking to take care of them. He was responsible for their growth and maturity. Followers should care for their leaders, of course (Acts 6:2-4). But there are times when that just isn't possible or doesn't happen. And at those times leaders should not abandon their followers. Nothing should break the bonds of Christian fellowship, and certainly not money. Neither leaders nor followers should dwell on money. Neither wealth nor poverty are categories of salvation.

Continuing this theme Paul wrote, "And I will very gladly spend and be spent for your souls, even if loving you more and more, I am loved the less" (v. 15). Paul did not need to be stroked and pimped—paid for his services. He would deliver to them what he had received from the Lord (1 Corinthians 11:23) because doing so gave his own life great joy, meaning and purpose. He also knew that the love of Jesus Christ, once delivered, was not resistible. Paul knew that all that the Father had given to Christ would in fact come to Him" (John 6:37), that "he who began a good work in you (them) will bring it to completion at the day of Jesus Christ" (Philippians 1:6).

It wasn't that they had no choice except to come to Christ. Rather, only in Christ did they actually have the choice, and being in Christ they would most certainly make the right choice. It was only a matter of time. So, Paul would do whatever it took to move the gospel forward in their midst, even if they didn't appreciate him for it in the short run.

CRAFTY

Paul then turned to deal with a particular accusation against him.

"But granting that I myself did not burden you, I was crafty, you say, and got the better of you by deceit" (v. 16). Paul had been charged with tricking some of the Corinthians into believing him. This is a particularly nasty charge and exceedingly difficult to refute because it switches the burden of proof from Paul to those whom he supposedly deceived. Paul could argue about himself all day without being able to refute those who said that they had deceived themselves by buying into Paul's teachings.

None of Paul's arguments applied to those who said that they had deceived themselves. This argument was not about Paul's integrity but about the gullibility of those he taught. By putting the burden of the proof on their own gullibility, they took it off of Paul. They shifted the argument from Paul's defense to their own self-deception. If the problem is my own self-deception, then your argument is immaterial.

Calvin said of this verse, "For it is customary for the wicked impudently to impute to the servants of God, whatever they would themselves do, if they had it in their power."[46] This is a common practice because people easily believe that other people are just like they themselves are. We all do this all the time. But here it was particularly pernicious because it relegated the message of Paul to the wiles of Satan, the original crafty deceiver. This is closely related to the one unforgivable sin against the Holy Spirit (Matthew 12:31) because it attempts to undermine the power of the Holy Spirit in Paul's gospel message. It is a projection of the evil in one's own heart upon others, as if such evil were the substance of what is sometimes called common sense.

Here we see an evil use of eisegesis in that it projects one's own evil upon others. Eisegesis is the imposition of meaning on something. And where that meaning is evil, evil is imposed. I have previously discussed a use of eisegesis that is necessary to a faithful reading of scripture.[47] There we saw that the correct use of eisegesis involves the imposition of one's own faithfulness into the reading of Scripture in such a way as to reveal the assumptions of faithfulness and veracity that underly the text. In other words, it takes faithfulness to see faithfulness because if one is not faithful himself, he has no idea what faithfulness even looks like. And therefore cannot recognize it, even if he were to trip over it. Christians recognize others who are like-minded—faithful—because the Holy Spirit in them recognizes the Holy Spirit in others.

LIKE LIKES LIKE

But this same dynamic works for the forces of Satan, as well. Evil

---

46 *Calvin's Commentaries*, Volume XX, Baker Book House, 1993, p. 387.
47 *Eisegesis & Exegesis*, p. 71.

recognizes evil in the same way. It takes one to know one. Criminals recognize other criminals in a crowd, not always, not perfectly, but generally. Unfaithfulness projects itself onto the world, just as faithfulness does. Consequently, Satan is able to use this same kind of argument (process, dynamic, eisegesis) to further his cause, and he does so effectively.

However, the eisegesis process works only to group like kind with like kind, the faithful with the faithful and the unfaithful with the unfaithful—not always, not perfectly, but generally. The old saying is true, birds of a feather do flock together. And so this process of eisegesis ultimately serves God's purpose of separating the sheep and the goats, the lost and the saved. In the final analysis those who agree with one another make alliances that benefit the Lord at harvest, when the wheat and the tares are gathered together but separated from one another and dealt with in different ways. The wheat and the tares, the sheep and the goats are self-selecting groups. Like attracts like.

The practice of eisegesis cannot be avoided because it is nothing other than reading a text (or situation) through one's own perspective, one's own set of values or presuppositions. We all see and interpret the world through a particular perspective or lens, through a particular set of values and assumptions. And we cannot do otherwise. Thus, the most honest thing we can do regarding this fact is to acknowledge it and put our values and presuppositions on the table for all to see. This process of presupposition recognition can also be called confessing our faith (or admitting our lack of faith). But the heart of the matter is not faith versus no faith. The real issue is the object of our faith.

To have faith in the only God that actually is (Deuteronomy 4:9, Isaiah 45:5-6), is to have faith in Jesus Christ (Mark 12:32, Acts 4:12, Galatians 5:10), His only Son and the only mediator between God and man (1 Timothy 2:5).

There is no escape from God's sovereignty, if there was, He wouldn't be sovereign.

37. DISSONANCE

Did I take advantage of you through any of those whom I sent to you?
I urged Titus to go, and sent the brother with him. Did Titus take
advantage of you? Did we not act in the same spirit? Did we not take
the same steps? Have you been thinking all along that we have been
defending ourselves to you? It is in the sight of God that we have been
speaking in Christ, and all for your upbuilding, beloved. For I fear that
perhaps when I come I may find you not as I wish, and that you may
find me not as you wish—that perhaps there may be quarreling,
jealousy, anger, hostility, slander, gossip, conceit, and disorder. I fear
that when I come again my God may humble me before you, and I
may have to mourn over many of those who sinned earlier and have
not repented of the impurity, sexual immorality, and sensuality that
they have practiced.   *—2 Corinthians 12:17-21*

Continuing in the same vein, Paul appealed to the consistency of the message that he and the apostles preached. "Did I take advantage of you through any of those whom I sent to you? I urged Titus to go, and sent the brother with him. Did Titus take advantage of you? Did we not act in the same spirit? Did we not take the same steps?" (vs. 17-18). Because God is perfect, He does not change (Malachi 3:6). God has always saved people in the same way—by grace alone through faith alone. Paul's whole argument was not that God was doing a new thing through Christ, but that Christ was the fulfillment of what God had been doing for thousands of years.

Christ had come, but His coming was not unanticipated. Christ had come in the fulfillment of Old Testament promises. Christ's coming did not change the Old Testament, but it most certainly put it in the proper context, which would indeed bring about many changes in God's church and in the world. But the message of God's salvation would remain, though after Christ it became a message of fulfillment rather than expectation.

Paul's point was that the message that he and the apostles had preached and taught was a unified message, a consistent message. So, if the message had changed somewhere along the line, the change was not the message that he and the other apostles had preached and taught.

However, not only did the apostles teach the same message, they lived the same gospel principles. Neither Paul nor the other apostles had tricked anyone about anything. They had taken advantage of no one. The AV reads, "Did I make a gain (*pleonekteō*) of you" (v. 17)? The Greek word means to overreach, to take advantage of. How did Paul gain from his ministry with them? They had given him much grief and difficulty, and he had paid his own way. Paul's ministry with the Corinthians did not contribute to Paul's personal bottom line. It cost him money to work with them.

Had Paul or the apostles tricked or deceived the Corinthians there would be some kind of personal gain that would serve as the motivation for the deceit. But there had been no such personal gain. They were not in it for themselves. They were promoting Christ, not themselves. That should have been clear from Paul's recitation of the personal difficulties, dangers and costs he faced as the result of his preaching of the gospel.

He named Titus, whom he had sent to minister among them. Had Titus taken advantage of them? Had Titus abused his authority? He was confident that Titus had not, that Titus was as faithful to the gospel of Jesus Christ, as he was. The other brother that Paul mentioned is traditionally considered to be Luke, the physician evangelist. Again, Paul's point was that they all acted in the same spirit and took the same steps.

The larger message and its application here is that all Christians should act in the same spirit and take the same steps. Unity of belief, motivation and action should be common among Christians. This is not an argument for cookie cutter Christianity, but for common faithfulness, common motivation and common purpose. The trinitarian character of the God we serve provides for the existence and expression of amazing individual diversity within the constraints of our common corporate faith and purpose. There is no danger that Christians will all be alike, apart from our common faithfulness and service to Jesus Christ.

Not About You

At verse 19 Paul introduced another concern: "Have you been

thinking all along that we have been defending ourselves to you?" If they had been thinking that Paul had been simply defending himself against the false apostles at Corinth, they were mistaken. Of course, Paul had been defending himself against the false apostles at Corinth, but he had not been doing that simply for their benefit. Paul was very aware that he had been speaking on behalf of the Lord and for the benefit of God's people, which included the Corinthians, but in no way would be limited to them.

Here we see that Paul was very much aware of his larger ministry to the greater church, a church which included all of the churches that were in existence at the time he wrote, but also included all churches in perpetuity. Paul was also writing to us and to our grandchildren, and to their yet unborn grandchildren, etc.

"It is in the sight of God that we have been speaking in Christ, and all for your upbuilding, beloved" (v. 19). Paul had been speaking and writing not just in their presence, but in the very presence of God. Because Paul needed to reach other born-again Christians with the Word of God, he had been speaking and writing, not merely to communicate to the Corinthians, not merely to the flesh and blood people who were in Corinth. He needed to reach the Holy Spirit within them— and, indeed, the Holy Spirit who resides in all Christians everywhere. The Spirit in him needed to speak to the Spirit in them (Psalm 42:7). In order to do that, Paul's words needed to accurately and correctly communicate the gospel, and the Corinthians would need to have "ears to hear" (Deuteronomy 29:4).

Christians need to realize that when they speak they speak in the presence of God—not just sometimes, not just at church or at Bible study, but always. God is always present and Christians always represent God in everything that they do and say. Paul knew that he was speaking in Christ in the sight of God. God was listening.

In addition Paul had been speaking for the upbuilding (*oikodomē*) of the beloved in Christ. *Oikodomē* is often translated as edify or edification. And as we have noted before, to edify someone is to make them understand something. And yet, there is more to edification than understanding.

The word *oikodomē* is composed of two words: *oikos* and *dōma*. *Oikos* means household and is sometimes used to describe the domicile in which a family resides, and sometimes refers to the family itself. The root of *dōma* means to build and refers to an edifice and sometimes to a rooftop in the sense that the roof suggests the completion of the building. Putting them together, *oikodomē* suggests the establishing and strengthening of a family unit, of family unity. And in this case, the family being God's family—the church, it suggests establishing and strengthening the church or body of Christ.

Paul had been defending himself as a means of edifying the body of Christ. Paul's defense was his testimony. Those who would benefit from Paul's defense—his testimony—were not just the Corinthians, but the whole of the Christian church. This means that Paul was aware of what he had been doing, that he had been speaking and witnessing to the whole of Christ's church, and not just to the Corinthians.

This is important to notice because Paul called attention to it. But also because those who speak on behalf of Christ speak, not just to those who are immediately before them, but they (must) speak from the Holy Spirit in themselves to the Holy Spirit in others. And the Holy Spirit transcends time and space.

The application of this insight is that speaking on behalf of Christ —preaching, witnessing, giving your testimony—must not be narrowly conceived to apply only to those who are the immediate recipients of one's words. Rather, we must speak as if ten thousand angels are listening, evaluating and reporting back to the Lord about the integrity of the gospel that is spoken of—because they are! If the Holy Spirit in others is to be reached, He must be reached with or through the Holy Spirit in one's self. The Holy Spirit in me speaks to the Holy Spirit in you and recognizes His own truth. The accuracy and integrity of the message is preserved by the Holy Spirit for the Holy Spirit, who Himself establishes the communication link, receives and verifies the communication. It is not that the Holy Spirit can be in more than one place at a time, but that He transcends time and space.

NOT BEYOND HELP

Paul continued, "For I fear that perhaps when I come I may find you not as I wish, and that you may find me not as you wish—that perhaps there may be quarreling, jealousy, anger, hostility, slander, gossip, conceit, and disorder" (v. 20). Here Paul suggests that both he and the Corinthians may be disappointed with each other because neither of them were likely to live up to their expectations of one another.

If you review what Paul has said in his letters to the Corinthians you will see that he has set the bar of Christian faithfulness, understanding and behavior quite high. So high that it is out of the reach of everyone, including Paul himself. Actually, it was not Paul who had set the bar, but Jesus. Paul had simply delivered to them what had been delivered to him.

And the bar was set high on purpose, but not so that we cannot reach it. Rather, it has been set high so that we cannot reach it *apart from Christ*. It cannot be reached apart from the grace of God who lifts us up in Christ, not only to reach the bar but to surpass it (John 14:12).

Paul was aware that just as some of the Corinthians would repent upon hearing Paul's concerns others would remain unrepentant. Some people are impervious to the gospel, not because they are stronger than God, but because they are willfully obdurate. God will prove His superiority to their willfulness by bringing them to judgment before the cross of Christ. No one will escape this judgment.

It is instructive to note that not even the preaching of Paul could dissuade some of the false believers from their false beliefs. And if Paul was not able to do so, then it should be no surprise that we can't dissuade various sinners in our day, either.

Paul was concerned that his letters to the Corinthians had raised the bar of faithfulness so high that division and dissension were sure to result. He warned them that "quarreling, jealousy, anger, hostility, slander, gossip, conceit, and disorder" (v. 20) would follow on the heels of their mutual disappointment with one another—him with them, and them with him.

We should not be surprised when heathens behave like heathens. But Paul was saying here that, because the church was not perfect, because both true believers and false believers attended the same churches that we should not be surprised when Christians get caught up in sin and act like the sinners they are. Oh, there should be less of it in the churches—eventually. There should be less of it over time, as Christians grow in grace and maturity. But until the church reaches perfection, it should come as no surprise that Christians get caught up in "quarreling, jealousy, anger, hostility, slander, gossip, conceit, and disorder" (v. 20) just like other people do.

Finally, said Paul, "I fear that when I come again my God may humble me before you, and I may have to mourn over many of those who sinned earlier and have not repented of the impurity, sexual immorality, and sensuality that they have practiced" (v. 21). Paul feared two things: 1) that God would humble him, and 2) that he would have to mourn over many unrepentant sinners.

NOT APPRECIATE

What did Paul mean by being humbled (*tapeinoō*) by God? He meant that he would be brought down a notch or two in their presence, that some of the Corinthians would not appreciate nor condone Paul's message. He was afraid that many of them would not understand or appreciate the real message or gospel of Jesus Christ. Particularly in comparison to the successful message of the false apostles who had grown the church at Corinth by pandering to godlessness. Paul's reputation with the Corinthians would likely suffer because of his effort to purify the church of false beliefs and if necessary of false believers. It was likely that the false apostles would make every effort to humiliate Paul publicly, as they had already been doing.

This last verse suggests that Paul may have been girding up his loins (preparing himself) for the conflict that awaited him at Corinth. Success does not yield the floor willingly, even when it is wrong. Success will fight to the death to maintain itself. Many, probably most, of the false apostles, who had gained success by believing and teaching as they did, would not easily alter their positions. Doing so would ruin their success.

Paul was also afraid that he would have to mourn over those who would not repent—the successful but false apostles. Here we see that Paul was not about to change his mind or his tactics regarding the character of the gospel, or his promotion of it. Paul would not relent the position that he had made regarding Christ's call to faithfulness, growth, maturity and sanctification that would result in increased purity, that would strive toward the high calling of Christ. Individuals who would grow in Christ would themselves also grow in moral purity, and that growth would spur similar growth in others. Like is not only attracted to like, but like encourages the development of like. Or, if you prefer: monkey see, monkey do.

If the momentum of that moral purity were somehow stymied in any one person, it would effect the growth of moral purity in others because people are mutually interrelated. Therefore, Paul would set the model for emulation. He would move forward, growing in Christ and holding to the position—the vision—that Christ had given him, come what may. Paul's vision of the role of Christ in the salvation of the world—Christ's cultural centrality and Christ's trinitarian character—would not and could not be changed. Paul knew that his own faithful steadfastness to the gospel of Jesus Christ would in fact create, not mere tensions in the church, but knock-down, drag-out fights and divisions. That was his fear!

Paul had been concerned about those who had "not repented of the impurity, sexual immorality, and sensuality that they have practiced" (v. 21). The character of the high calling communicated by Paul suggested many subtleties of belief and behavior, but in the final analysis Paul returned to the most base of the sins that he had been countering—impurity (*akatharsia*), sexual immorality and sensuality.

The AV translated the first as *uncleanness*. The word points to the impurity of lustful, luxurious, and profligate living, to the impure motives that are attached to such living. Paul was arguing against the temptation to compromise one's principles or excuse behavior that should not be tolerated. Both uncleanness and impurity suggest the value of the discipline of being separate, of not running with the wolves, of not *hangin' with the 'hood*—supporting what is popular simply because it is popular. Paul's denigration of impurity suggests the value of not mixing with the wrong kinds of people (2 Corinthians 6:17).

Of course, complete separation is neither possible nor advised. The separation that Paul called attention to is not so much a matter of physical separation, but of maintaining Christian values and comportment regardless of who you are with. Part of the high calling of Christ involves maintaining the integrity and consistency of Christian character. Being a Christian means being a Christian all the time.

No Discernment

Paul's mention of sexual immorality (*porneia*), or "fornication" in the AV, hearkens back to reports that there was sexual immorality among them, "of a kind that is not tolerated even among pagans" (1 Corinthians 5:1). While there are subtleties of sin that are sometimes hard to discern, sin ultimately produces various kinds of ungodly behavior.

It seems that the faithful Corinthians hadn't noticed the subtle theological errors of their false leaders, but only when they were overwhelmed with blatant sin did they begin to notice that something was wrong. It began when Chloe's people had reported to Paul that there had been "quarreling among (the) brothers" (1 Corinthians 1:11). The quarreling was ostensibly about church leadership. Some touted Paul's leadership, some Apollos', some Cephas' and others claimed to follow Christ. Church leaders were going different directions, teaching different things. And as it turned out they were justifying different behaviors, and behind those differing behaviors were different belief systems.

This came more clearly to light when the sexual immorality (*porneia*) was reported. Paul knew that by the time that errors in belief erupted in gross and blatant sin, especially when church leaders had been compromised by such gross sin, things were pretty far down the proverbial pike. While the reports may have suggested that the problem was that various church leaders needed to be replaced because they had been caught in some gross sin, Paul knew that there was more to the problem than the errant leaders.

Paul knew that the leaders were capable of spinning fairly sophisticated theological justifications of their sins in a way that not only excused them, but made their sins appear to be positive expressions of freedom, even favorable character traits. Even in our day, sexual promiscuity is touted to be a fountain of artistic creativity and personal freedom. It is even taught as if it is an expression of freedom in Christ, as if Christ Himself taught and practiced such variants of so-called spiritual freedom. Paul knew the power of self-justification because he had been a well-educated Pharisee, and the Pharisees were masters of such justification. Indeed, the justification of sin is a time honored religious art that is well-documented across the globe.

LEADERS/FOLLOWERS

The reports that had come to Paul left him with two problems: 1) the problem of the sinful leaders, and 2) the more subtle problem of the tainted followers who had been exposed to the errant thinking of the sinful leaders, and particularly those followers who had accepted to one degree or another the errant thinking of those sinful leaders, those who had compromised their theology, those whose understanding of the gospel had changed with exposure to the errant leaders. The errant leaders were one problem, and the misguided followers—especially those who didn't think that it was all that serious—posed another problem.

Paul knew that it was unlikely that the leaders, who had been hardened by sin, would change their minds and repent. He mourned for them, for the difficulty that would ensue to remove them from their office, and for their souls. But Paul also knew that there would be more to this problem than replacing the leaders because the leaders had infected the congregation with errant thinking, with misguided theology. Dealing with that problem would be more difficult and the results would be less clear cut.

And this is why Paul had gone into such a long, theological treatment of the problem with the Corinthians. Paul hadn't simply addressed the problem of fornication, but had launched into various discussions that would treat the more subtle errors that, left unchecked, would eventually manifest in sin of one kind or another. Paul discussed baptism, marriage, divorce, head coverings, the Lord's Supper, spiritual gifts, love, the resurrection, money, forgiveness, excommunication, etc., and tried to show them how the trinitarian character of Christ and those in Christ was the source of the interweaving of all of these various things together into a unity.

Paul knew that if church leaders had broken out in blatant sexual sin while remaining in their leadership positions, the theology and practice of the church generally would require correction top to bottom because the reality of the Trinity caused all of these various things to be interrelated. Consequently, Paul mourned over many, not just those who had been involved in sexual immorality, but those who had been involved in all of the various errors of the Corinthian church. And Paul included in verse 21 the sins of impurity and sensuality (*aselgeia*)—translated in the AV as lasciviousness, which also means wantonness.

The root of the problem was a lack of regeneration, which resulted in a lack of interest in the things of God, which led to the failure to learn or care about the ways of God, which left such people without the desire or practice of personal discipline. The entire structure of the church had been compromised, top to bottom. So Paul had addressed it all. He mourned for those lost leaders who would not repent, but he also mourned for those lost followers who saw nothing wrong with the behavior or teaching of the false apostles and who would themselves not repent either. He mourned for the false teaching that had begun there and would continue among the willfully unrepentant there and down through the ages.

Paul had hoped to nip the Corinthian problem in the bud, but he found that the bud had already flowered and gone to seed in Corinth. And so he mourned for those who had not repented, and for those who would not repent in Corinth, and down through the ages. Paul knew that worldly success would not willingly yield to the corrections of God's wisdom in Christ without a fight.

In verse 21 Paul was thinking about yet another visit to Corinth to help straighten them out, and the unpleasant fight that awaited him.

38. Traction

This is the third time I am coming to you. Every charge must be established by the evidence of two or three witnesses. I warned those who sinned before and all the others, and I warn them now while absent, as I did when present on my second visit, that if I come again I will not spare them—since you seek proof that Christ is speaking in me. He is not weak in dealing with you, but is powerful among you. For he was crucified in weakness, but lives by the power of God. For we also are weak in him, but in dealing with you we will live with him by the power of God. Examine yourselves, to see whether you are in the faith. Test yourselves. Or do you not realize this about yourselves, that Jesus Christ is in you?—unless indeed you fail to meet the test! I hope you will find out that we have not failed the test.

—2 Corinthians 13:1-6

P aul had written and personally visited Corinth at least twice now, yet the problem persisted. The AV reads, "In the mouth of two or three witnesses every word shall be established" (v. 1). Paul was not speaking about their charges against him, but of his charges against them. He was using the biblical form of establishing charges, intensifying his threat to bring action against the false apostles (Deuteronomy19:15, Matthew 18:16). Paul was proceeding judicially and not using under the table methods like gossip and rumor mongering. Scripture everywhere denounces such methods of manipulation, and insists that God's people operate above the table in all things. These kinds of matters need to be open to public inspection in order that justice may be served.

The other witnesses are not named, so we don't have any information about them. This is the last letter that we have regarding Paul's involvement at Corinth, so the story will not be completed. Loose ends will be left dangling. The tenor of Paul's language suggests that he was frustrated because the problem had not been resolved by his previous letters and visits. He thought that he had provided sufficient instruction to settle the matter without having to be personally involved.

"I warned those who sinned before and all the others" (v. 2), he said, suggesting that there were two guilty parties: 1) those who had done the actual sinning—various leaders, and 2) those who put up with it—various followers. It is significant that his warning covered both groups. The application is that church purity requires that sinners stop sinning and that others in the church not tolerate sin in their midst. This, however, does not mean that churches should aggressively hunt down and punish sinners. Pressing too hard on the elimination of sin will decimate the church roles. Rather, proper biblical discipline must always be engaged, and if we are err, it should be on the side of love and mercy. The procedures of discipline should proceed according to Matthew 18:15-17, beginning privately and escalating into formal, public charges and procedures. And all discipline should be exercised with the intention of the restitution of the errant parties to faithfulness and fellowship through repentance and forgiveness.

Jurisdictional boundaries should also be respected. Matters of personal conscience can—and should—be freely discussed, but there is no recourse for matters of personal conscience beyond the efforts of discussion and persuasion. Family matters, which include sexuality and family relationships should be handled within families. Heads of households can seek counsel, but adjudication of family issues is first and foremost a family matter. Church issues and unresolved family issues that bleed into the church are then handled by church elders. In all of these things, discipline should always honor God's love and mercy, and never our desire for vindication or revenge.

According to Paul's model, those who tolerate known sin share in the sin and the guilt. The idea here is that we are not free to ignore sin in the church. It must be dealt with, lest it fester and cause even more ruin among the fellowship and in the wider society. So, to gossip about sinners is to be guilty of sin. Again, the process of church discipline is not meant to serve the punishment of the guilty or the pride or prejudice of others. The process is to serve the unity and purity of the church by increasing genuine love and concern among the members.

Paul's warning here demonstrates that the escalation of the process should be gradual, that people should not just jump to formal accusations but should exhaust all informal means of rectification before engaging formal discipline procedures. This appears to be his final warning that, unless the situation was rectified, such rectification being either the confession and repentance of those involved or their resignation from the fellowship, Paul would engage formal procedures by bringing witnesses.

ESCALATION

His leniency and patience were coming to an end. His threat "to not spare" (*pheidomai*—v. 1) them was not a threat of violence. Paul was not threatening to beat them up or to kill them or to bring any harm upon them. Rather, Paul's threat was to invoke the power of God to aid the cause of the gospel in Corinth. And how would he do that? By escalating the process of bringing formal charges against them that would bring their sin to the light of Christ through the power of God.

The idea is that we human beings need to settle such matters ourselves, before things escalate to the point that God brings His judgment to bear. If we can put things right and keep the sin from growing, we can keep the matter out of God's court. People always have some control of their own behavior. So, it always makes judicial sense to settle matters at the lowest possible level because higher courts bring about greater consequences. Jesus said, "why do you not judge for yourselves what is right? As you go with your accuser before the magistrate, make an effort to settle with him on the way, lest he drag you to the judge, and the judge hand you over to the officer, and the officer put you in prison" (Luke 12:57-58).

In verse 3 Paul provided the Corinthians with the means to adjudicate the matter without any further involvement on his part by engaging the power of God. His threat was that if he had to "come again" (v. 2), he would come with formal charges and regional representatives that comprised the highest church courts at the time, other apostles who would bring witness against the erring parties. The Corinthian sins were serious and the church was a wreck. This was their last opportunity to sort it out themselves, which was the preferred method, lest Paul bring in more witnesses and engage a higher court.

Verse 3 authorized the Corinthian church to remedy the problem themselves, which (again) was the preferred method. They could prove Paul's perspective by engaging the power of God among themselves. The proof that Christ was actually speaking through Paul would be found in the exercise of power and authority that Paul had given to the Corinthians through the instructions provided in his letters. Paul's letters to the Corinthians provided everything they needed to fix their own problems. Why? Because Christ had been speaking through Paul. The proof would be in the proverbial pudding, in the application of Christ's wisdom through Paul.

Engaging Paul's instructions—corrections, his perspective—would be powerful among them. Paul said "among *you*" (v. 3), the *you* is plural. Church is a team sport. So, to get good at it, we have to get the whole team involved. Every member of the team needs to play his or her position. The positions are important, and people can't just play any position they want. Nor can everyone play the same position. Rather, team members need to play their assigned positions. God has gifted each member and makes appropriate assignments based upon His gifts. We also need to keep in mind that every position doesn't play the same way. Different positions play differently. The bottom line is that every position needs to be played to the best of one's ability.

WEAKNESS

Speaking of Christ, Paul said, "He is not weak in dealing with you, but is powerful among you" (v. 3). Paul had been boasting in his own weakness. He mentioned weakness a lot, and showed how the Lord uses human weakness to advance His cause. So, it comes as no surprise that Paul mentioned weakness again at this point. He needed to clarify that, while Christ shines in our weakness, Christ Himself is not weak. Christ is powerful. So, our display of personal weakness in Christ is not a display of Christ's weakness. It is a display of Christ's power and strength.

Yes, Christ "was crucified in weakness" (*astheneia*—v. 4). Paul used the most common Greek word for weakness because Christ's crucifixion was a demonstration of His humanity. Christ shared our weakness. He was fully human, though not sinful. Though Christ shared our human weakness, He was spiritually strong. And like us, He was not strong in His own strength, but in God's. Similarly, we share a likeness with God and Christ. Christians are strong, not in their own strength, but in Christ's. Christ is the mediator of God's strength. The power of God is mediated through the strength of Christ, and engaged through simple faith.

It doesn't take great human strength to have faith. Faithfulness is not a function of our strength, but of our weakness. Therefore, it is available to all. Faithfulness is not a function of human superiority or human strength or human intelligence or human anything. Rather, faithfulness is a function of the power of God's grace.

Again, while Christ "was crucified in weakness," He "lives by the power of God" (v. 4). Christ's weakness (Matthew 23:12, Philippians 2:8) was filled with the power and strength of God through faith alone, just as our weakness is filled with the power and strength of Christ through faith alone. Though Christ died on the cross, He lives in eternity. That's the model. That was Paul's model, and Paul is our model.

Paul then offered this clarification, "For we also are weak in him, but in dealing with you we will live with him by the power of God" (v. 4). Paul acknowledged the weakness of the Corinthians—and all Christians, but said that God's power would manifest among Christians as they dealt with each other or related to one another by the power of God. The power of God is that by which or through which Christians are to deal with one another. And what is the power of God? Paul wrote to the Romans, "For I am not ashamed of the gospel, for it is the power of God for salvation to everyone who believes" (Romans 1:16). The power of God is the gospel, the good news of salvation in Christ.

And how are Christians to deal with one another regarding the power of God? Through the application of the gospel, first to ourselves and then to one another. We are to deal with one another through the application of the Word of God to the structures and forms of Christian relationships, by applying what Paul had been teaching the Corinthians in his letters. Paul had been clarifying and extending the way of Christ (1 Corinthians 12:31; Acts 16:17, 18:25-26, 22:4; Hebrews 10:20).

CLARITY & FOCUS

Paul couldn't be more clear, and yet many Corinthians and legions of others down through the ages have misunderstood him at this very point. How can it be that Paul's clarity could be misunderstood? Because understanding Scripture is not a function of its clarity. All Scripture is clear to those who understand it. Understanding Scripture is a function of regeneration, of imposing the proper presuppositions upon Scripture, of faith, of the assumption that Scripture is true and it applies to one's self personally, of correct eisegesis.[48]

Of this concern, the Westminster Confession of Faith teaches that "our full persuasion and assurance of the infallible truth and divine authority thereof, is from the inward work of the Holy Spirit bearing witness by and with the Word in our hearts" (1:5). Apart from the inward work of the Holy Spirit there is no faith, nor any real or true understanding of Scripture. Without faith Scripture cannot be properly understood. Understanding rests upon faith.

Toward this end Paul wrote, "Examine yourselves, to see whether you are in the faith. Test yourselves. Or do you not realize this about yourselves, that Jesus Christ is in you?—unless indeed you fail to meet the test!" (v. 5). What sort of examination (peirazō) was Paul talking about? Notice that Paul did not suggest that Christians should find the faith in themselves, but rather that they should find themselves in the

---

48 *Eisegesis & Exegesis*, p. 71.

faith. We are not to look for a residue or deposit of faith in our own hearts. But rather, we are to look to see if our hearts are caught up in the faith of Jesus Christ.

The object under consideration is not generic faithfulness, not simply trusting in something beyond ourselves, not faith in something nebulous or unknown, but loyalty to a particular faith, to *the* faith. The Greek contains a definite article. Paul had in mind a particular faith. The particular faith that Paul referred to here was the faith that facilitated the "power of God" (v. 4). It was faith in the power of God, but not directly because God's power and authority had been given to Jesus Christ.

So, the power of God, from the point that His power and authority were given to Christ, has been mediated through Christ. So, the particular faith to which Paul alluded was Christ's faith. Christians are to have faith in Christ's faithfulness, to trust in the propitiation of Christ on the cross. Christ's faithfulness, which led to the cross, propitiated God. It appeased Him, it made peace with God. Christ's faithfulness, which fulfilled the Old Testament prophecies and satisfied God's demand for justice in the face of human sin, turned God's wrath to mercy for those who are in Christ.

We are to trust in the mercy that Christ's faithfulness has provided. The main element of this faith is not that it resides in our hearts—though it does. Rather, the main element of this faith is that Christ's propitiation was sufficient, that Christ's faithfulness, which led Him to the cross, was not merely a real, historical event, but that it was *the* defining event for all human history. Christ's self-sacrifice on the cross was the watershed event of all human history.

Again, it is not that this faith resides in our hearts—though it does. Rather, it is that our hearts reside in this faith. The faith is greater than our hearts. Our hearts cannot contain or encompass it. While it is true that the faith is in our hearts, it is more accurate to say that our hearts are in the faith.

And yet, in the very next phrase Paul suggested that Christ does (or should) be in us, as if Christ Himself does reside in the hearts of Christians—because He does! Even so, these things—Christ in us and us in Christ—are not two separate things.

If I were to glue a nickel to a sheet of paper, I could say that the nickel is stuck to the paper, or that the paper is stuck to the nickel. Once the glue dries, the nickel and the paper are bound together as one thing. Once glued, these two things become one. They are inseparable. But we cannot forget the glue, for without the glue the bonding of the paper and the nickel would not be possible. So, in fact these two things are actually three—the nickel, the paper and the glue. And yet, they are fused into one thing, a unity—or more accurately, a tri-unity.

This example is not quite trinitarian. It fails to fully represent the unity of the Godhead in the spiritual sense of the Trinity. The Trinity is more like a triangle, where each corner or angle is unique and entirely dependent upon the other angles for its existence as a triangle. Each unique angle defines a unique point and yet apart from each point or angle there could not be a triangle. The unique angles and points are bound together in the identity of each angle separately and of the triangle as a whole. The triangle is three things yet one thing at the same time. Language is inadequate for a complete description, but sufficient for an adequate understanding.

This faith that Paul referred to is trinitarian faith—not the mere intellectual belief in an abstract idea of the Trinity, but the actual reality of the trinitarian character of Christian faith. It is grace through faith that puts the heart of the believer in Christ, and that simultaneously puts Christ in the heart of the believer. And the means of this accomplishment, this mutual intertwining of Christ and believer, is the Holy Spirit through regeneration. The Holy Spirit is like the glue (sort of) in that it is the glue that is the bonding agent that interpenetrates Christ and believer. The Holy Spirit glues Christ and the believer together in unity.

TEST

Paul then calls Christians to test (*dokimazō*) themselves. The AV translates it as *prove*. We are to prove ourselves faithful. Such proof is both a discernment and an activity. It calls us to not simply see if it is true, but to actively prove it, to act it out, to test it in the sense of engaging it.

"Or do you not realize this about yourselves, that Jesus Christ is in you?—unless indeed you fail to meet the test!" (v. 5). The burden of proof is upon the believer. Tests can be passed or failed. We are not to test one another, at least not here. Here Paul calls each believer to examine himself. The Corinthians were to test their own hearts, their own individual faith, to personally engage in faithfulness to the gospel as Paul had been teaching them. Paul called them to apply what he had been teaching them and see for themselves whether it was the true gospel, which is the power of God for salvation.

By exercising faithfulness within the church, they would unleash the power of God, by grace through faith (Ephesians 2:8), through the power and presence of the Holy Spirit through regeneration. Believers would be brought into unity in Christ, and unbelievers would either be converted or separated out from the body of Christ. The test or proof was doing as Paul directed. The proof was in the pudding, in the tasting, in the experience or exercise of faithfulness within the body of Christ.

And yet, Paul's command to test ourselves may be interpreted individually or corporately, and likely involves both. Examination or proof of faith surely begins with self-examination, but it doesn't end there because in order to perform a thorough examination we must involve others. Self-delusion is too easy and too common to limit our examination to self-examination. Yet, Paul did not likely mean that we should provide paper and pencil examinations like we do in our schools. There is nothing wrong with testing our intellectual knowledge, of course, but Paul did not intend to limit his meaning to intellectual knowledge. Of course, there is an intellectual component to the faith, but there is more to the faith than intellectuality.

We are to prove ourselves both individually and corporately as the church, as the body of Christ. We are to engage our faith individually, but also corporately. Because Christ calls us to love one another, that love needs to be real, to be proven, to involve other people. It needs to be tested, to be engaged, to be enacted because, again, the proof is in the pudding. And the way we prove ourselves as true members of the true church is to truly engage Paul's instructions, individually and corporately.

Of course, no test is a real test unless it can be failed. If failure is not an option, then testing is irrelevant. Because Christ is real, unity in Christ is real. Because Christ is real, Christ's church is real, faithfulness is real. Therefore, failure is also a real possibility. People will fail, churches will fail. As the resurrected Christ said to the church at Ephesus, "Remember therefore from where you have fallen; repent, and do the works you did at first. If not, I will come to you and remove your lampstand from its place, unless you repent" (Revelation 2:5). Faithfulness is dependent upon the light of Christ, and apart from faithfulness, the light of Christ will be removed.

The first step toward faithfulness is always acknowledgment of sin and repentance in the light of Christ. Sin always dogs us. It's always a factor in this life. And the light of Christ reveals our sin. So, repentance is always appropriate.

To fail the test is to be a *reprobate* (*adokimos*), as translated in the AV. In the ancient world all money was made from metal, which was heated until liquid, poured into molds and allowed to cool. When the coins were cooled, it was necessary to smooth off the uneven edges. If you have ever poured your own led soldiers or led bullets, you know that the seams left by the mold require some smoothing down. Excess metal was shaved from the sides of ancient coins. In one century, more than eighty laws were passed in Athens, to stop the practice of further shaving down the coins already in circulation. Some money changers were men of integrity, and would not accept counterfeit money. They were men of honor who put only genuine full weighted coins into circulation. Such men were called *dokimos* or approved. The Greek word translated reprobate is *adokimos* or not approved.

"I hope you will find out that we have not failed the test (*adokimos*)" (v. 6). Paul's hope was that the Corinthians would put his teaching into practice, and by doing that they would find out more fully that Paul's teaching was indeed the word of God, that it was true and that Paul and the apostles were true apostles. Paul's point was that their own engagement of his teaching would provide the proof that he had been speaking the truth. This was Paul's hope, and Paul's hope is our calling.

39. Final Exam

But we pray to God that you may not do wrong—not that we may appear to have met the test, but that you may do what is right, though we may seem to have failed. For we cannot do anything against the truth, but only for the truth. For we are glad when we are weak and you are strong. Your restoration is what we pray for. For this reason I write these things while I am away from you, that when I come I may not have to be severe in my use of the authority that the Lord has given me for building up and not for tearing down. Finally, brothers, rejoice. Aim for restoration, comfort one another, agree with one another, live in peace; and the God of love and peace will be with you. Greet one another with a holy kiss. All the saints greet you. The grace of the Lord Jesus Christ and the love of God and the fellowship of the Holy Spirit be with you all.   *—2 Corinthians 13:7-14*

A gauntlet of sorts had been thrown down before the Corinthians. They were being tested—not by Paul, but by God. It was a test of faith. Would the Corinthians pass the test? Would they continue in the faith once delivered to the saints (Jude 1:3)? Paul did not want them to get it wrong (*kakos*). He didn't want them to fail the test, to do evil, as several translations render it.

He was not concerned about himself. He didn't want them to do good so that he would look good because he was their teacher. No. He wanted them to do well for their own sake, not for his. The fact that he mentioned this at all, suggests that he was aware that he had been or would be criticized for being concerned about himself, as if he was in it for what he could get from it, for personal gain. We've seen this criticism of Paul before. But that was not Paul's motivation.

He wanted them to get the faith right for their own good, for the benefit that it would be for them and for the rest of the church. Paul prayed that they would get it right, "not (so) that we may appear to have met the test, but that you may do what is right, though we may seem to have failed" (v. 7). Regardless of what of they or anyone else thought about Paul and the apostles, he wanted them to be faithful for Christ's sake.

Those who opposed Paul painted him in the colors of failure. They accused him of being a weak and ineffective speaker. And compared to their idea of success—their large, wealthy, influential church, Paul did look like a failure. If the measure of success was that of the false apostles, Paul was a failure. But, Paul argued, their understanding of success was based upon falsehood. The wisdom of their success was foolishness in God's eyes. According to God's measure, the false apostles had produced the real failure—a large, shiny, well-funded failure. Paul didn't care if he looked like a failure to those who had been captivated by worldly foolishness because he knew that they had it wrong, not him.

"For we cannot do anything against the truth, but only for the truth" (v. 8). Paul was concerned for the truth (*alētheia*). Everything he did was in its service. I suspect that he felt so bad about what he had done as a Pharisee, that he was working overtime to make up for it. Because he had worked so hard against Christianity, he probably felt like he had to make up for it by working even harder for it. He understood himself, not to be working to promote a particular perspective or a particular religion, but to be working for the truth itself. Being a spokesman for Christianity was exactly the same as being a spokesman for the truth. He was a servant of Christ, who is the Truth incarnate.

WEAKNESS

God used the truth about Paul's situation, as He uses every truth about every situation, for His own purposes. This is important because the truth was that Paul was tired and weak. He had spoken a lot about weakness because he had learned a lot from his own weakness. Strength tends to make people prideful. Winners strut and swagger. But weakness provides a lesson in humility. Losers are more likely to develop better character qualities like humility and deference.

"For we are glad when we are weak and you are strong" (v. 9). It wasn't that Paul preferred weakness over strength, but that he was very much aware of his own weakness, and was glad that he wasn't able to force himself or his views upon the Corinthians. God had brought him face to face with his own weakness—that's what God does. In order for the Corinthians to recover the gospel, they would need to engage the process of recovery themselves. If a strong leader were to impose the gospel perspective upon them, their recovery would eventually fail because it would not be *their* perspective. Every generation—

indeed, every person—needs to own the gospel for him- or herself. The changes that needed to happen at Corinth needed to happen to all of the people, not just a few of them.

Paul was not dismissing the importance of Christian leadership. Rather, he was emphasizing that leadership is not the whole package. Good leadership is essential for churches to be faithful, but leadership alone is not sufficient. There is more to a church than its leadership. The leaders need to be faithful, of course, but the followers also need to be faithful. There is a relationship of mutual dependence between leaders and followers. Sometimes strong leadership can help a church and sometimes it can harm a church.

If the leaders are strong but unfaithful, they can drive the church into unfaithfulness. Conversely, when the leaders are strong and faithful, they can steer the church away from the ditches. But at some point the followers must engage in personal faithfulness themselves. The leaders cannot and should not try to do it all. Rather, the art of leadership is nurturing the gifts of the saints from bud to flower to fruit.

This was the situation in Corinth. Paul had successfully opposed the false leaders by reasserting the biblical vision of faithfulness through his preaching and his letters. The Corinthian church at this point did not need strong leadership from outside of the congregation to impose order and discipline. Paul was already serving in that role. At this point the church needed the members—the followers—to recognize how the church had gone astray and assert their own faithfulness from below, if you will. Paul had sufficiently reasserted the vision of faithfulness, which is the primary function of leadership, and it was time now for the followers to follow by engaging the vision themselves.

Paul had shown the faithlessness of the false leaders, and out of God's design and Paul's weakness, vacancies in the Corinthian leadership had occurred or would soon be available. As the false leaders left their positions, new leaders would be needed, and Paul had no intention of filling local leadership positions with non-locals. He did not want to assign an existing apostle to a local leadership position at Corinth. Rather, it was time for the leadership of the local church to emerge from their own membership. He wanted new leaders to rise up from the followers. He wanted the Corinthians to exercise their own gifts of the Spirit, which would be less likely if Paul or one of the other apostles took a leadership position.

Paul's weakness provided a model for church leadership. Jesus taught that His "power is made perfect in weakness" (2 Corinthians 12:9). Paul's weakness was not an obstacle against Christ's power, but a vehicle for it. Christ's power was available to all of the Corinthians because it was not manifest on the basis of personal strength, but because it manifests best in the midst of personal weakness. Personal weakness is not a deterrent of faithfulness. To the contrary, faithfulness is designed for the weak. The first step toward faithfulness is always the acknowledgement of our own weakness, of our own failures and sins.

It's not that those who are strong cannot be faithful—they can! But not apart from confronting their own weaknesses. When a strong person is faithful, when a strong person confronts his weaknesses, those weaknesses can still be stronger than the strengths of most Christians, which makes it easy for the rest of us to attribute his faithfulness to personal strength and natural superiority. Thus, people can easily but mistakenly think that they are not strong enough to be faithful. People too often mistakenly think that faithfulness requires some sort of personal superiority—but that is not the gospel of grace! Paul was not deterred by his own weaknesses. Rather, by confessing his own weaknesses, he was modeling the proper gospel response.

Worldly leaders are afraid of appearing weak, but Paul wasn't. Worldly leadership is a matter of being the top dog in a dog-eat-dog world, as the old adage goes. But that wasn't Paul's concern. The false leaders were undoubtedly from the dog-eat-dog school of social leadership. Paul wasn't. He opposed it because Christ opposed it. So, Paul was glad to be weak, glad to demonstrate how his own personal weaknesses would better allow the power of Christ to manifest in their midst.

MOTIVATION

"But we pray also for this, your perfection" (v. 9), Paul added. He prayed because he was concerned for their restoration, for the reclamation of the gospel of Jesus Christ in their midst by locals, by the whole of the Corinthian church. He had done all he could do, the rest was up to them—up to Christ through them, actually. So, he prayed for the completion of what God had begun among them. He prayed for their perfection, for their faithfulness, for their sanctification. He didn't want to have to use his authority to impose measures of faithfulness upon them. He wanted them to do it themselves.

"For this reason I write these things while I am away from you, that when I come I may not have to be severe (*apotomōs*) in my use of the authority that the Lord has given me for building up and not for tearing down" (v. 10).

Paul did not want to have to "use (the) sharpness" (AV) God had given him. He didn't want to have to cut the false apostles out of the flock. He didn't want to have to exercise discipline against them as a top-down measure of church authority. He didn't want to bring the Corinthian church to the court of the apostles. He didn't want to bring the false apostles to trial. When a breach gets that far, when a matter ends up in court, it seldom turns out well. Courts create winners and losers, and Paul was after repentance and restitution for all involved. He wanted the Corinthians to deal with their own problems. If genuine restitution was going to happen, each party of the dispute had gospel obligations. The false apostles needed to repent, and the faithful Corinthians needed to forgive. He couldn't do it for them, they needed to do it themselves. He prayed for their restoration, not their punishment. He didn't want to have to play the church cop.

He wanted the church to engage in self-discipline. Each member should be engaged in self-discipline, and the church fellowship itself should be engaged in corporate self-discipline. Whatever discipline is needed is best exercised in the most immediate context. Whoever is closest to the problem is the best person to fix it. People need to learn to solve their own problems. Again, the closer the solution is to the problem, the better the result will be. Greater authorities are available up the chain of command, but the ideal is not to engage them unless necessary. Start without them. Go directly to the sinning brother.

Paul had the authority to come in and do what was needed. But he would rather that the Corinthians do it themselves. That's the ideal. That's the model of church leadership that Paul gave to the Corinthians. Paul had used his strength to reassert the vision of faithfulness for the Corinthians. Then, he trusted the Holy Spirit to use that vision to accomplish God's purposes without the heavy hand of additional authority. The additional authority was there if it was needed, but the better route was self-discipline. In fact, self-discipline is not simply a better method of growing a church, it's really the most effective way to do it.

Heavy-handed top-down authority has its purposes. There are times when it is necessary to maintain order or to maintain an orthodox vision of faithfulness among people. But the actual success of the gospel comes only when it issues from the bottom up, when the people in the pews get it. Gospel success comes when the weak are not oppressed by the strong, when the weak are allowed—enabled, encouraged—to exercise genuine gospel faithfulness on their own. Not alone, not apart from the fellowship of the community, but without the domination of the weak by the strong. Churches are strong when the weak are no longer taken advantage of. When the power of Christ can be seen among the weak, we can be sure of the faithfulness of the fellowship.

Of course, care must also be taken so that the weak do not gang up and dominate and suppress the strong, either. The ideal is not democratic totalitarianism. The ideal is self-discipline, self-government, not domination of anyone by any individual or group. The domination of one person or group over another never works. Domination always requires the suppression of freedom and the stifling of the spirit. Domination is not the model. Rather, Paul was lobbying for representative cooperation in the midst of self-discipline. Go back and look at the vision of Christianity that Paul gave to the Corinthians. Look at both letters. That's the model. Not any one part of it, but the whole thing in its trinitarian and mutually interrelated fullness.

FIVE PRIORITIES

Paul then gave his final instruction to the Corinthians, "Finally, brothers, rejoice. Aim for restoration, comfort one another, agree with one another, live in peace; and the God of love and peace will be with you" (v. 11). We might think of this as Paul's five-fold vision for Christianity, five priorities that should occupy all Christians.

First, rejoice (chairō)! The AV translated the word as "farewell," and if we understand it to simply mean goodbye, we are mistaken. A better understanding is "be well." The word literally means to be full of cheer, to be calmly happy or well off. Rejoice is to be preferred. It is the same word that Paul used when he said to the Philippians (4:4), "Rejoice in the Lord always; again I say, Rejoice."

Christians can have joy in all things because joy is not dependent upon our circumstances. While happiness involves a feeling of delight that is dependent upon our circumstances, joy does not. Happiness requires that we be in a situation that delights us, joy does not. Joy is not dependent upon our situation or our circumstances. Joy involves a feeling of delight that is not dependent upon our setting. Joy stands above our circumstances and takes delight in God regardless of our situation.

That is why Paul could rejoice in the midst of affliction. Paul could act with great boldness toward the Corinthians and be filled with comfort in the midst of affliction and weakness. Paul was not disappointed because of the difficulties he had experienced in his service to Jesus Christ. Rather, he overflowed with joy (2 Corinthians 7:4)—not because of his difficulties, but in spite of them. His joy, the joy of Christ, was not dependent upon his circumstances. Joy trumps affliction.

Second, Paul told them to "aim for restoration" (katartizō—v. 11). Here the AV translated it, "be perfect." The word means to completely fix or thoroughly restore. It is important to remember that perfection in Christ is the long range goal of Christianity. We are to aim for perfection in Christ, not that we will attain it anytime soon, but that if we don't aim at it we'll never hit it. And again, while Paul did not say so here, he didn't mean that we are to hold others to our idea of perfection. Rather, we are all to hold ourselves to Christ's idea of perfection.

Third, we are to "comfort one another" (v. 11). Paul spent a lot of time talking about comfort in chapters one and seven of Second Corinthians. Rather than repeating all that here, let me again suggest that you review it. As Christ has comforted us in the midst of affliction, filling us with the joy of the Lord, so we are to comfort others, to share the joy of the Lord with others regardless of their situation—or ours.

Fourth, we are to "agree with one another" (v. 11). The AV got it right here, "be of one mind." It is not that I'm to agree with you or that you are to agree with me, but that we are all to agree with Christ. As Paul said to the Philippians (1:27), "let your manner of life be worthy of the gospel of Christ, so that whether I come and see you or am absent, I may hear of you that you are standing firm in one spirit, with one mind striving side by side for the faith of the gospel." Our unity is in Christ, not in ourselves, not in our churches, not in our denominations—but in Christ alone. Even if we agree with one another, if we fail to agree with Christ we will be unfaithful and not in Christian unity. Christ alone is the standard of Christian unity.[49]

Fifth, Paul told the Corinthians, and all Christians by extension, to "live in peace" (*eirēneuō*—v. 11). Such peace requires the kind of universal prosperity among God's people that comes from mutual love and service. My prosperity cannot come at the expense of yours, nor yours at the expense of mine. Rather, we must find ways for everyone to prosper. This does not mean that we should all be rich, nor that we should strive for financial equality. Neither of these are possible. Rather, we should strive for a state of quiet and tranquility in joy.

We cannot eliminate conflict, and I don't think that the Lord plans to, either. The Lord uses conflict for our sanctification. The Lord has in mind that we learn to settle our conflicts peaceably. We need to learn this, not in order to end conflict, but because conflict will always be with us. It is the process of the resolution of conflict that provides personal opportunities for repentance and forgiveness that are essential to our sanctification. God's peace means freedom from oppression and violence, but not the end of conflict. It requires that our methods of conflict resolution be found in the Word of Jesus Christ, in the love of Christ, through the Spirit of Christ.

---

49 It is the *alone* part of *Christ alone* that is the source of Christian unity. Christian unity is found in our common commitment to *sola Christus*.

Conflict arises from our differences. And our differences arise because we are each unique persons. Our uniqueness, our individuality, our personal identity will never end. So, we need to learn to deal with our differences peaceably, and dealing with them in the trinitarianism of Christ is the only way to honor both the differences of individuality and the likenesses of commonality.

In the exercise of these things will the God of love and peace be with God's people. This is the calling of every Christian. These are the things that we are to be occupied with. This is the occupation of Christian dominion (Genesis 1:28).

Paul then said that we should "greet one another with a holy kiss" (v. 12). We don't do that in American churches, but this practice continues in many nations of the world. I suspect that this instruction is much like the wearing of head coverings. Paul recommended the holy kiss as a cultural practice because of its symbolism. Where the symbolism of head coverings was authority, the symbolism of the holy kiss is love, fellowship.

We are to express our love for one another. We are to speak of it, of course. But speaking of it is not sufficient. James agreed with Paul, "and one of you says to them, 'Go in peace, be warmed and filled,' without giving them the things needed for the body, what good is that?" (James 2:16). James' point (and Paul's) was that our love needs to be shown, acted out. It is not enough to think affectionate thoughts. We must show our affection.

At the same time, we must not let our affection run wild. We must not be dominated by our feelings. So Paul gave a particular instruction to greet one another with a holy kiss. *Do this,* he said, *no more and no less.*

Of course our affections must be genuine and heart-felt, but not overdone, not overly emphasized. Paul would not approach this issue legalistically, by demanding one peck or two, on one cheek or both, neither insisting on a good back slap or a gentle embrace. The manner is not as important as the intent. Rather, our greetings should be genuinely affectionate, and our love genuine.

How we exercise our greetings is more a function of personal and cultural expression and is not to be imposed upon others. Then again, if the method doesn't matter, there is no reason to disregard Paul's recommendation.

"All the saints (*hagios*) greet you" (v. 12), continued Paul. Most of the time *hagios* is translated as holy. By using the word here Paul acknowledged the reality and the unity of the greater fellowship of believers. The biblical ideal is for all Christians to be saints. However, this does not mean that all church members are saints. I wish they were, and I'm sure that Paul also wished it, but he knew better (Romans 9:6). Being a saint is the calling of all church members, but the reality is that not all church members live up to their calling.

To be holy is to be sanctified, or in our case, to be in the process of sanctification. To be holy is to be growing in Christian maturity, the maturity of Christian morality. To be holy is also to be set apart unto the Lord, to be set apart from what is not holy. It usually means that Christians don't run with the proverbial crowd, that Christians separate themselves from people who are not actively engaged in the pursuit of holiness, that Christians "seek first the kingdom of God and His righteousness" (Matthew 6:33).

HOLY HUDDLE

This gets tricky to explain. We are not called into a Christian ghetto or apart from the culture in which we live. And yet we are called to holiness—to growth and maturity in Christ—in the midst of our circumstances. God does in fact want His people to be engaged in a holy huddle, where, like a football team planning a play, we make our plans apart from the enemy, apart from Satan, apart from people who are not engaged in the pursuit of holiness. We are not to remain in huddle formation, of course. Once our plans are made, we are to execute them in the world, among the worldly.

The point here is that there is a time for huddling and a time for execution, and we are to engage both. So, we need to know the difference. We need to know when to do one and when to do the other. But we are most decidedly not to make our plans with the ungodly. We are not to invite Satan into our plan-making huddle. This means that we are to do everything we can to exclude the ungodly—the immature in the faith—from church leadership. Church leadership is for the saints alone, not for the unsanctified, not for the immature, not for the ungodly.

By bringing the greeting of the saints to Corinth, Paul was telling them that the saints in Corinth had the support of the saints elsewhere, that the spiritual influence of the saints everywhere was actively engaged in helping the saints in Corinth accomplish the purposes of God through the instructions of Paul. Because there is strength in numbers, Paul was telling the Corinthian saints that they were not alone.

Paul, then closed with a trinitarian benediction, "The grace of the Lord Jesus Christ and the love of God and the fellowship of the Holy Spirit be with you all" (v. 14). Grace, love and fellowship. Christ, God and the Holy Spirit. These are the things that make people Christian.

The church of Jesus Christ is located wherever these things are found. May they be found in abundance everywhere. May they be here among us, with you who are reading this, and among all our friends and neighbors. And may we not merely find these things, but may we ourselves be actively engaged in promoting them for Christ's sake, for the sake of the world. May the change that the world so desperately needs begin here with us.

"The grace of the Lord Jesus Christ and the love of God and the fellowship of the Holy Spirit be with you all" (v. 14).

SCRIPTURE INDEX

ALPHABETICAL INDEX

Books by Phillip A. Ross

It's About Time! — The Time Is Now

40 pages. 2008.

This book is about thinking about God, the gospel, and Jesus Christ. We all need to make more time to do that. It is for the Mid-Ohio River Valley, but it is also for every valley where people live. It comes to a valley perspective from a valley perspective. This booklet is not about a mountaintop experience nor is it from a mountaintop perspective. Rather, it is from the "street," down in the valley where people actually live. It is not sad or morose, but it is serious —and it's about sin, yours and mine. It is an invitation to think more deeply about the things that we deeply care about, the things we believe. It's about Jesus.

These essays were originally written in 1998 as a short sermon series during Advent. They are not the usual Advent presentation of well-worn platitudes and biblical pablum. Unlike too many of my peers, I can't stomach that kind of stuff. To me, warm milk not only tastes bad, but it makes me sleepy.

This booklet is about the time in which we live. Hopefully, you will find it to be timely in your own life, as well. Time is a funny thing. We all live in it. Most of us are slaves to it, driven by appointments and schedules that must be kept. Asking people to think about time is like asking a fish to think about water—with one important difference. As far as we know, fish can't think at all, at least not in the way that we define thinking. I will ask you to think about time, about how much time you have, how much you need, and what you do with it.

Engagement—Establishing Relationship in Christ

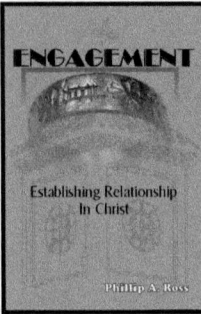

104 pages, 1996, 2008.

The material in this book is not my usual fare, but was an attempt to put my best understanding of Scripture and salvation in Christ into a succinct format for a church that did not know me. It is not a expositional book study, but is more of a topical study intended to speak to the needs of contemporary people by uncovering various biblical truths and at the same time revealing various contemporary misunderstandings about the Bible and salvation.

As you will come to understand, it created quite a stir among those who heard it. But it did not generate church renewal or revival, at least not in the way that anyone would notice, not in what are considered to be the measures of renewal and revival. Rather, many hearers found it quite disturbing, and I then found myself in defensive mode as it seems to have raised more questions that it answered.

What you will see here is a synopsis of the historic, Protestant, Reformed position. If it seems unusual it is more likely because this theological position has been all but abandoned by the vast majority of contemporary Christians and their churches over the past 20, 50 or 100 years, depending on where you live and what circles you fellowship in.

The Big Ten—A Study of the Ten Commandments

105 pages, 2001, 2008.

We live in an age of increasing lawlessness. It is not simply that there is a void of law, far from it. Quite the opposite is actually true. There is an overwhelming preponderance of laws, the size, scope and complexity of which world has never before seen. The body of law for any modern country, and in particular the United States—the most litigious society in history—is phenomenal. So, how can I say that we live in an age of increasing lawlessness?

What is in view here is not human law, but God's law. Just to speak the phrase brings a chill upon many a backbone. People don't like to talk about God's law. To do so is to be branded a fundamentalist, legalist, theonomist and/or extremist, all in the most vile sense of the words. For the most part contemporary Christians believe that they have arrived at a time in history that is beyond the application of any Old Testament laws, and in many cases, a time that is beyond all biblical law. People have converted the gospel of grace to mean a gospel without law—without obligation or responsibility.

The good news that is preached in too many pulpits today is lawlessness, couched in terms of a gospel of positive thinking, of upbeat moralisms intended to make life better, richer, fuller, more meaningful, and happier. In order to justify the human distaste for biblical law, people—Christians among them—no longer speak of God's law or the human obligation to it, not even in Bible study or worship.

However, the Bible is not a divided witness. It is a whole, a unity. God's Word, God's testimony is completely true.

The Wisdom of Jesus Christ in the Book of Proverbs

414 pages, 2006.

This study of Proverbs is an attempt to uncover the biblical message of Proverbs verse by verse in the light of Jesus Christ. We cannot pretend to be other than Christians who live on the redemption side of the Cross, while Proverbs was written on the anticipation side of the Cross. Nonetheless, the Christian faith is founded on the eternal consistency of God. God does not change. The God of Solomon, the author (and editor) of Proverbs, is the same God spoken of in the New Testament. In fact, the God of Solomon is Jesus Christ by the power of the Holy Spirit. Thus, the present work acknowledges this fact of faith and applies it by reading Proverbs in the light of Jesus Christ.

Marking God's Word—Understanding Jesus

324 pages, 2006.

Contemporary Western churches are a wreck, regardless of denominational affiliation or lack thereof. Mainline churches have been in serious decline for 50 years. The so-called contemporary churches are simply picking up transfer growth from other churches. Saying that there is a problem is one thing, but clearly defining the problem is something else. That something else is the subject of Marking God's Word. Clearly, there is much confusion in and out of the church about Christianity. Is confusion about the gospel of Jesus Christ new to the Modern and/or Postmodern world? That is the question that has haunted this treatment of Mark. *Marking God's Word* will help you see the gospel with new eyes, from a perspective that is obscured by sin and selfishness. Yet, this is not a new perspective. Rather, it is an old perspective that has a long and noble history of reformation and revival. Come, see Christ again, for the first time.

ACTS OF FAITH—KINGDOM ADVANCEMENT

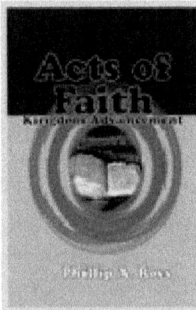

326 pages, 2007.

Acts of the Apostles continues the story of Jesus after His death. The story of the misunderstanding of the gospel among those who personally knew Jesus continues in the ministry of Paul. Paul, who was knocked off his high horse and thrown to the ground against his will and born again by the power of the Holy Spirit, came to see that he had been completely blind, and had his eyes miraculously opened. Paul – formerly the chief enemy of Christ, who became the chief disciple—took up the ministry and perspective of Jesus and began preaching the message of Christ to anyone who would listen. But Paul had the same difficulties that Jesus had—people thought he was crazy, that he didn't know what he was talking about, that he had gotten the gospel mes-sage wrong. Paul was hounded to death by the enemies of Christ, just as Jesus had been. Again, what is discovered in Acts of Faith is not a new perspective on Paul, but a very old one—the forgotten perspective of God's remnant.

INFORMAL CHRISTIANITY—REFINING CHRIST'S CHURCH

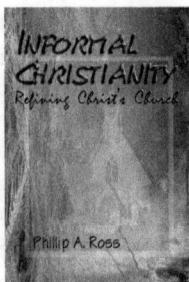

136 pages, 2007.

Informal Christianity reviews the personal and informal realities involved in a personal relationship with Jesus Christ that provide the foundation of Christianity. Where the internal and subjective realities of regeneration are absent from the lives of church members, churches find themselves on a foundation of sand. Such churches turn away from the heart of Christianity — doctrine and theology — to focus on peripheral concerns of administration and maintenance. Christians and churches that do not enthusiastically embrace biblical doctrine and theology as the life-blood of faithfulness, tend to spend their time and energy polishing the outside of the cup (Matthew 23:25). Such efforts concern themselves with church growth — noses and nickels — rather than Christian maturity (Ephesians 4:13).

Informal Christianity aims to drive a nail through the heart of such trivial indulgence on the part of those who fail to live up to the potential of their Christian calling because such a failure amounts to the denial of the power and presence of the Holy Spirit in their own lives. Yes, the flesh is weak, no one is disputing that. But "the spirit indeed is willing" (Matthew 26:41). Christians "receive power when the Holy Spirit has come upon" (Acts 1:8) them. Such power is the "strength that God supplies" (1 Peter 4:11). To wallow in administrative trivialities is to deny the power of God (Mark 12:24) and to deny one's citizenship in the Kingdom of God.

While great effort is being poured into the administrative expansion of churches (church growth), the very heart of personal faithfulness is being ignored, denied, denigrated and trivialized by the very principles that have been adopted to generate such growth. The proper priorities and first things (Matthew 6:33) are giving way to the "wisdom of men" (1 Corinthians 2:5). Informal Christianity cuts through the trees that have become veritable logs in the eyes of contemporary Christians to reveal again the forest of faithfulness in which the life of Christianity dwells.

PRACTICALLY CHRISTIAN—APPLYING JAMES TODAY

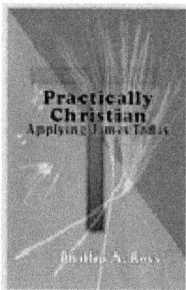

135 pages, 2006.

Practically Christian offers a fresh and insightful application of the ancient Christian epistle of James to the contemporary American Evangelical world. Against the Antinomian backdrop of a Christianity shaped by the Church Growth Movement, Practically Christian puts teeth into Christianity, pressing for a practical realism in order to re-store some theological balance and sanity to the practice of the faith.

"*Practically Christian offers a fresh and insightful application of the ancient Christian epistle to the contemporary American evangelical world. Against the Antinomian backdrop of a Christianity shaped by the church growth movement, Ross puts teeth into Christianity, pressing for a practical realism in order to restore some theological balance and sanity. His book is by no means dull reading or trite, but is replete with fresh anecdotes illustrating the salient points he is conveying. I found his exposition of James 1:2-4 to be especially instructive and profound, and on that basis alone the book was worth reading. Ross's commitment to Reformed doctrine is quite obvious throughout. Many parts of the book I wish I had written myself!"* —David C. Brand, Pastor and author

ARSY VARSY—RECLAIMING THE GOSPEL

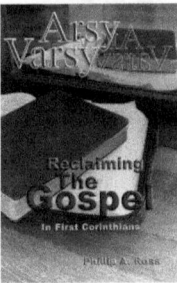

399 pages, 2008.

"Corinth was a city of wealth and culture, seated at the crossroads of the Roman Empire, where all the trade and commerce of the empire passed through. It was a city of beauty, a resort city, located in a very beautiful area, but it was also a city of prostitution and of passion. It was devoted to trade and commerce, but also to the worship of the goddess of sex" (*The Corinthian Crisis*, by Ray Steadman).

Paul had a problem with the Christians at Corinth. They were a large, successful church. They were growing leaps and bounds. They thought they were doing great. But not Paul. Paul found that they had substituted the wisdom of the world (the philosophy and culture of the Greeks) for the wisdom of Christ (the philosophy and culture of the Bible). This volume contrasts the folly of Greek (and ultimately modern American) worldly wisdom with the gospel of Christ. Stones are turned over and small-minded creatures that thrive in the dark scatter in the light of Christ.

Ross brings Paul's struggle to light with clarity and passion that leaves the worldly no where to hide in this trinitarian treatment to First Corinthians.

THE WORK AT ZION—A RECKONING

Two-volume set, 772 pages, 1996.

The Work at Zion is the journal of a spiritual conversion that turned a ministry upside down. This collection of sermons details a preacher's rediscovery of classic, historical, Protestant Christianity in the midst of apathy and apostasy. The logical conclusion of modern Christianity is brought to a head and set in stark contrast to God's Word.

Sin is always the key to receiving Jesus. When people do not believe themselves to be sinners, they perceive no need for Jesus. The modern secular world has done everything it can to eradicate sin from modern awareness. Secular psychologists and educators insist that sin is outdated, that the doctrine of the Fall overly emphasizes the negative, to the detriment of personal self-esteem... But this modern, secular theory runs directly counter to the teaching and testimony of scripture. Scripture shows us that the confession of personal sinfulness is a prerequisite for salvation in Christ.

Books can be purchased through your favorite bookstore, on the Internet at www.pilgrim-platform.org or by calling 877-805-0676.

www.ingramcontent.com/pod-product-compliance
Lightning Source LLC
LaVergne TN
LVHW051452080426
835509LV00017B/1744